The Anteater's Guide to Writing and Rhetoric

COMPOSITION PROGRAM
UNIVERSITY OF CALIFORNIA, IRVINE

THIRD EDITION

General Editor
Tira Palmquist

Lead Chapter Editors
Jonathan Alexander
Bobbie Allen
Lorene Delany-Ullman
Kat Eason
Lynda Haas
Peg Hesketh
Kelsey Layos
Cathy Palmer
Tira Palmquist
Joy Parker

Contributors
Michael Andreasen
Sylvia Bass
Shohreh Bozorgmehri
Hillary Branman
Emily Brauer
Chieh Chieng
Michelle Cho
Margaux Cowden
Keith Danner
Sonja Djuricin
Lisa Douglass
Jaya Dubey
Kim Gerrard
Alberto Gullaba
Leah Kaminski
Scott Eric Kaufman
David Lacy

Kathie Levin
Daniel Matlock
Ralph McLaughlin
Josef Nguyen
Collier Nogues
Abraham Romney
Alex Sartor
Matthew Seybold
Elaina Taylor
Eric Titterud
Andrew Tonkovich
I-Lien Tsay
Briandy Walden
Jeff Wilson

Cover Art
Nasser Mufti

Course Directors: Bobbie Allen, Lynda Haas, Tira Palmquist
Director of Composition: Daniel M. Gross
Campus Writing Coordinator: Jonathan Alexander

HAYDEN
HM
McNEIL

Printed in the United States of America

10 9 8 7 6 5 4 3 2 1

ISBN 978-0-7380-4390-6

Hayden-McNeil Publishing
14903 Pilot Drive
Plymouth, MI 48170
www.hmpublishing.com

HaasL 4390-6 F11 (Anteater's Guide to Writing and Rhetoric)

Table of Contents

Preface

A Word of Welcome from the Director:

What we mean by "good writing" depends—radically—on the situation. In the humanities we usually find the agency of the active voice preferable, whereas in science writing the passive voice is generally preferred; students who arrive on campus with the rule that one can't use the first-person pronoun in academic writing may be thrown by their anthropology course that makes room for the "I" of auto-ethnography; new students of poetry may wonder just for a moment why the creative punctuation that served Gertrude Stein so well in *Tender Buttons* produced less satisfactory results on their Psychology midterm.

Therefore our Composition Program, housed in the English Department, teaches students not just a single set of rules for writing in one situation, but rather **rhetorical know-how**, which is to say we want our students to exit the Program with the understanding that any communication situation requires that they consider the people involved, the conventions, and of course the purpose.

Thus in 39A, 37, and 39B students focus on critical reading and rhetorical analysis of texts across a variety of genres and media. In 39C students research current cultural, scientific, and social issues with an eye toward writing in the disciplines and beyond, in the public sphere. All of our courses consider writing in a larger communication context that includes digital literacy and speech. Put succinctly, then, when you finish our program you will be on your way to becoming a master rhetorician, in the best sense of the word!

Sincerely,

Daniel M. Gross
Associate Professor of English
Director of Composition

June 2011

Acknowledgements

It seems fitting that we end each year creating a new edition of the *Anteater's Guide to Writing and Rhetoric*. After all, in creating this *Guide*, we practice the principles of writing and revising, peer editing, and practicing our rhetorical know-how. In other words, it's only right that we practice what we preach.

Then, the guide is a truly collaborative affair. Our contributors include course directors, TAs, lecturers, librarians, and other specialists on campus. We have a remarkable group of instructors (and writers and editors) who have helped with each successive edition, and I cannot calculate how much easier my work has been because of their efforts.

What's not included on this list of contributors, but that deserves noting here, are the instructors and students in our program who have provided samples, comments, suggestions, and (perhaps most importantly) inspiration for the guide. To those individuals—thank you! The *Guide* is for you, after all. We hope you find it as helpful and practical as we intended it to be.

I'd be remiss, though, if I didn't take the time to thank a few particularly hard-working individuals. Thanks, first, to Daniel Gross, Director of Composition, for his careful attention to our chapters and excellent suggestions for revisions. Then, thanks to Nasser Mufti, for creating the new cover art. Nasser, in addition to being an excellent instructor in our program, is a fabulous graphic designer. Thanks for making us look good!

To my team of crack proofreaders and editors—Lynda Haas, Kat Eason, Collier Nogues, Leah Kaminski, Keith Danner, Hillary Branman—another round of applause. Your patience and good humor made the journey much more enjoyable.

Tira Palmquist
General Editor
June 2011

Chapter 1

RHETORIC

WELCOME to UC Irvine. You've come a long way in your educational career to get here, so congratulations on being admitted to one of the largest and most prestigious university systems in the country! A group of teachers from the Composition Program collaborated to create this book, which you will find to be an indispensable companion to the work you do in your classes.

Composition courses at UCI are designed to do a few things. First, they help you figure out how to establish a strong voice in the discourse community of the research university generally, and then in your chosen field specifically, where many of the conventions for academic argumentation are shared. Composition courses won't, however, teach you the rules to master *every* communication situation you'll encounter at UCI and beyond—that would be impossible! They will teach you how to approach any new communication situation by asking the right questions about the relevant conventions, expectations, and opportunities for writing and speaking effectively. Finally, Composition courses will help you develop rhetorical *flexibility* that should serve you outside of the immediate university context, in your professional, civic, and everyday lives.

1.1   Why Writing Is Important to You

Writing is a human activity—a profound act and a highly specialized form of communication, if you consider all that is involved. Scholars who study writing have observed that people at all stages of intellectual pursuit continue to grow and change as writers. This is because writing is not quite like your other educational pursuits. There is no real "content" to be memorized, no formula to follow, and no list to tell you how to get it right—each situation is a unique interaction between you and your reader.

Since writing is a specialized form of communication, let's consider it as part of this larger category for a moment. Every interaction is a little bit different, so you rely (perhaps unconsciously) on what you already know about communication, and about what has and has not worked in the past. What might be the right thing to say in one situation (for example, talking with your mother) might be the entirely wrong thing to say in another situation (for example, talking with your professor). Based on your memory of past interactions and your knowledge of the message and audience, you must make a judgment about what words to choose, what tone is most appropriate, and how to frame the information you'd like to communicate.

writing is a form of communic.

When it comes to communication via writing, your primary frame of reference may be your experience writing in high school classes. Chances are your writing there was like this: you read and studied a text (a novel, poem, essay, section of a textbook, etc.) and then were asked to write an essay or report about that text for an audience of one: your teacher. The purpose was usually to show that you had read and understood the material; also important was to show that you understood enough about the kind of "standard" English required for school that you could write with few errors in grammar, punctuation, and mechanics. You may have written a lot of in-class essays in order to prepare you for written essay exams like the AP, IB, SAT Writing, or UC's own AWPE. Writing at school meant writing for the grade.

In your composition courses, you'll still be receiving a grade, but we hope to broaden your horizons to think of writing differently: instead of thinking only of the grade, we hope you'll see this as a vital process deeply connected to your personal and professional goals. We hope to build on your high school experiences and introduce you to new genres and media for reading and writing, new purposes, and new audiences. This new attitude about writing will prepare you to move on to communicating in the context of your major field of study (your academic discipline) more effectively.

Once you've completed your college education, you'll still need to be an effective writer and communicator—though, of course, when you get to that point, there will no longer be a grade. However, being an effective communicator extends far beyond simply getting good grades, and is arguably an important part of being an active citizen or member of a community. If you need to be further convinced that learning to become a better writer is important, consider these recent findings of the National Council on Writing. This federally funded organization interviewed executives from every sector of the American workplace to ask them what place writing plays in the context of their company. The final report, "Writing: A Ticket to Work or a Ticket Out," found that for the majority of professional jobs, writing is a threshold skill:

Writing Is Necessary to be Hired or Promoted. More than eighty percent of the responding companies said that writing was taken into account as part of the hiring process. "Poorly written application materials would be extremely prejudicial," said one respondent. "Such applicants would not be considered for any position." Then, half of all companies take writing into account when making promotion decisions.

Writing Is Required in the Workplace. Two-thirds of salaried employees in large American companies have some writing responsibility. "All employees must have writing ability . . . Manufacturing documentation, operating procedures, reporting problems, lab safety, waste-disposal operations—all have to be crystal clear," said one human resources director.

More than half of all responding companies report that they "frequently" or "almost always" produce technical reports (59 percent), formal reports (62 percent), and memos and correspondence (70 percent). Communication through e-mail and PowerPoint presentations is almost universal. "Because of e-mail, more employees have to write more often. Also, a lot more has to be documented," said one respondent.

1.2   Why Rhetoric?

As you progress through your undergraduate degree and enter your desired profession, you will be asked to write in a variety of genres and media: a lab report,
an instruction manual, a white paper, an analytic essay, a scientific report, a
research grant proposal, a graduate school application letter, a PowerPoint about
your work for colleagues from other offices within your company, a memo to
an executive justifying the cost of a new hire in your department—and the list
could go on and on.

There's no way a few 10-week writing courses could teach you everything you'd
need to know in order to successfully complete every communication task you'll
ever face. And even if we did have the time to cover all the different forms your
writing might take, we could never know enough about all the future contexts
in which you'll be communicating and the audiences for which you'll be writing in order to teach you how to approach each one.

What we can teach you is the basic components of any communicative situation. We'll show you how to read texts closely in order to understand what makes
them effective or ineffective pieces of communication, and then we'll give you
ample practice applying what you've learned about successful texts to your own
attempts at writing and communication.

1.2.1   What Is Rhetoric?

When you're trying to figure out what makes an act of communication effective
or ineffective, you're thinking about **rhetoric**. The word "rhetoric" comes from
ancient Greek and originally referred to effective oratory—public speaking that
moved, influenced, or persuaded the listeners.
During the fifth and fourth centuries B.C.E.
in Athens, rhetoric became recognized as a facility with written and spoken language used
for political deliberations, legal arguments,
and public occasions. You might have a heard
someone using the term "rhetoric" with a negative connotation, and this sense of the word
has its roots in history, too—those orators who
could be paid to speak well about anything.

Today, though, we think of rhetoric as a comprehensive "art," or set of techniques, for effective communication. Aristotle, the Greek philosopher and teacher whose writing did much

[handwritten annotation at top:] rhetoric = using the art of language to communicate an idea * persuasiveness

to solidify the art, defined rhetoric as "the ability, in each particular case, to see the available means of persuasion." Throughout your composition courses, you'll hear this ability called rhetorical knowledge or **rhetorical know-how**, where the former refers to your conceptual understanding of rhetoric and the latter refers to your practical ability.

Rhetoric concerns not only the production of a communicative text, but also its reception by an audience within a particular context. A rhetor is someone who is aware of the elements of any given communication situation and who is thinking about the best way to be effective within that situation.

1.2.2   Everything Is Situated

All rhetorical acts are situated; or, put differently, every communicative act takes place within a specific context—within a particular place and time. Because the context is unavoidable (and, in a sense, invisible), we get to the point where we don't even think about it—for example, we know that we live in SoCal in the early 21st century, but that knowledge is so second nature to us that we are much like fish in water. Because we have always lived and breathed within the water, we take it for granted.

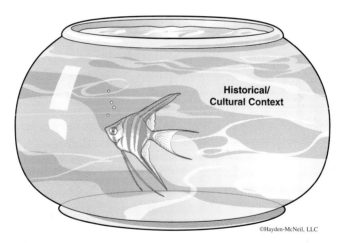

Historical/
Cultural Context

©Hayden-McNeil, LLC

To be a good rhetorician, you must become *aware* of the water—always thinking about context, not only when you communicate (as speaker, writer, rhetor), but also when you act as the audience of someone else's communication (when you read, watch, listen). In your composition courses, we'll keep reminding you to consider the broad context of time and place, and also the narrower context of the particular communication situation you find yourself in at any one moment in time.

You can only become more rhetorical in your thinking through a lot of practice—conditioning yourself to remain aware of what's going on in each different communication situation and to make informed decisions about how to act based on what you know about that situation. Your composition courses will give you ample practice at writing and communicating in a variety of situations, for different audiences and purposes.

1.3   The Rhetorical Situation

Rhetorical theory in ancient Greece as well as in contemporary times has analyzed communicative acts by breaking them up into their constitutive elements. Though you will spend time with your instructor complicating this analytic process so it approaches real-world experience, these traditional concepts and categories are a helpful first step.

The Rhetorical Situation

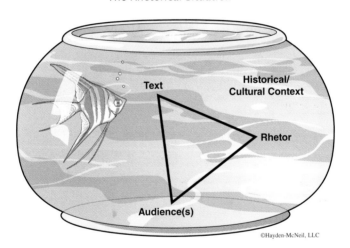

©Hayden-McNeil, LLC

Think of communication as an action involving a triangle of elements: the **rhetor** (the person or people attempting to communicate, like writers, speakers, artists, or directors), the **audience** (the readers, listeners, or viewers), and the text itself (including what form the communication takes—the **genre**, and the means used to transmit the message—the **medium**). And to fully describe the situation, don't forget **context**: all acts of communication take place within a particular historical and cultural environment.

1.3.1   The Rhetor

Two things to consider when thinking about the **rhetor** (the one responsible for composing the communication) are **purpose** and **ethos**. In your composition courses, you'll be asked to look at the rhetor from both ends of the communicative act—when you read, you'll consider the purpose and ethos of the writer, and when you are the communicator, the writer, the composer, we'll ask you to think about your own purposes and how you can construct an effective ethos.

A. The Rhetor's Purpose(s)

Although each reason for communicating is slightly different depending on immediate context, here are some general purposes to consider. In many cases, rhetors have a combination of these purposes for composing:

emphasis on audience

Persuasive. An emphasis on the **audience** (reader, listener, watcher) is characteristic of persuasive texts. Advertising, political speeches, legal speeches such as closing arguments, and editorials are all examples of persuasive writing. Much of the time, persuasion is a secondary purpose in a predominantly expressive, informative, or stylistic text. Several assignments in your composition courses will ask you to convince the audience to adopt your interpretation or solution. Instead of trying to persuade through emotion or sheer force, for instance, academic writers typically persuade by way of a logical sequence of statements called an **argument**.

emphasis on text

Informative. When the focus is on the **text (or message of the text)**, the purpose is informative. This is a very common purpose for communication and can be identified in definitions, descriptions, problem solutions, and research of almost every type, news articles, reports, web sites, summaries, technical articles, diagnoses of illness, and many other types of texts.

emphasis on rhetor

Expressive. When the emphasis is on the **rhetor** (speaker, writer, singer, musician, artist, etc.), the purpose can be called **expressive**. As a rhetor, the point is to share your feelings or thoughts through the text. As a reader of expressive texts, any objective measure of the message is less important than your own attitudes, perspectives, and context. Expressive communication can come from a single author or from a group. Some examples in writing are personal diaries, blogs, manifestos, poetry, prayers, and religious credos. Purely expressive communications are not very common in academic writing contexts, although personal perspective, belief, and commitment often underlie academic arguments. Other forms of communication that are generally expressive in purpose are music, dance, and art.

Literary or Stylistic. This is another purpose focused on the text. Sometimes we communicate in order to explore and exploit the possibilities of the **genre** and **medium** of the **text** itself. Although most often tied to the expressive purpose, stylistic texts go further than pure expression, reining it in to fit a particular form or style. We call this purpose literary or stylistic and put short stories, novels, films, TV shows, poems, songs, and visual art into this category. To some degree, every communicative act involves some self-conscious assertion of style.

B. The Rhetor's Ethos (Character, Persona)

You may not recognize the term used for this element of rhetorical action because it comes from ancient Greek and is not used very much in everyday conversation; however, by the end of your composition sequence, you'll have heard about it plenty of times.

Ethos refers to the way a communicator represents herself to an audience. It could refer to the person doing the communicating in a real setting or it could refer to how a particular character in a fictional text represents himself to the audience; in fact, ethos is sometimes translated as "character." Get into the habit of analyzing the ethos of any rhetor or character who is communicating when you read, listen, or watch, and also get into the habit of thinking about your own ethos each time you prepare to communicate.

Because ethos is discussed at length throughout this text, we will only note here that you *do* create a sense of yourself in every communicative act (not only in formal writing, but also in everyday conversations with your friends) and this persona or character can be shaped and adjusted for each occasion. In other words, there is no single, stable version of "you" that will be effective in all communication contexts.

In your composition courses, you'll have several opportunities to practice creating an effective ethos; we'll ask you to speak and write for different audiences and with different purposes, so that you'll gain practice with assuming roles that are appropriate to the rhetorical situation. Your persona will be more or less opinionated, more or less formal, artful, flamboyant, or technical in your use of language. In your formal essay writing, you'll also start learning how to create an **academic ethos.** As you progress through your university coursework, the performance of academic ethos will become so familiar to you that you'll probably start to take it for granted. It will become another feature of your rhetorical know-how.

You may also be asked to write as though you were someone else as a way to practice fine-tuning your ethos. For example, you may be asked to take different sides of an argument, or to write as though you were in dialogue with someone with a different view. Although there will be an element of artificiality in these exercises, studying at the university is a continual process of imagining yourself into new roles: as a rhetorician, a writer, a scientist, a sociologist, a citizen who makes informed decisions about political issues, and ultimately, as a professional.

The ancient rhetorician Isocrates wrote that practicing the responsibilities and rhetorical habits of exemplary people is the best training for becoming knowledgeable and ethical. Trying on different voices or personae in your writing can help you develop an awareness of and a sensitivity to the multiple perspectives that you'll come into contact with, not only in an academic setting, but in all areas of life.

tolerance
being involved w/ the world

1.3.2 The Audience

How a rhetor approaches the composition of a text is shaped in relation to the audience or reader. To go back to your previous experience as a high school student, you probably thought of your teacher as the primary audience for your writing. Sometimes, students characterize their teachers as arbitrary individuals, reading and grading papers based on personal idiosyncrasies of taste. Of course, we are each unique as readers and listeners, and each teacher will have special interests.

A. The Discourse Community

discussing + learning from the ideas of others

Now that you're part of the university, it will be much more useful for you to think of each teacher as a representative of a **discourse community**. "Discourse" is just another word for communication—discourse about a subject is a conversation about it; a community is a group of people who have something in common. So then, a discourse community is a group of people who have some communication practices in common.

For example, your high school comprised a particular discourse community—there were ways of communicating that were unique to students, teachers, and administrators who spent their weekdays at that location, as part of that institution. UC Irvine is another broad discourse community: everyone who is part of the UCI community knows things that are particular to communication here. If I said to you, "It's easy to find—it's straight across Aldrich Park," you'd know what I meant; but if I gave that direction to a student from Boston University who has never been to Irvine, he'd have no clue.

Disciplines across universities comprise discourse communities, both broad and narrow in membership. Scientists, in general, form a broad scientific discourse community—but there are smaller discourse communities within the sciences—those who specialize in psychology, environmental studies, computers, chemistry, and many more. Your composition teachers come from the general discipline of the **humanities**, which means they all share an interest in the way humans have communicated, created meaning, and shared knowledge throughout history, but they also come from narrower discourse communities of poets, fiction writers, rhetoric and composition specialists, historians, and those who study particular fields of literature.

Your composition class is also a discourse community: a group of people who will come to share some ways of communicating. We'll capitalize on the community of your classroom by asking you to frequently address them in speech and in writing. Composing for this particular audience will give you the practice you need to target audiences in general. Your classmates are also your colleagues in the academic community as well as the smaller UCI community. Don't discount the **class community** assignments like blogs and forums as "busy work"—these are important exercises for enhancing your rhetorical know-how.

Discourse communities aren't restricted to academics: if you are passionate about a sport, say football, then you probably know how to talk about football when you are around other football fans. If you're a cook, you probably know special terminology that is particular to foodies (and if you're a short-order cook, your way of talking about food and cooking is different from a sous-chef at a high-priced restaurant). Or if you're a World of Warcraft player, you know there are ways of speaking about that experience that only other WoW players understand.

When you prepare to compose a text, it helps to think about the discourse community or communities your audience belongs to. But, through your writing, you also engage in the process of shaping your readers into the kind of audience you *want* them to be. Contemporary rhetoricians refer to this process as "invoking an audience."

B. Demographics and Psychographics

It might help you to think about audience the way an advertising agency does—in terms of demographics and psychographics. What categories do the audience members fit into within the larger society (demographics) and what do they think or believe (psychographics)? Demographics are things like nationality, locale, gender, race, economic class, age, educational background, and occupation—traits that typically can be measured in a census. Psychographics are things like specific interests, cultural beliefs, political affiliation, religion, or other values in a given community.

While psychographics can be harder to measure, the advertising industry dedicates much of its resources trying to understand the personality traits of consumers. According to a recent study in *Advertising Age*, your favorite television programs reveal a lot about your attitude and outlook. Some of the findings:

Char!

- Fans of the show *Glee* are 41% more likely to be open-minded and empathetic. Gleeks enjoy new experiences and often seek out creative outlets in a quest for an authentic lifestyle. They are receptive to certain brands of French bottled water and compact German sports cars.

- Fans of *The Real Housewives of Orange County* are 33% more likely to be argumentative, hot-tempered individuals who aren't afraid of taking charge and hurting the feelings of others. They value honesty above all, and are more likely to buy teeth-whitening strips.

Of course these findings are only generalizations based on statistical group tendencies (not all fans of *Real Housewives* like to argue). Yet studies like these illustrate the advertising industry's desire for a rich and profound grasp of audience.

In order to read rhetorically you have to be able to think outside your own culture (and your likes/dislikes) and become aware of the original intended audience. This requires a bit of research and a strong imagination. Keep in mind that some texts may appeal to multiple audiences by including several elements which each function separately to address subsets of a broader audience.

As you can see, there's much to think about where audience is concerned—and we haven't even touched on the ways audience should be considered when you are reading a text critically and rhetorically (see Chapter 2 for an extended discussion about that). The main point to keep in mind now is that there is no such thing as a "general audience." All writing and speaking is directed to someone in particular, and it is one of the responsibilities of the effective writer to think about that rhetorical feature of the communication act.

1.3.3 The Text
In your past experiences with reading and writing in school, you probably spent most of your time dealing with the text itself—what was happening, or what that meant, or why it should be considered of "literary merit." In your composition classes, you'll still be asked to work with a number of texts—but once again, we hope to broaden the horizon of texts you'll encounter.

In high school, your writing instruction was generally connected to English or American Literature classes, and therefore, the kinds of texts you worked with were largely literary—novels, short stories, poems, and plays. If you took AP Language, then you also worked with nonfiction texts such as essays and articles.

Although in your composition courses your teachers will be interested in litera-ture, the primary goal of the courses is not to teach you more about literature, but instead, to teach you how to think rhetorically about all the different kinds of texts you'll encounter in the future. Rhetoric occurs in and is a part of every text, from the dialogues of a classical philosopher to a conversation between you and a friend—or a novel, a film, a web site, a painting, a comic book, a song on the radio, or a scholarly essay. All of these are texts in which rhetoric is at play, and so all of them are fair game for rhetorical analysis. Throughout the 39 sequence, you'll read, analyze, and compose many different genres of texts, in various media. For more on this, see Chapter 2.

1.4   The Lower-Division Writing Sequence

This guide covers the entire sequence of first-year writing courses—WR 37, 39A, 39B, 39C, and FIP—each of which has distinctive goals. The particular path you follow through the sequence will depend upon your writing ability when you enter UCI.

Some of you will begin with **39A, Introduction to Writing and Rhetoric** (Chapter 5). This course offers an introduction to the basic range of reading and writing assignments you will find in the other courses.

The emphasis in **WR 37, 39B, Critical Reading and Rhetoric** (Chapter 6), is reading-based writing. In this course you will read more closely and critically than you would in non-academic settings, and call upon your judgment to inter-pret the methods of a diverse set of rhetors.

The final course in the first-year sequence, **39C, Argument and Research** (Chapter 7), is the most specialized. In it, you will focus on using research to become expert on a unique topic by reading and writing about it throughout the quarter.

Alternatively, you may choose to participate in **FIP**—the **First-Year Integrated Program**—reading and writing about topics within a specific discipline or disci-plines (Chapter 8). Students who complete the FIP sequence receive credit for 39C, but must still take 39B.

As you move from course to course, we will try to help you understand how concepts and practices you worked with in the previous course will assist you in the next one. And your instructors will also try to help you keep in mind the next stages in your university writing development: writing in other disciplines and upper-division writing for your major.

Some tasks are repeated from course to course to help you build competence. For example, you will be asked in each course to **summarize** something you have read. To be able to recount the essential points of a reading selection in your own words is a writing task you will be required to perform in every major and beyond the university in workplace writing.

Another activity you will perform repeatedly, but in different contexts and for different purposes, is **analysis**. This is a frequently used, all-purpose category of writing and thinking. Analysis means to take something apart and examine each part, as well as how the parts relate to each other to make it work (or not). When you are given a writing assignment that asks for analysis, read carefully for more specific instructions about what type of analysis is necessary. You should be ready to encounter these tasks again and again in your course of study and beyond; the challenge will be to determine how to use your previous experiences with these modes of thinking and writing while adapting them to new circumstances, new subject matter and new disciplinary expectations. For more on different ways to develop your writing, see Chapter 4.

Assignments in the first-year writing sequence will help you to isolate and practice different modes of thinking and writing, as well as combine them, as most people must repeatedly do in academic, public, and professional communication. You will benefit from discovering where and how various ways of thinking come into play in academic, public, and professional writing, and you'll gain more confidence in employing them for your own purposes.

1.4.1 Tech Literacy

Something you'll encounter in every first-year writing class is the use of technology in both reading and writing. You've grown up part of a generation who has always had technology as part of your life—you probably don't even remember a time when there weren't computers in every home. Since our purpose in these classes is to teach you how to think rhetorically when reading and composing texts of all kinds, you will also encounter technologically-based texts, sometimes called "emerging genres," like blogs, forums, and wikis.

In all the 39 series courses, you'll be introduced to an online writing environment called "The Writing Studio." The studio, although housed on servers at Colorado State University (where it was first created by Professor Mike Palmquist), has been co-developed since its early days (in 2005) by faculty from the UCI Composition Program.

Each section of composition has its own unique home at the studio, and each class home is a closed database—only members of the class can see what is posted there. You'll be able to find everything you need for your course at your section's home page: a calendar of assignments, the course syllabus, a description of and rubric for each assignment, materials that will provide tips for your coursework, and files or links to required reading for the course. You'll also be able to upload files to your studio home, create a blog and share it with your classmates, participate in forum discussions by posting entries, and collaborate with your colleagues by producing online texts in the wikis.

1.4.2 Student Learning Outcomes

Learning to write is a complex process, both individual and social, that takes place over time with continued practice and informed guidance. Therefore, it is important to understand that these outcomes cannot be learned in reduced or simple ways. Mastering these outcomes requires you to understand your own composing process and to be aware of your own progress.

As you move beyond first-year composition, your writing abilities will not merely improve. Rather, they'll diversify along disciplinary and professional lines, moving into whole new levels where expected outcomes expand, multiply, and diverge. Please study the learning objectives for all composition courses in the table below; if you have questions about them, ask your instructor. When you have progressed into your upper-division coursework (which will occur sooner than you think!), perhaps you'll take the time to look back at these learning outcomes to reflect on how far you've come.

Student Learning Outcomes By the end of the first year of composition, you should be able to:	
Rhetorical Knowledge	• Focus on a purpose
	• Respond to the needs of different audiences
	• Respond appropriately to different kinds of rhetorical situations
	• Use conventions of format and structure appropriate to the rhetorical situation
	• Adopt appropriate voice, tone, and level of formality
	• Understand how genres shape reading and writing
	• Write in several genres
Composing Processes	• Be aware that it usually takes multiple drafts to create and complete a successful text
	• Develop flexible strategies for generating, revising, editing, and proofreading
	• Understand writing as an open process that permits you to use later invention and re-thinking to revise your work
	• Understand the collaborative and social aspects of writing processes
	• Learn to critique your own and others' works
	• Learn to balance the advantages of relying on others with the responsibility of doing your part
	• Use a variety of technologies to address a range of audiences

(continued)

Critical Thinking, Reading, and Writing	• Use writing and reading for inquiry, learning, thinking, and communicating • Understand a writing assignment as a series of tasks, including finding, evaluating, analyzing, and synthesizing appropriate primary and secondary sources • Integrate your own ideas with those of others • Understand the relationships among language, knowledge, and power
Knowledge of Conventions	• Learn common formats for different kinds of texts • Develop knowledge of genre conventions ranging from structure and paragraphing to tone and mechanics • Practice appropriate means of documenting your work • Control surface features such as syntax, grammar, punctuation, and spelling
Composing in Electronic Environments	• Use electronic environments for drafting, reviewing, revising, editing, and sharing texts • Locate, evaluate, organize, and use research material collected from electronic sources, including scholarly library databases; other official databases (e.g., federal government databases); and informal electronic networks and internet sources • Understand and exploit the differences in the rhetorical strategies available for both print and electronic texts

Chapter 2

METHODS FOR READING

We **live in** a cultural environment where images and messages are constantly present—we might even say that in current American society, we are continuously bombarded with texts that compel us to read them.

Right now you're reading a text, the kind stacked in the bookstore, what teachers mean when they ask you to bring your text to class. Immediately we want to expand our definition of what a *text* is. The term comes from a Latin word, *texere*, "to weave," as in a textile, woven maybe for warmth, maybe for decoration. For any number of reasons, authors compose texts by weaving their instincts, impulses, habits, and desires into a material object. It significantly broadens our definition to think of a text as something—anything—deliberately made by human hands to accomplish a goal. Here are some of the many texts you might read in just one day: nutritional info on the back of your cereal box, an email from your mom about coming home for the weekend, billboard signs as you drive on the highway, visual messages advertising products on TV, text messages from your best friend, a syllabus from your Math professor, rottentomatoes.com film reviews of a movie you might go see this weekend, a *New University* editorial about recycling on campus, instructions on how to use your newest iPhone app, ads flashing on the edges of your Facebook page.

2.1   Paying Attention

Reading is one of your most important communication skills because texts are ubiquitous—they are everywhere around you. Because you are a part of a media-saturated culture, being a careful and efficient reader is essential for success—not only in college, but also throughout life. If we define a text as anything that can be read and/or interpreted, even people are texts; we compose ourselves to others. Ratty or classy, your classmate's shirt sends a message for you to read. When you ask for an extension on an assignment, your professor's facial expression is a composition for you to interpret. That tree you pass as you walk through campus: is that a text? If, like so much in Irvine, it was planned and planted to accomplish a goal (maybe photosynthesis, maybe beauty), then, yes, that tree is a text.

In everyday life, a large part of being a good reader is just **paying attention**—reminding yourself that when you encounter texts (even people), you are responsible to read and interpret. You've probably heard the familiar saying of the ancient Greek philosopher, Socrates: "The unexamined life is not worth living." Your response and responsibility to the texts all around you are part of your life—you can glance at texts and then move on, or you can stop and examine them long enough to understand what it is they are demanding of you.

Developing Reading Methods. In addition to the texts you encounter every day, while at the university (and very likely as part of your profession afterwards) you'll have to learn to become a good reader of specialized, difficult, and formal texts. You'll be asked to read these in order to help you gain the knowledge you need in that particular subject area: textbooks, articles, scholarly books, web sites, and more. For these kinds of discipline-specific texts, you need to do more than just pay attention (although that is essential too). You'll have to **develop an attitude about reading as a process and a practice**, and you'll have to discover and develop what are for you the best methods for reading and understanding demanding texts.

2.2   Critical Thinking and Critical Reading

Definition. The word "critical" has a rather negative connotation. We think of people being critical in the sense of *finding fault* (say, your parents being critical about your taste in clothes or music). But when we use the term "critical" in the context of "critical reading" or "critical thinking," we mean something a bit more like the scientific term "critical mass." The *Sci-Tech Encyclopedia* defines **critical mass** as "the amount of fissile material (uranium-233, uranium-235, or plutonium-239) that supports a self-sustaining nuclear chain reaction." Critical mass is reached when the right components are all in place, and once critical mass is achieved, change (nuclear reaction) will happen.

No, we're not saying that **critical thinking** is like nuclear fission. But we are saying that critical thinking is accomplished when you have amassed enough knowledge about a topic (the components) in order to make an informed interpretation of it or decision about it (the change). For example, you might have gone to see the last *Harry Potter* film because some of your friends said it was good; you watched, you were impressed with some of the special effects, it was a fun way to spend a few hours, and then you pretty much forgot about it. That would not be a "critical reading" of the film. A **critical reading** would mean you not only watched the film but also studied it with an agenda of better understanding the context in which you experienced it, what the text (or author, director) was trying to say, how the message was communicated to viewers, and how it was received/interpreted by its audience (other perspectives besides your own).

[handwritten margin note: something should do more often]

Some Reading Methods You'll Practice. In your composition courses, you'll learn some tried-and-true methods for starting your practice of reading all texts critically: observe the text closely, taking careful notes and making sure not to miss anything (you'll probably have to read/watch/listen more than once); identify what kind of text it is and what conventions it uses; summarize the most important ideas and arguments; choose portions to analyze even more closely; find out more information about who made it, for what purpose, and for what audience; talk about your analysis and interpretation with classmates; write about it, read some peers' ideas about it, and reflect on all the knowledge you have amassed.

After the process of methodical and serious study, you will have reached critical mass: you'll be prepared to make some very informed statements about that text. Critical reading means not just memorizing information and storing it away (and likely forgetting it)—it requires **critical engagement** with the text or topic. If you think this process sounds a little bit like the scientific method, you're right—critical thinking is a scientific activity.

2.3   Where You Stand

In Chapter 1, you learned that UCI's composition courses have been designed to give you the practice you need to develop **rhetorical know-how**. The first step to thinking like a rhetorician is to understand your own situation, even as it applies to texts you read: Why are you reading and what do you hope to gain from

reading? What demands does the text make upon you as a reader and respond-
er? Where you stand within the reading context is your own rhetorical situation.

If you are reading an email from your mom or watching a TV commercial for
the ShamWow, you will surely practice a different set of reading methods than
if you're reading a chapter of your Econ textbook in order to take a test. Or, with
people-texts—you probably don't listen to a story told by your roommate the
same way you listen to a lecture by your favorite professor. This means you're already unconsciously practicing rhetorical reading methods. Now you just need
to become more deliberate—you have to consciously acquire the habit of contextualizing everything you read.

2.4   Where the Text Stands

Once you've consciously thought about why you're reading a text, the next step
for reading rhetorically is to remember that **all texts are situated**. Where the
text stands within history and culture, who constructed it, why, how, and for
whom—this is the text's rhetorical situation.

Reading for Rhetorical Situation

1. What is the rhetor's primary purpose for composing this text? How does he
   hope the audience will react?

2. What is the primary message communicated?

3. Who is the original intended audience? What might be some of the common expectations of this audience?

4. Are there secondary or unintended audiences to consider?

5. What is the historical time period in which the text was composed?

6. What is the cultural background of the rhetor and her initial audience?
   Consider geographic location, gender, ethnicity, shared beliefs, and discourse communities.

7. What have others said or written about this text or its subject?

If you read the text itself with these questions in mind, you'll be able to find
some of the answers. However, you'll have to do a bit of directed research and
reading outside of the text to get fully developed answers about rhetorical situation. The Headnotes assignment in WR 39B is designed to help you practice

research and reading for the text's rhetorical situation. In WR 39C, you'll have ample practice with reading texts rhetorically—when you are researching in order to use sources in your own writing, you must carefully evaluate each source for rhetorical situation to make sure that it's a wise choice to quote in your scholarly essay.

2.5   Identify Medium

Besides studying how texts are situated, the rhetorical reader analyzes how texts are constructed. What form does the message take and how does that form play a part in the rhetorical effect on the audience? The first step in the analysis of how a text creates meaning is to identify the rhetor's method of delivery—medium and genre(s).

Thought. A **medium** is a means of communication, the delivery vehicle for an act of communication. In a way, **thinking** is the foundational medium for all communication—although the communication going on in thinking is between you and yourself, an engagement with language is happening and as a result, meaning is created. Language is inherently social (it was created and exists as a way of communicating between people, members of a society), and so when we think using language, that practice is inherently social.

Audio. Another medium for communicating, the first one you formally learned how to manipulate, is **speaking**. When we speak, we realize that it's a different medium than our internal monologue; note how we often filter things that we say. We don't—or shouldn't!—say everything we think.

Before writing was widely practiced, human societies relied on speaking—these pre-writing cultures are often called "oral cultures." The grand epic poems of early western civilization like *The Tale of Gilgamesh*, *The Iliad* and *The Odyssey*, and *Beowulf* all began as stories told around the fireside, oral performances that were memorized by the speaker for an immediate audience. Eventually, as cultures developed the practice of writing, these poems were written down and passed on as literature.

Although speaking has never gone out of style, technology has enabled us to expand orality as a medium for mass communication. Before the days of television, families used to huddle around their radios to listen to radio plays and serials like *The Phantom*, or listen to the latest news reports from around the world. Radio broadcasts, podcasts, spoken word, audio books, and music are all types of current texts in the **audio** (aural) medium.

Writing is the next communicative medium that you learned about, probably around the time you started school. Writing is a medium that has allowed humanity to achieve our greatest accomplishments; without writing, we would not have our current disciplines of mathematics, science, technology, or literature. Written text, since it can be archived (unlike the transitory nature of thinking and speaking) is a much more formalized and stylized medium, including vastly different genres, all with their own specific conventions.

Visual. You know the old saying "a picture is worth a thousand words." Cliché that may be, but before alphabets, people who had sticks of charcoal found a nice flat cave wall to record the story of The Great (or not so great) Mammoth Hunt. Then when alphabets did develop, some of the earliest ones were like pictures—hieroglyphs. Chinese characters, still highly suggestive of images, are evolved from early hieroglyphs; this illustrates how writing is technically a subset of the **visual** medium.

As technology developed (from cave walls to parchment, then paper, paint, ink, cameras, film, digital) so too did our types of visual communication. Still photography, maps, paintings, drawings, sculptures, and textile arts such as tapestries are all examples of visual texts that can be read critically and rhetorically.

Mixed Media. Combining more than one medium in order to communicate is nothing new: Romans drew obscene words and pictures on the city walls, Medieval monks illuminated their manuscripts, and Hollywood figured out how to add sound to silent film. When texts use more than one medium to communicate, we call them **multi-modal.** Today we're accustomed to having several media combined in one communication: film and television, music videos, graphic novels, animation, video games, and web sites are all multi-modal. Conversations between you and a friend are also multi-modal: you use your friend's facial expressions and body language to help interpret the meaning of what is spoken.

2.6   Identify Genre

Once you've determined the medium for an act of communication, the next step is to identify genre. Broadly defined, a **genre** is a category. Genre is a way to categorize a text through its form (format, structure, style) and content (its subject matter). In order to be able to critically read and analyze a text, it is vital that you be able to categorize it by genre—just like if you want to be a biologist, it's crucial for you to know what differentiates a mammal from a fish.

Once you know the genre of a text, you will also be able to make some predictions about what to expect from it, because texts from the same genre (category) will generally have many of the same features (conventions—more on those in the next section). Because you've been reading texts since you were a young child, you've already accumulated quite a bit of knowledge about genres, but you might have never thought about them so specifically. For example, if you are watching a TV crime drama (like *CSI*), you expect that by the end of the episode, they'll probably solve the case (unless it's a "To Be Continued..." show). Or, if you're listening to KROQ on the radio, you expect to hear music, specifically alternative rock. Should you hear jazz, or worse, a detailed report on the Dow Jones Industrial Average, you would feel betrayed.

Form Specific. Texts within the same genre always have some elements of form, structure, and style that are the same. Poems are usually written in lines and stanzas, and poems look different in formatting than prose. Novels usually have narrators and are divided in chapters or sections. A song usually has a chorus. Plays have Acts, and screenplays use capital letters to designate a character name. An essay always has an introduction, body of discussion, and conclusion. A film usually starts with titles and credits. When you first play a video game, the early levels are usually easier, meant to train you. These are all conventions of form that are specific to a genre.

Content Specific. Some genres are identifiable by their content. For example, there are several genres of film that you're probably familiar with: action adventure, romance, comedy, horror, science fiction, fantasy, thriller, mystery, etc. You'll also find many of these same genres in fiction—although because a written text (novel) and a multi-modal text (film) are different media, some elements might be different, too. Or maybe you're more familiar with content-specific genres in music (you probably have genre categories on your MP3 player)—rap, blues, R&B, rock, alternative, country, pop, etc.

Audience Specific. Some genres are pleasurable or appropriate to a particular audience. The audience might be drawn to the themes or style of a certain genre, or consider it appropriate to certain ages or genders in society (a "chick flick," for instance). For whatever reason, the genre audience knows what to expect from texts in this genre—and this enables them to take particular pleasures in the text, those of recognition, repetition, and of predicted resolution. Pleasure may also be drawn from differences. Some audience members might identify with the characters, themes, or styles in generic texts and may shape their own identity in response; for example, think about the different modes of dress that go along with different musical genres: emo, metal, or country.

Sometimes genres are born out of the necessity for communication within a specific community. For example, the essay, a "short nonfiction literary composition," is a written genre that first appeared in 1597 in the work of Francis Bacon (who was probably imitating Montaigne, a French Renaissance scholar). The **academic essay** has its own particular conventions for form and content because it is written specifically for an academic (scholarly) audience.

Moreover, different academic disciplines favor different conventions of form, structure and content in their disciplinary academic writing practices. This is an extension of the idea that genres are often audience-specific—the audiences in this case are the members of the different academic disciplines. In your composition courses, part of UCI's general education requirements, you'll learn some of the most prominent features of general academic writing. As you progress into your upper-division courses and take your required "W" course, you'll begin to learn more about the particular conventions of your chosen discipline.

Although you need to distinguish between form-, content-, and audience-driven genres, you should also remember that these categories can overlap—they are leaky containers. For example, although a romance film is a distinguishable genre of the film medium because of its content (narrating the story of lovers), it is also worth noting that the romance film will inevitably draw a particular type of viewer: someone who enjoys the content of romance films. Sometimes, genres begin in one medium and are then adapted into another medium; for example, the epic genre began as oral poetry—but now you can also find epic novels, films, and even TV mini-series (in each incarnation, the genres will have some overlap in how they're defined, but there may be significant differences, too). The overlap and leakiness is ultimately a good thing—if you are asked to critically read a text, one thing you can always do is look for the ways that the text is and is not fulfilling the definitions for its genre. The practice of thinking about texts according to genre even has a name: "genre theory."

Thinking about texts according to genre

2.7   Understanding Conventions

Elements included in a particular medium or genre, including form and content, generally adhere to a certain set of **conventions** aimed at the expectations of a particular audience. Those who regularly read, watch or listen to a certain medium/genre come to expect certain elements, techniques or devices as "conventional." For example, if you have ever watched the popular TV show *24* (medium: television, genres: drama, action) you know that each episode tells the story of one hour in a day, and you expect to see the minutes of that hour counting down between segments, decreasing numbers against a black screen. Or, if you're used to watching "scary movies"(medium: film, genre: horror), you know that at the end, the monster may be defeated, but it will probably come back again—it's a convention of modern horror films that evil is never really defeated.

conventions make film predictable

Conventions are also often attached to the form and content of a particular medium. For example, you've watched enough television to know that during prime time (8–11 PM), networks usually format programming into 30 minute and 60 minute shows. Additionally, the content of programs during the day is quite different from what's offered in the evening. These are both conventions of the television medium.

Knowing (or finding out) the expected conventions of genre and medium is part of gaining critical awareness about how a text constructs meaning, and a crucial first step for creating an informed interpretation of the text's message(s). For example, if you were asked to evaluate an academic essay and you responded by criticizing it for using lots of complicated words and being overly structured in its approach, you'd look pretty silly to someone who knows that formalized, discipline-specific word choice and clearly logical organizational devices are conventions used in almost all academic essays. In other words, your interpretation would be misinformed and thus, rejected by your audience.

Conventions are rhetorical devices: a rhetor uses the expected conventions of an audience precisely because they are expected. By providing what is familiar, the rhetor creates a connection with his readers. When an audience knows what to

expect and then the expectation is fulfilled, they feel confident that they understand and want to keep reading. This engagement between rhetor and audience
within the text is the goal of all communication.

Critical Reading: A Rhetorical Methodology

1. Identify your rhetorical situation for reading. Why are you reading this text, what do you expect from it, and how will your own bias color your reading?

2. Identify the rhetorical situation of the text. Where does it stand within history and culture? Who constructed it, why, and for whom?

3. As part of understanding the text's construction, identify the medium (media) by which the text is communicated; how are the medium, rhetorical situation, and message related?

4. Identify the genre(s) in which the text has been composed; what conventions of form and content are expected of texts in this genre?

5. How does the text follow, play with, or reject these conventions?

The Next Step: Analyzing the text—for more, see Chapters 4 (on analysis), 6 (on rhetorical analysis), and 7 (on historical analysis)

Postmodern art and literature will often play with an audience's conventional expectations. A novelist might begin with a narrator who seems reliable and accurate, but later reveal additional information that proves the narrator unreliable and inconstant. This gesture doesn't lose the connection established by the familiar conventions—to understand the "play" involved, the audience has to understand the conventions in the first place. In other words, you have to know the rules before you can break them (or, you have to know the rules before you can enjoy reading a text in which someone else is breaking them).

The Next Step. After you've identified and understood how the text is situated and the basic category in which it was constructed, you're ready to dive in for a really close reading. In this part of the process, you should read the text closely, not only to understand its message (what it means), but also to understand how that message is constructed and how it elicits audience response (how it means). You'll want to identify specific devices or strategies within the text that create a connection with the audience and convince the audience to feel, think, act or respond in a certain way. This close, critical, rhetorical reading is what you'll be learning to do in WR 39B.

A Note on the Rest of this Chapter. The remainder of this chapter will discuss some of the media, genres, and conventions you'll encounter every day and in the 39 series of courses. These sections are arranged according to medium: audio, written, visual, multi-modal. You probably won't be asked to read the following sections all at once, but rather, consult them as starting places when you are assigned to read or compose a text in a particular medium and genre. The catalogs that follow are not exhaustive. Not every medium will be mentioned, not every genre, and nowhere near every associated convention. When you need to know more about any one medium or genre, you'll have to search for more information (ask your instructor, a librarian, or Google).

Nor are the categories absolute. When you read a text critically, analyze the ways it repeats and transgresses the conventions of a medium or genre. When a text follows generic conventions purely, ask how the author uses that genre to accomplish his or her goal. When a generic text swerves from convention, ask why the author uses difference to control the meaning of a text and the response of an audience. It is always interesting, finally, when a genre associated with one medium appears in a different medium: do the conventions of the genre survive this innovation? Not all texts fit neatly into categories constructed by critics or academics, nor should you expect them to.

2.8   Methods for Reading Audio Texts

What we *listen* to can be read rhetorically, but you'll need to give your full attention to listening. In other words, you have to engage an audio text with careful, open-minded listening. Popular audio genres today include radio broadcasts, podcasts, spoken texts, stand-up comedy, and music.

2.8.1   Speeches

Similar to writers, speakers make rhetorical choices about their subject, audience, point-of-view, purpose, and message. Speeches and addresses are written texts as well as auditory, since a speaker typically prepares her speech as a written text. The script and the actual performance are two different texts—same message, different media (writing/speaking).

In all acts of oral communication, various uses of the voice—pace, pitch, intonation, volume, stress or emphasis, pause, and rhythm—cue the listener and contribute to an engagement between audience and speaker. If you are present at a speech or at a comedy club, the rhetor's use of body language is also central to your understanding of the communication. Nonverbal language includes the use of gesture, facial expressions, stance, eye contact, and movement. Use of visual aids or props also figures into how we interpret what we hear in a speech.

The beginning of the speech, or hook, must engage the audience's interest and attention. Typically, a speaker begins by trying to establish common ground between himself and his audience. Speeches and addresses are clearly organized with lots of verbal signpost transitions so that the audience can follow along easily. The main points of a formal speech are often emphasized by the use of compelling examples and anecdotes.

Speechwriters use concrete language, parallel sentence constructions, and repetition of important words and phrases as a way to communicate abstract ideas. At the end of a speech or address, the orator usually leaves the audience with something to remember, think about, or do.

2.8.2   Radio

Similar to television, radio broadcasts operate at both local and national levels. Radio stations have specialized genres such as music, talk shows, sports events, public affairs, and news.

A primary function of the reporter in radio news or the Disk Jockey (DJ) on a music station is to guide the listener, to ensure that the listener knows what he is listening to—much like the narrator in a novel. In music programming, DJs often become "air personalities" and their popularity is tied to how well they connect with their specific audience. Likewise, radio news reporters may be known for the way they deliver their newscasts—this is part of their ethos.

2.8.3   Podcasts

This emerging genre uses audio over the internet to provide radio-style talk and music, but podcasts are more distinctive, specialized, and personal than radio. Annalee Newitz, writing for Wired.com, says podcasting "promises a future where anyone can make radio, instead of just listen to it." Podcasts consist of digital audio (or video) files, which are available as MP3 downloads via web syndication, and can be distributed worldwide.

The variety of topics covered in podcasts is enormous—in fact, there are no restrictions on topic or purpose. There are, however, a few basic conventions. First, the podcaster might create a written outline of what he or she plans to record. Some might even write word-for-word scripts. In most podcasts, the podcaster introduces or prefaces the material, and he or she may periodically provide commentary in order to keep listeners engaged. Podcasters might record once, or they might edit the sound clips in post-production. Podcasters share specific audio content with a focused audience (listeners must subscribe to the podcast in order to hear it); that means they must think carefully about their rhetorical situation and audience expectations.

2.8.4 Stand-Up Comedy

Comedians directly address audiences in a monologue by telling jokes and amusing anecdotes. Their monologues are scripted and memorized for performance. Comedians, as a part of their routines, develop particular comedic voices and personalities. For example, they may tell jokes in character. During the course of the monologue, stand-up comedians have to handle hecklers, and adjust their routine to specific audiences.

Many comedians have a catch phrase that becomes their trademark. Timing is critical to the performance of stand-up comedy, and a comic pauses to enhance the timing of a joke. Comedians will also frequently banter with the audience. Sometimes comedians will verbally attack or insult hecklers.

Most jokes have a setup and a punch line. There are a several kinds of jokes or gags: ad-lib, improvisation, one-liners, callbacks, inside jokes, running gags, sight gags, topical jokes, and closing lines. Ad-lib and improvisation are similar in that the joke or bit is made up within a scripted monologue. One-liners are just that—one or two sentence jokes. Callbacks refer to jokes previously told during the monologue, but are told in a different context. Inside jokes are aimed at select group of people. Running gags are jokes that keep recurring and sight gags are jokes based on props. The closing line is the final joke of the monologue, and the comedian usually expects to get the biggest laugh with this gag.

Jon Stewart, who hosts *The Daily Show with Jon Stewart*, is a master at topical jokes, which are jokes based on current events. Stewart pokes fun at politicians and government officials and the news events they participate in at a national level.

2.8.5 Music

Classifying music into genres is often seen as controversial and problematic because music genres are complex and in flux. Some musicians consider generic classification to be arbitrary and reductive. None of us listens (reads) every kind of music in the same way—we each possess different grammars and lexicons. Perhaps more than with any other medium, our personal tastes are dictated by our nostalgia. A piece of music, like a smell, often unconsciously stimulates memories and emotions in ways that books and films do not. These reactions are usually deeply subjective, which exacerbates the difficulty of reading music rhetorically. For this reason, it is often valuable to analyze music comparatively. Try to focus on tangible aspects of the aural experience, instead of ambiguous adjectival descriptions like "soulful," "inspired," or "hard."

Why, specifically, are songs by Shania Twain, Johnny Cash, and Garth Brooks all called "country"? What qualities and conventions do they share? In addition to lyrics, pay attention to tempo and texture. What is the instrumentation of the ensemble? Which "voices" are melodic (dominant) and harmonic (supporting)?

Some genres, like reggae or salsa, are defined by the rhythms they employ. How are these rhythms achieved? Are they syncopated, swung, or straight-ahead? Who is responsible for maintaining this rhythm? Is it the bass, percussion, guitar, or some combination?

What is the form of the composition? Technical terms like "blues," "ballad," or "fugue" refer to actual characteristics of a song's construction. Also, is there a chorus, a refrain, or a cadenza? The better you can imagine the music as it would be written on a page, the more accurately you can correlate it to other pieces with which it shares conventions and therefore make an argument about its genre.

2.9   Methods for Reading Written Texts

You've been reading words on pages for most of your life, and you probably think you're pretty good at it. But the way you've been taught to read in English classes has been literary, with a focus on the language of a text and what it says. Reading rhetorically changes the focus of our reading from **what** a text means to **how** a text creates that meaning.

2.9.1   Poetic

A. Poetry

Beyond our expectation that a poem will impress us with its use of language, when we read poetry we expect conventions of form such as the physical appearance of line breaks (unlike prose, which is written in sentences clear across the page to the margin). This is not to say that the lines of poetry do not accumulate into sentences—they frequently do. And those lines may be arranged into stanzas, a common organizational structure in poems. In fact, a coherent, unified structure (e.g., repetitive, narrative, or logical structure) is another basic convention of poetry.

When reading poems, we also expect some significant theme or content to be conveyed. Edgar Allen Poe once defined poetry as "the rhythmical creation of beauty in words." We've all read love poems at one time or another such as Shakespeare's Sonnet 18 or the deeply passionate poetry of Emily Dickinson. Most poems are meant to give us the experience, to show (not tell) through the use of devices such as imagery, figurative language, and the musical qualities of language.

When reading poetry, you'll want to think about which sub-genre the poem belongs to: is it a song-like poem written in the first person? Then, it's a lyric poem. Does the poem tell a story? Then, it's a narrative poem. Or is the poem written in third person from the point-of-view of a character or persona? Then, it's a dramatic monologue. Long narrative poems, like *Beowulf*, are often epics in which a heroic figure is placed within a historical event, usually war, and the hero must complete a quest or some other mythic or legendary achievement that is central to the traditions and beliefs of his culture.

While these sub-genres are a convenient way to categorize poetry, poems do cross genres—that is, a poem may be lyrical in language, but also tell a story. An example of a cross-genre is prose poetry, which is a poem that exhibits the basic conventions of poetry—musicality in language and a significant message within a unified, coherent structure; however, the poem is not written in lines, but as prose. Once you've determined where the poem may be categorized in terms of sub-genre, you'll be able to examine the poem more thoroughly for how well it meets the conventions of that sub-genre.

An additional approach to reading poetry is to read the poem for stylistic elements, and then evaluate these elements in light of the rhetorical situation. A poet's style includes his or her use of vocabulary, sentence structure, figures of speech, allusions, tone, voice, point-of-view, and structure.

Poetry, although written, is also an oral art, written words meant to be spoken (or sung). So a poet's style will often include her unique use of sound devices—rhymes, alliteration, consonance, assonance, and repetition. Read the poem aloud, and listen for the musical effect of language—poets use sound and rhythm as techniques to create a more visceral experience in the reader.

B. Music Lyrics

When we sing along to songs, we're not only enjoying the work of the musicians, but also the work of the songwriter or song lyricist. We appreciate poetry and song lyrics for their artistic merit because constructing this kind of text takes skill, craft, and inspiration.

Both poetry and song lyrics use sound devices rhetorically: end-rhymes, internal rhymes, and near rhymes. Both also use imagery, allusions, figures of speech, and narratives to create an emotional response in their audiences. Song lyrics differ from poetry in that they are sung by a human voice or voices and integrated with music (though some lyrics can stand on their own as poetry). The words attach to a melody for easy remembering by the listener. Poems are written on the page, and the music of poems, while achieved through language similar to song lyrics, doesn't have the added effect of musical instrumentation. And poems tend to be more complex in form and content than song lyrics.

The conventions of song lyrics, in part, depend upon the genre of music: pop songs, country, rock, R&B/soul, hip hop, rap, and heavy metal, etc. All appeal to different audiences, and the lyrics associated with those genres use language and content differently to convey the message.

Frequently music fans ask artists: which came first, the music or the lyrics? So, think about the rhetor—in songwriting, the song lyricist is not always a member of the band or the entertainer who sings the song. Yet, when the song is performed, the band/entertainer is the rhetor since the performance of the song is also an act of communication.

Reading Song Lyrics

1. Listen to the song with the written lyrics in front of you so that you can take note of how the melodies work with the chorus, verse, and bridge. Note which order these three structural elements appear in the song.

2. Find the verses and the chorus. The verse usually begins the song and provides listeners with information about the situation, emotions, or people in the song. The chorus is that catchy melody you'll hear three or four or more times during the song. Many songs have a bridge: a transitional melody between the verses and chorus. One popular song structure is as follows: verse / verse / bridge / chorus / verse / bridge / chorus.

3. Read the lyrics as if they are a poem. Notice how rhyme and repetition are used to create rhythm without the music. Is there a clear narrative? Do the images link together to form a story? Or do the lyrics primarily convey an emotional theme? To further your understanding, look into the background of the rhetor or songwriter—this will often shed important light on things you might miss on first reading.

4. Now listen to the song again, paying close attention to the instrumentation. How does the repetition, variation, and rhythm of the melody emphasize/de-emphasize the lyrics? What instruments are being played? Which instrument(s) make the most prominent or striking sounds? How does this sound work in conjunction with the words of the song? What happens at the hook? How do the dynamics of how each section is played (the intensity or lack thereof) influence your emotional response?

2.9.2 Fiction

Works of fiction are works of the imagination—although most writers draw from their own real-life experiences, fiction texts are presented as having no resemblance to real characters or events. Novels, novellas (a short novel), and short stories are all recognizable sub-genres of fiction that you might study in your composition courses. Some basic conventions used in fiction are a narrator, plot, complication, resolution, climax, character, exposition, setting and atmosphere, point-of-view, and structure.

A. Novels

These longer narratives can be divided into content-specific sub-genres such as romance, western, science fiction, fantasy, true crime, mystery, magical realism, horror, gothic, young adult, adventure, historical, and the epistolary novel. Novels have also changed over the years since they first appeared in the late 1600s or early 1700s (there is debate about which text could be called the first novel), so you could divide them into sub-genres depending on historical and cultural environment.

Each sub-genre carries with it a set of conventions expected by readers (although many of the sub-genres can overlap, as well). For example, the Romance Writers of America contend that romance novels follow two basic conventions: a central love story and an emotionally satisfying and optimistic ending. Mystery novels challenge readers to solve the crime or puzzling event before the detective explains it at the end. According to the Horror Writers Association, horror fiction might deal with the mundane or the supernatural, but as long as it elicits fear or dread in the reader, it's considered horror.

Even within a specific sub-genre, the definition of conventions may vary by author. For example, take two famous science fiction authors: Isaac Asimov and Ray Bradbury. Asimov defines science fiction as "that branch of literature which is concerned with the impact of scientific advance upon human beings," while Bradbury's definition is the "sociological studies of the future, things that the writer believes are going to happen by putting two and two together."

Once you've established how a novel is situated (its historical and cultural context, the author, audience, genre and conventions), concentrate on how it constructs meaning, and how it appeals to the reader to understand and accept that meaning. Novels will not have explicit thesis statements, but they do have themes. When you're trying to identify theme, ask yourself "what did I learn from this story?" or "what's the story about?" Often you'll find more than one answer to the question. To read rhetorically, you need to think about not only what it means, but *how* a text gets its theme across to the audience.

Let's take a look at Mary Shelley's *Frankenstein*. Some people classify it as a horror novel (because, of course, there is a monster who skulks around killing people). Others call it science fiction (because Victor uses science to create his monster). If we choose to read the novel as sci-fi, then we might say that a dominant theme is a warning about the terrible consequences when scientists try to play God and transgress against nature. But if we read the novel as horror, we might focus instead on the techniques Shelley uses to frighten or unsettle her readers, or how she uses the juxtaposition of the monster and Victor to make us question what constitutes monstrosity.

A rhetorically situated reading might also consider how the novel's historical context affects the way themes play out in the narrative, or how your interpretation as a modern reader might differ from Shelley's original early-nineteenth-century readers. We might also look at the kinds of imagery Shelly uses to describe nature, her characterization of Victor and the monster, or the way in which she describes the creation of the monster, in order to talk about how Shelley creates meaning. Figuring out *how* a text works, in addition to *what* it means, is reading rhetorically.

Reading Fiction

1. Identify the themes at work in the novel or story. Ask yourself: what was this story about? What did I learn from this story? Make a list.

2. What is the genre? Is there more than one genre? In what ways does the story or novel fulfill genre conventions? In what ways does it subvert or change them?

3. Are there any recurring literary or rhetorical techniques (images, metaphors, juxtaposition, irony, etc) in the narrative? How do those devices work in relation to the theme(s)?

4. Who was the original audience? What did they expect?

5. Did the main character undergo a transformation? What was lost or gained by this change? If none occurred, what else was lost or gained from the story that affects the character? What was the rhetor's intention in letting readers see this transformation or lack thereof?

B. Short Stories

Although the short story shares many of the novel's conventions, it is necessarily simpler in structure and, as the name indicates, shorter in length. A short story will usually deal with one theme, one character (or only a few), and one situation or issue, rather than the multiple themes and sub-plots possible in a novel. Short stories are usually episodic (like episodes of a TV show), and it is clear that the characters' lives continue outside of the story's narrative.

Short stories are not simpler (read: easier, less rhetorically sophisticated) than other types of fiction. Sometimes quite the opposite! A short story that focuses on a single event can become a metaphor for the much larger issue. So for instance, a short story like Neil Gaiman's "Changes," about a doctor who invents the cure for cancer, becomes a metaphor and a commentary on how our society interacts with scientific progress. Jack London's "To Build A Fire" becomes both the story of one man's attempt to survive in the Arctic and a critique of how humans approach nature and the wilderness.

When you read a short story, ask yourself the same sorts of questions that you do with a novel. You'll probably have to research and read other sources besides the story itself to get full answers. What is this story about? Who was the original audience? How does the author get her meaning across to the audience? Why, for instance, does Jack London choose not to name the characters in "To Build A Fire"? What themes did London generally write about? Why would London's early 20th century audience have been interested in the story of a man versus wilderness? How does the story defy or subvert the audience's expectations of how a story should end? The answers to both *what* a story does, and *how* it works, will help you with rhetorical analysis.

2.9.3   Nonfiction

Nonfiction is prose other than fiction—quite a large genre, with several sub-genres. However, don't confuse nonfiction with truth (and fiction with the false): in letters, diaries, journals, blog entries, and to a certain extent memoir and autobiography, the rhetor's intention is often to reveal feelings or thoughts, sometimes without much regard to objectivity or truth.

A. Letters

Letters may be composed as informal communication between friends and relatives or as formal communication, such as an introduction to an résumé or a letter of complaint about a service or product. You are probably already familiar with the conventions of letters: the letter format with an address and signature, how the level of formality in language differs based on audience, and the order of the information (introduction, body, and closing). For example, a business letter is typically written in formal and concise language and formatted in a block style with a heading, date, inside address, salutation, body, closing, and if necessary, notations. However, a letter to Grandma usually just begins "Dear Grandma." The top address is usually ignored unless there is pre-printed stationery involved.

B. Journals and Diaries

These genres are both usually self-expressive types of nonfiction in which the writer records daily events, thoughts, and feelings to be read only by the writer herself. However, sometimes more formal records such as business ledgers can also be considered diaries because they provide a day-to-day archive of information. **Field Notes** are a specific type of diary or journal that is usually connected to scientific observation.

C. Blogs

Blogs, or "web-logs," were made possible by the development of the internet—this is an "emerging genre" that although based on the older genres like diaries and journals, takes on new practices and conventions because of the internet medium. Despite their original purpose, blogs began in relative isolation. You could sign up for an account with a service like Blogger and host your blog on their site or your own, but the interface wasn't much different than your average text-based web page. Later on, blog software added comments features, and blog communities like Live Journal appeared, where users could easily link to each other's blogs, comment, and join blog communities.

Many blogs now are organized not around a single user, but around topics like politics, feminism, motherhood, military service, or technology. A group of writers will generate content, and the blog's readership will argue, discuss, and otherwise carry on the conversation in the comments section of each post. The Huffington Post, Obsidian Wings, and RedState are examples of collective blogs.

Because blogs can be personal or public, audience consideration will have something to do with the form and content of the text itself. For instance, a public blogger might incorporate a provocative headline to attract readers. The blog itself may be written in shorter paragraphs since reading digital text is easier to comprehend in smaller chunks. Key points in the blog may be highlighted for quicker access (and tagged as keywords for search engines), and hyperlinks are usually provided for background source material. Also, making use of the multimodal nature of the internet, blogs often contain images, graphics, and sound files, too.

D. Memoir and Autobiography

A **memoir** focuses on a brief period of time or a series of related events, whereas **autobiography** spans a lifetime. Both can also be described as part travelogue, essay, journal and diary. As a convention, memoir and autobiography tell stories that are crafted using literary techniques and devices, but usually sound like the writer is speaking. Written in first person, the writer is the protagonist of his/her own memoir or autobiography. The events of the writer's life are reconstructed, and especially in memoir, the writer contemplates the meaning of the events in retrospect. Like any good story, memoir and autobiography will have an underlying theme woven throughout text. Sometimes the writing of a memoir can be a therapeutic experience for the writer, especially when the memoir is about a highly emotional crisis or survival against all odds. When rhetorically reading memoirs and autobiography, try to distinguish between the two.

Memoir and autobiography writers often use literary techniques—plot, characterization, dialogue, setting, etc. Some literary techniques, for example, anecdotes, dialogue or imagery, can be read rhetorically and evaluated based on how well these techniques emotionally affect a rhetor's audience by tapping into their common needs, values, and beliefs.

E. Journalism

Although journalism began as a "periodic" genre designed to report on current events and issues in daily, weekly, and monthly print formats, the electronic age has ushered in an even more immediate, less regionally connected form of journalism—one that has fostered greater speed and flexibility in the production and delivery of the text to an ever more technologically sophisticated audience. Nevertheless, whether it is published online or in traditional newspapers, journalism is still divided by those who produce it into *three* main classes—news, features, and opinions—with important rhetorical distinctions that determine the form and function of each.

News stories are generally straightforward, timely reports of what happened—plane crashes, election results, basketball game outcomes, box office totals for a movie release, summaries of newly released census data, economic indicators, or health statistics. They are usually written in the third person, objective point-of-view. They are intended to inform and are expected to present concrete and specific details that are neutral in diction and tone. News articles are commonly structured in an inverted pyramid: the most important material is placed at the beginning of the article, which allows readers to quickly learn what they want to know about a news event, and it allows editors to cut the least important information if they are pressed for space.

Feature stories attempt to provide additional behind-the-scenes or "follow-up" information, often with a "human interest" angle, about the people, places, and events making the news. The language of feature articles tends to be more descriptive, even figurative. One organizational structure common to feature articles is chronological or narrative. Similar to fictional stories, features that are narrative include scenes, anecdotes, characters (real people) and dialogue to build toward a climax. Also like fictional stories, these types of features, which are often called "human interest stories," tend to use more descriptive, or figurative language, and they can be written in either the third or first person point-of-view.

Another type of journalistic structure is the hourglass, which combines elements from the inverted pyramid and the narrative structures and is often used for an in-depth follow-up of a news event. In the hourglass, the most important material is placed at the beginning, followed by a transition, and a chronological retelling of the events. Investigative news stories like those that revealed the cover up behind the Watergate break-in use the hourglass structure. Features that examine what led up to the arrest or trial of a notorious murder suspect, or the mysterious—for example, the disappearance of a popular young outdoorsman—also may be written in the hourglass structure. Like the hybrids that they are, the language and point-of-view can be either more or less objective or descriptive than straight news or features, and they can be written in either third or first person.

Opinion pieces offer a critical analysis of or comment on a newsworthy event or issue, or advocate for or against a news-related policy or position. Most opinion pieces tend to be short, and structured along the lines of persuasive essay with an introduction, several body paragraphs that develop an argument using supporting evidence, and a conclusion. Opinion pieces vary in tone, point-of-view, and diction, depending on the type.

For instance, **editorials** are unsigned institutional opinions; they are constructed in the first person plural point-of-view known as the "editorial we" because they are written by a committee, or Editorial Board, and generally reflect the views of the publisher or corporate owner. Editorials can take strong positions on public policy issues, controversial social trends, and legislative and regulatory initiatives, going so far as to make voter recommendations in upcoming elections. They can also comment, sometimes humorously, on the less serious actions of public figure or the odd cultural anomaly. Whatever the topic, however, the diction tends to be measured, rather than impassioned. Authoritative, but seldom dogmatic.

A **column**, on the other hand, is written under the byline of a staff writer, regular contributor, or guest columnist. It is always written in the first person and reflects only the views of the writer, and not the publication at large. In fact, **Op-Ed** columns in traditional newspapers appear opposite the editorial page and often represent political or cultural views that are in direct opposition to those reflected by publication's Editorial Board. Depending on the style and intent of the individual columnist, the diction may be colloquial or erudite, and the tone may be straightforward or sarcastic or anything in between.

Understanding the purpose of a particular class of journalism (whether it's intended primarily to inform, entertain, or persuade) can help you read the text more rhetorically. It can also help you recognize the conventions of each of the various categories of journalism, which can make you more aware of not only what is being said, but how it's been said and why. These are key considerations that can help you critically evaluate the news sources you may turn to for background information on the complex current events and the opinions that form around them, as part of the research you will do in 39C.

Remember the miraculous crash-landing of a passenger jet on the Hudson River? As soon as the plane went down, general or breaking news articles reported what happened, and where, when, why, and who was affected—what journalists refer to as the Five W's.

Almost immediately afterward, feature articles began to embellish the basic, but still fact-based narrative. Stories on the heroic pilot—his training, his personal life, recollections of friends and colleagues—were written to put a human face on the near tragedy. Additional information was provided through backgrounders on related issues such other recent crashes and near crashes involving flocks of birds or water landings, the safety record of the airline involved, and the sorts of equipment and expertise that goes into the investigation of an airline crash.

Finally, opinion began to emerge in news analyses, editorials and columns—commenting on what went wrong to cause the crash (or what went right, in this case, to avert a disaster), praising the training of the pilot, and even calling for stricter regulations for airlines that operate in migratory bird flyways—in response to the facts surrounding the crash and its aftermath.

Of course, even within these general classes, stories may be further divided by purpose and subject and placed within another set of subdivisions that includes sports, business, arts and entertainment, and lifestyle, in addition to general news.

Like all genres in all mediums, there is some overlap in categories and classes. A report on the box-office failure of a film biopic about a popular sports figure, for example, might fall under either business, entertainment, or even sports news, depending on its emphasis, while an interview with the movie's star would likely be categorized as an entertainment feature, unless the interview focuses on the star's misguided decision to personally finance the film, which could put it in the business section.

Similarly, a story that covers the viral spread of a pirated copy of the film could be considered a news or feature story and might land in the entertainment, business, or technology section of a newspaper. On the other hand, a review of the film is considered an opinion piece and is published under the entertainment banner.

In addition to purpose and subject matter, journalism texts are further situated by publication cycles and audience expectations. *The Town Crier*, a tiny weekly newspaper with a regional readership, may focus its news coverage of an outbreak of Swine Flu on reports of area school closures and confirmed cases among local residents over the previous week, while *The New York Times*, a large general circulation daily newspaper, may take a broader, but more time-sensitive look at the social, political, and economic impact of the current pandemic on the local, national and international stage.

Ultimately, where a particular piece of journalism is situated along the rhetorical continuum can be as fluid as it purports to be.

UC Irvine's Literary Journalism program defines the term **literary journalism** as "nonfiction prose that has transcended the limits of daily journalism. This is prose that has evolved into a distinct branch of literature, prose that adopts the aims and techniques of the finest fiction." Literary journalism is also called creative nonfiction or narrative nonfiction. Although it's a form based in fact and accuracy, this genre is usually written with candor and in an intimate voice. As a hybrid genre, it crosses and blurs the boundaries separating fiction, journalism, memoir, history, and autobiography. Similar to novels and short stories, the thesis or message in a literary journalistic essay is more often implied than explicit. For instance, an author may develop a thesis over the course of an entire essay, rather than succinctly stating it in the introductory paragraph.

F. Magazines

Also called **periodicals** because they are published at regular intervals, magazines are divided into audience and content specific sub-genres: scholarly journals, public affairs magazines, trade magazines, and popular magazines. Each of these targets specific audiences with a particular focus on subject matter. To critically read a periodical or magazine article, first identify the sub-genre and audience—this will help you identify the publication's purpose and know what conventions to expect. Then look at the author herself—what is her agenda, how does it fit in with the purpose of the publication, and how is her communication shaped for rhetorical situation?

Scholarly journals contain peer-reviewed essays and articles, scientific reports, and book reviews. If you compare a scholarly journal to a publication more targeted to a popular audience, you'll notice some presentation differences right away: scholarly journals are much plainer. For example, they won't include glossy four-color pictures, but will instead be mostly text-based. Scholars who write for this genre target a specific audience within an academic discipline, so the style of writing is highly specialized and specific to that discourse community. Some well-known scholarly journals are *The Harvard Business Review, The Journal of the American Medical Association* (JAMA), *Journal of Social Sciences,* and *Psychological Review.* You usually have to use the library databases to access these texts.

Many of the articles you'll find in scholarly journals will be preceded by an abstract—read this very closely because it will always tell you the author's main thesis or message. The language of scholarly articles (diction and style) will be formal and there will probably be many words and concepts that you won't understand at first. Don't feel overwhelmed—just get what you can, and look up some of the words you don't recognize. The only way for you become more familiar with the language of a discipline (i.e., become a member of that discourse community) is to commit the time it takes to read texts within it.

Scholarly articles are highly organized, usually with headers, and often you'll find "topic sentences" that will summarize the paragraph or section to come—this convention makes it relatively easy to scan the article for major points.

Although different disciplines will follow their own particular conventions of format (like how they cite sources), almost all will contain a lengthy "Works Cited" at the end (also called "References" or "Bibliography"), where you can quickly see the sources that have influenced the writer of the article. If you are conducting research connected to the topic of an academic article, you should always use the Works Cited as a way to find better or more credible sources. Your understanding of a topic will improve significantly if you read what the experts are reading.

Public affairs magazines are published by "for profit" commercial presses, and include long, well-researched articles aimed at professionals. Often these magazines will also include reviews of books, theater, film, and the arts. Editors review manuscripts submitted by staff writers, freelancers, and scholars. These periodicals may have a political bias—left, center, or right. Examples include *Foreign Affairs*, *Harper's*, and *The Atlantic Monthly*.

Commercial, "for profit" presses also publish trade magazines, which focus on a profession or trade like advertising, architecture, or retailing. Staff writers and industry specialists write articles with an aim towards the practitioners of a trade and their job concerns. Trades may post job listings, and generally advocate for the trade or profession. Advertisements in trade magazines are directed towards people in the specific field. Examples include *Inside Higher Education*, *Architectural Record*, *Advertising Age*, and *The Hollywood Reporter*.

The magazines that you buy at your local supermarket or bookstore are popular magazines: *Maxim*, *People*, *Entertainment Weekly*, and *Sports Illustrated*. Owned by large conglomerates or corporations, these magazines are glossy and illustrated with color photographs, contain many advertisements, and include short articles that focus on the special interests of the target audience. The authors are usually staff writers for the magazine or freelance writers. Seldom is the information in magazines documented. Although the general purpose of this genre is "amusement" (which literally means the absence of thought), you can still read these texts critically, with an eye to how they reflect and interpret the mainstream cultures in which they appear.

G. Textbooks

At this very moment you are reading a genre of nonfiction—the textbook. The purpose of this textbook, and all others, is to teach and inform. Obviously, there is a wide range of textbooks as there is a wide range of courses within a university, college or any other educational institution.

As a student, you probably want to learn something from this textbook and be engaged by the presentation of the material, as well. In most textbooks you expect to find a structured organization of chapters with subject headings, an index, a glossary, an appendix or two, study questions, study aids, and visual aids (maps, pictures, charts, diagrams and tables)—all aimed at imparting knowledge and helping you learn the material.

Reading a Textbook

1. Look over the table of contents. This will show you the overall organization of the course and help identify what's important.

2. Glance over any preface or foreword to see if you can determine its purpose.

3. Consider the title. This is often a significant statement about the book's "slant." Do you know something about the author?

4. Glance at the index. This is a listing of subject and pages upon which they can be found. You can tell from the percentage of known and unknown words how difficult the text will be for you. As a review for tests, you can easily look up unknown items since the page number is given.

5. Determine what other possibly useful materials are in the back of the book—before you need them. You don't have to read them now; just know that they exist. You might find footnotes from the chapters, illustrations, charts, or appendices.

6. Determine how a typical chapter is constructed. All of the other chapters will most likely follow the same conventions of structure. Use this knowledge when you have a reading assignment. Structure your approach accordingly.

H. Transactional Writing

Another type of nonfiction is used specifically in businesses, organizations, and communities. **Memos, emails, reports,** and **white papers** are typical modes of this nonfiction exchange, called **transactional writing**.

Much transactional writing is internal to the business or community. This type of writing may follow standards set by the business or organization, but most follow the conventions of business writing. Like all rhetorical situations, business writers consider audience and purpose when corresponding with co-workers, supervisors, managers, etc. Often the nature of the corporation or company will dictate the style and tone of the writing.

I. Academic Writing

Academic writing is a specialized genre that developed within the university setting as a way for scholars to share knowledge and research with other members of the same disciplinary community (see Scholarly Journals, page 41) and a means for teaching students how to enter the conversations of the academic disciplines. Scholarly writing follows different conventions of format according to discipline, but there are several fundamental conventions of American academic writing that persist throughout:

Academic writing is done by scholars for other scholars. Academic writers are always careful to establish themselves as insiders within their scholarly community; in other words, they consciously construct an **academic ethos** (credibility) within the essay. Part of establishing an academic ethos is illustrating expertise about a topic and convincing the audience that multiple perspectives were considered before advancing an argument (in other words, academic writers always show that they are critical thinkers and readers).

Academic diction is precise and specific to the disciplinary vocabulary. Academic writing is a conversation; each discipline, and each specialization within a discipline, is a "discourse community"—a group of scholars who are all interested in the same thing and who talk (discourse) about it. Discourse communities develop their own vocabularies for writing about the subject matter in their discipline.

Part of showing that you are part of a community is being able to use the language of the community. Therefore, academic diction (word choice) is always very precise (the right words) and specific (specialized knowledge words). When you're still learning how to read the conversation of a particular academic community, the insider language and technical nature of the diction will be difficult at first. Look up words whenever you can and try to remember the vocabulary and use it in your own conversations—this is the only way to become familiar enough with the language itself so that you too can become a member of that academic community.

Credible Sources. Academic writers build on the work of others by referring to **credible sources**. Because academic writing is a conversation between the members of a discourse community, you'll often find scholars referring to each other's works. Quoting from or referring to credible scholars shows that a writer understands what is important to the field and that she is an insider in that community. When you read academic discourse, don't skip over the quotes, paraphrases, and references to other writers—make note of the names and the titles of their work, and if you want to become an insider too, consider following them up and reading more.

Anticipating Objection. Academic writers may acknowledge a counterargument or concede a point. They often anticipate doubts or objections that a skeptical reader might have to their arguments. Giving the opposition a voice within her writing shows that the scholar has considered multiple viewpoints, which is part of being a critical thinker and necessary to establish her **academic ethos.**

Multiple Genres. Academic writers produce knowledge and report on research via many different genres. Some genres you'll probably encounter while at the university: essays, articles, book reviews, commentary, scientific study reports, lab reports, book-length monographs.

In the WR 39 series, you'll have the opportunity to practice reading and writing several academic essays. The scholarly journal article is basically an extended academic essay. As always, the particular conventions and vocabulary preferred will be discipline-specific, but most academic essays do have important facets in common: they are thesis-driven and logically structured.

Thesis Driven and Structured. Academic writing is highly structured, including a thesis. In some cultures, a thesis may be less important to the success of an essay, or the thesis is implied or delayed until the end of the essay. American academic essays are usually "thesis-driven," and the thesis is usually presented early in the essay. In other words, the thesis, which summarizes the purpose and the basic components of the essay, is usually found in the introduction of an academic essay. If you are looking at an academic article to find its main message, always scan the introduction first to look for the thesis.

The structure of an academic essay is usually linear; in other words, the points usually flow in a 1-2-3 type of logical arrangement. In longer essays, when sections are used, it is common that each section has its own thesis.

J. Assignment Prompts

An assignment prompt is a very special reading situation. It's a good idea to read a prompt several times, at different points in your process of answering the prompt. Reading the prompt at the outset of an assignment provides an initial sense of direction, but it helps to reread the prompt over time since the goals of the assignment will come into sharper focus as you discuss readings and examples in your classroom.

No matter what class the assignment is for, you can always start by answering a few general questions:

What Kinds of Tasks Are Required? Circle or underline the verbs in the instructions for your assignment since they indicate tasks that should inform your reading. In other words, those verbs let you know what your reading should enable you to do, whether it is to "define," "explain," "compare," "contrast," "relate," "analyze," "evaluate," "apply," etc.

What Kind of Support or Evidence Does the Assignment Require? Does it call for personal observations and experience? Does it ask for examples from texts that you are reading in class? Or does it require that you include outside information from research? If you have questions about what kind or what amount of support is appropriate, ask your instructor.

Who Is the Audience? How you write depends upon who your audience is. In your first-year writing classes, you'll be asked to write for a variety of audiences.

What Format and Writing Conventions Should I Follow? Handling the technical parts of the assignment with care helps to establish your credibility as an academic writer.

How Many Pages (or Words) Are Required? Page or word requirements provide an estimate of how much writing you will need to do to offer a focused and well-developed response to the assignment. It's important to recognize that following page requirements is not an end in itself but a means to an end—successfully accomplishing the goals of the assignment.

Reading an Assignment Prompt

1. Read and underline what you feel to be the most significant words or phrases in the directions given by the assignment.

2. What do you feel is the most important direction or goal of the prompt? If you feel that there is more than one main goal, list the secondary goals as well.

3. What practical things must you do to produce a solid response to this prompt? Try to list these as separate steps to be taken or draw a diagram (with boxes and arrows) of the steps you must complete to gather all the information you need to write this paper.

4. What separate points and/or kinds of evidence must each paragraph or section contain to respond fully to the prompt? How should these points and/or kinds of evidence be related and connected?

2.9.4 Drama

Drama has been around for as long as humans have lived in communities and shared their experiences with each other. The first dramas were probably recreations of what happened during the hunt, or to recognize a reoccurring natural phenomenon with a ritual (religious) dance. The Greeks gave us formal drama when they added spoken dialogue to a ritual performance enacted for Dionysus, the god of wine and agriculture. Aeschylus, Sophocles, Euripides, and Aristophanes were the first recorded Greek dramatists, and Aristotle classified the early conventions of tragedy (citing Sophocles as the best) in his *Poetics*.

Today we have stage plays, screenplays and teleplays (scripts) in many genres. Screenwriters intend for their scripts to be filmed or broadcast; playwrights and dramatists intend for their plays to be performed on stage in front of a live audience, but in all cases plays, drama usually starts as a written text. Screenplays, teleplays, and stage plays can be works of fiction, nonfiction prose, or even poetry.

A. Plays

Plays written for the stage follow the basic conventions of drama; some of these elements are similar to fiction. Plot is the dramatist's particular arrangement of the story in acts and scenes. Characters are revealed primarily through dialogue and action. Plays have settings, indications of the locale (time and place), and these are sometimes symbolic.

Traditionally, we say that plays follow a three-act structure: In the first act, the main conflict and characters are "exposed" or revealed. The second act is the longest, and is called the complication because "the plot thickens," peaking at the end. The third act is called the resolution—the conflict comes to some kind of conclusion. Contemporary plays, while still following the structure of conflict, rising action, climax, and resolution, now more often are written in the two-act format (or even in 90 minutes, with no intermission).

As written texts, plays may include a cast page, listing the cast of characters with a brief description of each. Also, there may be stage directions, the instructions in the text for the actors (entrances, exit, significant actions) and the stage crew (lights fade) as well as scene descriptions that work to set the scene of the play. Prior to the twentieth century, most plays were either tragedy or comedy, and each has its own thematic concerns.

Tragedy. According to Aristotle's *Poetics*, "tragedy is an imitation not of human beings but of action and life, of happiness and misery."

Some classical conventions of tragedy are: it takes place in a 24 hour period, the length of a day, it occurs in one setting, the plot entails a conflict between the protagonist (the tragic hero) and an external force such as another character or fate, the hero is someone of high or noble birth who in the course of the plot suffers a downfall, he suffers the downfall because he has a tragic flaw (such as hubris), he has an epiphany (a sudden realization, a moment of clarity) and the audience experiences catharsis (a purging of emotion). Commonly, tragedy involves the use of both ironic deeds and ironic speech. In high school, you probably studied some classical tragedies like *Oedipus Rex*—or you may have studied how Shakespeare followed most (but not all) of the classical conventions of tragedy in plays like *Romeo & Juliet, Hamlet, MacBeth, Julius Caesar, Othello,* or *King Lear.*

Comedy plays are amusing, entertaining, and also usually have something to teach us about the human condition. Romantic comedies typically have a love plot where a pair or pairs of characters run an obstacle course to the altar. Satiric comedies reveal the vice and folly of humanity, and focus more on a character who obstructs the amusement of others such as a public figure or institution.

Comedies use visual, verbal, and situational humor, and often the content of the plot is characterized by mistaken identities, coincidences, contradictions, and lots of complications and incongruities between how the characters see themselves and how they really are.

Whether romantic or satiric, comedies end happily—this is a convention of classic plays that has carried over to modern TV and film comedies. If you go to see a comedy, you do not expect a sad ending, and would probably be angry if there were one.

B. Screenplays and Teleplays

Although you might never have read a screenplay before, it is likely a text with which you are quite familiar. Behind every film and scripted television show is a screenplay that organizes the elements of a scene (the dialogue, the blocking, the camera movement) into a seamless viewing experience. In format, a screenplay resembles the script of a theatrical performance, but that resemblance is deceptive. Screenplays and teleplays are written to be directed and performed by many different artists, and in this respect, they are most like **speculative scripts**—that is, a script that has not been turned into a television show or film. Like plays, speculative scripts are written without knowledge of who will be cast in the film, nor do they contain detailed information about camerawork.

Most of the scripts you will read are modified **shooting scripts**, edited after production to reflect what ended up on screen. (An unmodified shooting script, like the one discussed below, is what the director followed while filming. It includes detailed information about the camerawork, but does not necessarily reflect the finished film because it has not been modified to correspond with any changes made during post-production.) Unlike plays and speculative scripts, then, shooting scripts are the record of the singular performance of a particular group of actors working under the supervision of a particular director.

Determining who is the rhetor of such a fundamentally collaborative project can be difficult; however, because the director is ultimately responsible for everything that appears on the small or big screen, you can attribute the rhetorical gestures present in the script to the director. If analyzing specific dialogue between characters, you'd be safe to attribute rhetorical agency to the screenwriter.

Scripts generally follow some linguistic and mechanical (punctuation) conventions that you won't see in other texts. For example, in other genres, words are normally written in ALL CAPS to add emphasis, but this is not necessarily the case in scripts, where the character's names (designating a line of dialogue) and camera/editing instructions are usually all caps. If you think about the reason for writing a script, it makes sense rhetorically for these words to be capitalized—this makes it easier for the actor, camera operator, director, or editor to quickly find the point of action in a scene. Scripts also conventionally include continuous numbering of scenes throughout and abbreviations for often used words that are only familiar to those within the film and TV community.

Sometimes (not often), directors write their own scripts (sometimes, even more rarely, they operate the camera and/or edit the film, too). In cases like these, you might expect to see more camera direction noted in the screenplay. Directors who both write and direct are called **auteurs.**

Consider this text from the opening scene of film auteur Paul Thomas Anderson's shooting script for *There Will Be Blood*:

EXT. NEW MEXICO DESERT – DAY – 1898

CAMERA looks up a steep trail. Half the frame filled with a hill in close distance, the other half is sky...over the top of the hill we see a prospector's PICK come up and then down...up and then down...up and then down...

CU. ANGLE. BEHIND THE MAN WITH THE PICK.

DANIEL C. PLAINVIEW (late '30s here) is, with pick and ax, in the middle of the day, in 110 degree heat in New Mexico, searching for SILVER. He has a shaft about fifteen feet deep at this point. Nearby is a MULE and a CART. He digs and digs and digs.

FRONT ANGLE. CU. DANIEL'S FACE

The script begins with exposition: the first scene is an exterior shot (EXT.), set during the day, in the desert, in the nineteenth century. CAMERA here is capitalized, because it indicates what Anderson wants to depict on screen and the angle of framing he has chosen to introduce his protagonist, Daniel C. Plainview. The camera "looks up" the trail, making what appears at the top of the trail more powerful. However, Anderson chooses to introduce the prospector via off-screen space: he exists in the diegesis but is not, in this first shot, visible in the frame.

Anderson then cuts to a close-up shot (CU), again indicating where he wants the camera positioned in all caps (ANGLE. BEHIND THE MAN WITH THE PICK). In this shot, we have still not seen the face of "the man with the pick." Anderson tells the narrative visually by slowly revealing more about the main character; in the next shot, also a close-up, this time a FRONT ANGLE, we finally see Daniel's face.

Scripts conventionally capitalize the names of characters; however, it is not conventional to capitalize the objects in a particular scene. Notice how the word "PICK" is capitalized in the first paragraph but not the second. In the first paragraph, Anderson uses capital letters to indicate that the pick appearing over the top of the hill is the most important element the frame; but in the second paragraph, as the pick becomes less important than what it is being used to dig for (SILVER), it is relegated to the lowercase.

2.10   Methods for Reading Visual Texts

From images of the hunt drawn on cave walls, Roman graffiti drawn on city walls, and Michelangelo's religious masterpieces on the ceiling of the Sistine Chapel, we have come full circle today to the work of "taggers" and street artists like Shepard Fairey. Visual representation has always been an important part of how human beings imagine, record, and interpret their world.

2.10.1   Visual Art

Each artist works within a medium (another usage of the word medium, but with a similar meaning): paints, water-colors, pastels, pens, pencils, clay, rock, wood, and even space. Marshall McLuhan's famous saying "the medium is the message" makes sense when applied to visual art: the same human model subject would be a totally different text as a painting than as a marble sculpture.

When you study what's going on in the frame of a visual text, make note of as many specific elements as possible: Who or what is in the foreground/background? Where does the light hit? Where are there shadows? Where is your eye drawn? What made it into the frame and what is didn't? Instead of an alphabet and words, visual texts use light and shadow, focus, color, perspective, size, texture, spatial arrangement, and design to create meaning.

Artistic conventions might be determined by the medium, a school of art (a community of artists using the same methods), the time period, or the artist's own unique vision. To critically read a visual art text, you'll probably have to do a bit of outside research as well as spending time observing the image itself.

While some artwork represents its subject realistically, most art created over the last century has displayed experimentation with many types of styles and approaches to representation that have radically expanded the way that the artist and audience might engage with the subject. For example, Marcel Duchamp's *Nude Descending a Staircase* (oil on canvas, 1912) challenges the viewer by representing not just a single moment in time but the progression of several moments in an almost filmic sense. (If you'd like to see this painting, search on Google with this string: "Duchamp nude descending staircase." You can also find it on Wikipedia under Duchamp). Within a single frame, we perceive the subject of this painting as she moves down the entire length of the stairs. Putting this artistic text into its historical and cultural context enhances our understanding. Not only was Duchamp influenced by the (then) new artistic medium of the motion picture, he displays the dynamics of the Futurists and the fragmenting of the human figure practiced by the Cubists (schools of art).

2.10.2   Photography

Photography is a relatively recent form of visual representation. The first daguerreotypes were created in 1839—after years of research and collaboration with scientific inventors, Louis DaGuerre used an early camera to expose an image directly onto a mirror-polished surface of silver coated with silver halide particles. Technology developed ways to capture the image on more accessible and portable papers, cameras became smaller, lenses stronger, and the art of photography became something anyone could do. Today, we can take photos on our digital cameras (or cell phones) and send them across the world in a matter of seconds.

Photographers use many of the same conventions as other visual artists to create meaning: light and shadow, focus, color, perspective, size, texture, spatial arrangement, and design. Photographers are also influenced by their school(s) of art, the time period, or their own unique vision. To read a photographic text rhetorically, follow the same basic method you've already learned: identify the rhetorical situation of the text, the medium for delivery, and the modes of construction—with all this critical knowledge, observe the image closely to make some conclusions about how all the elements in the frame work together to deliver a message or evoke a response from the viewer.

2.10.3   Graphic Novels (Comics)

The basic unit of analysis when dealing with a comic is the panel. The visual elements of a panel can be described using the same vocabulary used to describe a frame from a film: background and foreground, diegesis, high- or low-key lighting, etc. Pointing to the similarities between film and comics highlights what makes comics unique as a medium: the interaction of these visual components with the written word.

The word-picture relationship can be word-specific, in which the words convey the meaning and the images merely illustrate it (as in a children's book); duo-specific, in which the words and images both convey the same meaning (as when a picture of an irate man yelling is accompanied by a caption box that tells you the irate man is yelling); or interdependent, in which the words and images combine to convey a meaning neither is capable of conveying alone. Most of the comics you will read in your composition courses will rely heavily on interdependent word-picture combinations.

Comics are also unique in the manner in which they relate to time. No matter how the words in the panel interact with the visuals, there is a tension between the static image and the words in the caption box. Picture a panel that depicts a medium close-up of a young man in a bright orange shirt. A caption box extrudes from his open mouth and occupies the space above his left shoulder. The text inside it reads: "The bride? You wanna know about…the thing it is that happened to her? Because sure, I can tell you, but…"

All these words didn't spill from his mouth in the open-mouthed moment depicted in the panel. The words propel the narrative forward in time in such a way that we cannot be sure which word the panel depicts the man enunciating. It may not even be a word: the panel could be depicting the pause indicated by the ellipses. This tension between static image and narrative progress exists not only in panels, but also between them.

The empty area between panels is called the **gutter,** and in this in-between space, the reader is called upon to become an active participant in the creation of the text. Unlike a film, in which the twenty-three imperceptible gaps between the twenty-four frames flashed per second create the illusion of movement, the gutter produces breaks in the narrative that require interpretation to repair. If the panel following the one of the man in the bright orange shirt is a medium-long shot of a different, shabbily-dressed man in a prison garden holding an open stenographer's notebook and saying, "Yes, I want to hear about the bride," what inferences must the reader draw for those two panels to make sense? To begin with, the bright orange shirt in the first panel likely belongs to a prison-issue jumpsuit and the man across from him (as the reader infers from the comic equivalent of a shot/reverse shot) is a journalist interested in what this prisoner did to the woman they both refer to as "the bride." The act of making that inference—of bridging the gap between the first and second panel—is called **closure.** In this case, the closure is achieved via a subject-to-subject transition.

However, were the second panel to depict not a journalist, but a long shot of the man in the orange shirt unfolding a lawn chair next to a grill, the "prisoner" would be transformed into a man at a barbeque discussing an unfortunate incident at a wedding. If the third panel showed that same man placing a steak on the grill while continuing to discuss the wedding, closure between the second and third panels will have been achieved via an action-to-action transition, i.e. one in which consecutive panels depict the same subject undertaking a series of actions. If the next three panels track the path of the steak from the man's tongs to the grill's surface, the reader will be compelled by this moment-to-moment transition to create closure by associating the steak's slow-motion descent with whatever it was that happened at that wedding, such that it would not be surprising if in the fourth panel the steak was replaced by a bouquet of flowers of the sort brides toss at weddings. Because the reader knows that steaks don't often turn into flowers, it is safe to infer that the narrative has shifted to another place and time via a scene-to-scene transition.

But the assumption that this airborne bouquet is on its way into the arms of a single woman attending the wedding is not necessarily a safe one—an author could be exploiting this conventional image to confound the reader's expectations. In a subsequent panel, the "empty" space behind the falling flowers could be revealed to be the white satin of the wedding dress worn by a woman whose pained expression informs the reader why she dropped the bouquet.

If that panel were followed by another in which a younger, tuxedo-clad version of the orange-shirted man from the barbeque perches on the edge of a bed with his head in hands, then another panel depicting leaves falling outside a bustling travel agency, then another still of two empty chairs beneath an oversized umbrella on some Hawaiian beach, the reader is presented with a number of interpretive decisions. The transition from the jilted bride to her cold-footed fiancé could be interpreted as a scene-to-scene transition, as could the transition from the fiancé to the travel agency. However, because these panels depict the same moment in a series of different locations, we could argue that closure is achieved via an aspect-to-aspect transition.

The interpretive burden required to understand the intent of the author/rhetor of a comic is, as the previous paragraphs indicate, quite heavy—even though the experience of reading comics is so intuitive that many otherwise intelligent readers consider the medium juvenile. That so many comics chronicle the adventures of impossibly-muscled specimens of post-humanity in tights that reveal more than they conceal helps sustain this misperception. But as the story of the prisoner and/or the man who left his wife at the altar demonstrates, the content of a comic is not determined by the medium itself.

2.11   Methods for Reading Multi-Modal Texts

2.11.1   Film

Most of us can describe the plot of a film after watching it once, but how do we "read" and understand all of the elements that add up to produce the message of the film and the effect on its audience? When watching for entertainment, we don't normally pay attention to technical aspects of production such as camera angles, lighting, editing, or music selection. But if reading a film critically, these elements all become the rhetorical decisions and choices that make up the overall meaning of the text.

Thinking and writing about genre is an important practice in film and media studies; critics often discuss the characteristics of a genre and how a particular film fits into (or doesn't fit into) that definition.

Also, film theorists explore how film genres reflect the collective expressions of culture and historical time period: what frightens us (horror films)? What is criminal (gangster films)? What is heroic (superhero films)? What is alien? What will happen to us in the future (science fiction)? These genres, and the questions and themes embedded in them, are repeated in each generation—and as values change, the texts reflect that change. Scholars suggest that because genre films are a product of their socio-historical context, watching them becomes a shared ritual whereby that culture's predominant values are examined, and perhaps enforced. Exploring how a film results from or contributes to its cultural and historical context, or how it uses or refuses conventions expected by its audience are forms of rhetorical analysis.

A film text is the product of a highly collaborative process—so when you read or analyze a film, be aware that a group of people made it happen: screenwriter(s), actors, cinematographers, lighting specialists, set and costume designers, make-up artists, prop masters, sound editors, film editors, animators and designers of CGI special effects, and the composer—and this is by no means an exhaustive list (stick around to watch the credits roll in a theatre sometime to see how many people contribute to a film text). In action, adventure, and combat genre films, fitness trainers and fight choreographers also play a huge part in creating the images that make it onto the screen. What would the movie 300 be without the chiseled bodies of the Spartan soldiers—or a John Woo martial arts feature without the balletic choreography of the martial artists?

At the apex of this pyramid of talent stands the director, who usually makes final decisions about aesthetic and technical aspects of the film. However, directors often complain that they were not able to carry out their vision due to studios, producers, and their budgets—that's why you'll often see a DVD release called "the director's cut." This is the film the way she/he wanted it to be.

There are some basic conventions that apply to most all films: structurally, feature films have three acts and are about two hours in length, although some run longer. Conventions of format include the opening title sequence and the closing credit roll. Films are basically stage dramas delivered via the cinematic medium, so like stage drama, films come in many genres—drama, comedy, science fiction, historical (costume) dramas, action, horror, and so on. And of course, each genre has its own conventions and audiences who recognize them.

A. Drama

A film **drama** depicts situations where realistic characters deal with highly charged themes such as the death of a loved one, divorce, conflicts between parents and children, substance abuse, racial issues, or moral dilemmas of some kind. Some modern films still follow classical conventions of drama and tragedy, telling the story of a hero who makes a serious mistake, which, coupled with a character flaw or an act of fate, leads him to a well-deserved retribution or a sorrowful end.

For example, in *There Will Be Blood*, Daniel Plainview (Daniel Day-Lewis) uses all the charm, deceit, and guile at his disposal to buy land from poor landowners in Texas so that he can drill for the oil he knows is beneath their property. In the end, he is undone by his own greed and lack of concern for others, losing every meaningful human attachment he ever had. Before the film is over, Plainview has had an epiphany and the audience experiences catharsis: the ancient formula still works.

B. Comedy

A comedy is light-hearted and meant to create laughter and enjoyment in its viewers through comical misunderstandings, one-liners, and sympathy for a likeable but flawed character trying to find happiness. Comedy also has subgenres such as **romantic comedy**, **slapstick**, **black comedy**, (dark satirical comedy such as *Catch-22*), **screwball comedy**, **musical comedy**, and **parody**. Whether or not viewers "get" the humor in a film has a great deal to do with context—which is directly related to the audience's culture and/or sub-culture. For example, the many references to "kebobs" (shish kabobs) in director/screenwriter Richard Curtis's films *Knotting Hill* and *Love Actually* resonate more humorously with British than American audiences. The one-liners in many of Woody Allen's films, for example, jokes about psychiatrists, existentialism, and bad driving skills (New Yorkers seldom drive because of the great mass transit system), may not click with viewers who have always lived in the country.

C. Romance

The AMC Film site defines film **romance** as a genre that "shares some features with romantic dramas, romantic comedies, and sexual/erotic films. These are love stories, or affairs of the heart that center on passion, emotion, and the romantic, affectionate involvement of the main characters (usually a leading man and lady), and the journey that their love takes through courtship or marriage." While many types of films have some type of love attachment as part of their plot, the conventions of a romance film place this attachment at the center of the narrative. It drives every decision a character ultimately makes. Another convention in romance films is that they must have a happy ending, or at least one that is bittersweet. Films such as *Pride and Prejudice* and *Sense and Sensibility* based on the novels of Jane Austen, are strong examples of romance. The plots and subplots of each revolve around love, barriers to love, and the triumph of love.

D. Family

Family films are in a unique position; they try to appeal to both young children under the age of twelve and their parents. Ideally, said films have little violence, no overt sexuality, and no religious or controversial issues, one or two young characters with whom children can identify, and straightforward storylines that teach the difference between good and evil. While good for small children, such wholesome fare is pretty dull stuff for adults, and since parents are the ones bringing the kids to the theater, the filmmakers need to offer something for the adult crowd. A lot of times, this takes the form of humor with allusions to adult themes and experiences that children lack the context to understand, or some form of political satire or social commentary.

Shrek and its sequels are excellent examples of this kind of double-edged humor. To very young children, *Shrek* might just be an interesting story with talking animals and a likeable ogre, but to adults who understand the sexist and racist conventions of many fairy tales, where ogres are the villains and princesses just sit around waiting to be saved by Prince Charming, it is a wonderful commentary on racial tensions and female independence. Shrek may be big, green, and ugly, but he's a better man than Lord Farquaad or Prince Charming. And far from needing to be rescued by her prince, Fiona is more than capable of taking care of herself, as the audience sees when she and her friends are ambushed by Robin Hood and his Merry Men. While Shrek and Donkey look on in amazement, Fiona takes on Hood and his pals with bullet-time martial arts moves reminiscent of John Woo's Hong Kong cinema.

E. Horror

Horror films, drama for a particular audience, is a sub-genre that appeals to our desire to be entertained by being frightened, which creates a cycle of fear, shock, and catharsis. Horror plot conventions often focus on multiple murders (especially of teenagers), crazed villains and mental illness, haunted houses, and supernatural horror. The first popular horror films were based on 19th century gothic literature such as *Dracula, Frankenstein,* and *The Invisible Man.* More recent horror films, in contrast, often draw inspiration from the insecurities of life after cataclysmic events like WW II (and the atomic bomb), Vietnam War,

Watergate, AIDS, 9/11, and the Iraq War, giving rise to distinct but related sub-genres such as the horror-of-personality (*Psycho*), the horror-of-armageddon (*I am Legend*), and the horror-of-the demonic (*The Exorcist*).

F. Science Fiction

Science fiction is another sub-genre which can contain elements of horror, drama, and adventure films. Science fiction films may include aliens, space travel and outer space, or worlds (settings) in which scientific laws are subverted or altered by new technology. Sci-fi films may also explore the consequences and applications of contemporary science, such as nanotechnology or genetic engineering. While we can say that science fiction in general speculates about humanity's interaction with current or advanced science and technology, sci-fi films always reflect the culture and context in which they were made. Mid-20th century sci-fi, coming out of a **context** of McCarthyism and a strange blend of paranoia and triumphalism, concerned itself with humanity's battles with aliens, both seen (*War of the Worlds*), and unseen (*Invasion of the Body Snatchers*), in which the alien figures are a stand-in (symbolic) for all enemies of the contemporary culture.

Later science fiction films like *Blade Runner, The Matrix*, and *The Terminator* series show a more global concern, criticizing humanity's dependence on technology and showing us the implications of our so-called scientific progress. And still other science fiction films simply use a space or futuristic setting to recast a more universal narrative. *Star Wars* is a heroic action tale with timeless elements (young hero comes of age and defeats wicked villain) that happens to take place on spaceships. *Alien* is a classic gothic horror story—mostly unseen monster picks off the crew one by one aboard a darkly-lit vessel, isolated in space (where no one can hear you scream).

G. Superhero

Straight from the pages of the comic book, **superhero** films conventionally involve a costumed protagonist with some type of superpower such as the ability to fly, superhuman strength, X-ray vision, or the ability to shoot energy bolts. Superheroes generally share a compulsion or obligation to fight evil and to protect humanity. Every superhero has his or her nemesis, who is always defeated but often returns to fight again.

Another convention of the superhero film is a depiction of the protagonist's vulnerability, which increases the audience's feelings of identification with him or her. As Vasant Nath says on In.com, "The great irony of being special and still suffering from small everyday afflictions of the heart and mind sustains our interest in them. It makes them vulnerable and thus accessible to us, for who can deny vulnerability as a prime aspect of being human? Superheroes might take down stupendously powerful foes with their eyes closed, but when it comes to telling their love, or dealing with dark, childhood memories, they often fall by the wayside."

In the past one of the conventions of superhero movies was the happy ending where evil was vanquished and the nefarious plot to destroy Gotham City or the entire planet was thwarted. While films such as 1978's *Superman: The Movie* ended with a clear-cut, upbeat victory over evil, over the last two decades the conventions of the superhero genre have been shifting—now, imperfect, tormented protagonists with tragic childhoods or dark secrets have become more prevalent. Although treated much earlier in graphic novels, this trend began in film with Tim Burton's version of *Batman* (1989). Recently, *The Dark Knight* and *Watchmen* continue to redefine the superhero film genre, shifting the tone from optimism to uncertainty.

2.11.2 Television

TV is the most watched medium in the United States today. According to the latest A.C. Nielson data, a majority of Americans spend on average four hours a day watching. As viewers, we all have our favorite shows—and there are lots of genres to choose from—each with their own conventions and audience expectations. Although we usually think of TV as amusement, rhetorically reading TV texts, just like all other texts, can tell us a great deal about the values of the culture and historical time period in which they were broadcast. If you are interested in critically reading TV texts, you might look into taking a class in Media Studies.

The television medium itself is broken down into channels, and certain channel-types share conventions. For example, "Network programming" can be found on the channels of the major TV corporations: NBC, CBS, ABC, and FOX. "Cable programming" is found on channels like Comedy Central, Bravo, the CW, USA, and TNT. And "Premium programming" is found on channels such as HBO, Showtime, Cinemax, and Starz. Each of these programming media might broadcast a TV show genre discussed below, but the genre might differ in conventions according to its channel. For example, a drama presented on prime-time network TV (like CBS's *CSI*) shares some but not all characteristics with a drama on a premium channel (like HBO's *The Sopranos*).

A. Sitcom

The situation comedy (sitcom) is a half-hour series typically focused on everyday life. Sitcoms are based on a formula comprised of the premise for the show, characterization, humor, theme and structure.

The premise is the context (situation) that is established within the first few episodes, and which generally makes possible much of the comedy. The plot, often narrating two story lines, is resolvable within the thirty-minute episode, and like the comedy plays that came before it, ends happily. The two story lines are usually associated with different characters. Sitcoms conventionally have four to six recurring characters. The humor comes from character opposition or exaggerated responses to extreme situations. For example, in *Two and a Half Men* (according to Nielsen ratings, the most watched current sitcom on TV), the character Charlie Harper (Charlie Sheen) is opposite in personality, habits, and lifestyle to his brother Alan (Jon Cryer).

Structurally, a sitcom typically begins with a teaser, which is a quick, funny scene at the beginning of the episode followed by two acts and an epilogue. As a text, sitcoms deliver messages through every premise, characterization, episode theme, and joke. Even though they are most often filmed in front of a live audience, sitcoms also use canned "laugh tracks" placed at the right moments for further comedic effect. Some sitcoms break (or play with) with the traditions of the formula. For example, Larry David's *Curb Your Enthusiasm*, an HBO show now in its eighth season, was considered groundbreaking because it broke many of the conventions of the standard sitcom.

B. News

Television news is broadcast at both local and national levels. In the 1980s, when Ted Turner established CNN, the first 24-hour all-news network was born. News stories vary based on what network they're on, which channel, which program, and which newscaster reports. Typically, news programs try to appear authoritative, unbiased, and unflustered; however, differences in news reports between networks and local stations occur because of how a story is treated in terms of the length of time devoted to the topic, the news correspondent's perspective and interpretation of the event, and the thoroughness with which he addresses the event.

The purpose of news programs is to inform, yet programs will typically have consumer news or human-interest stories to lessen the severity of the unpleasantness reported in our 24/7 news cycle. These "newstainment" stories appeal strongly to local audience interests. Formal news stories cover politics, foreign affairs, and other events of serious import. Balance—a sense of fair play—is crucial in maintaining a news program's creditability, and by extension the network's credibility (the news is a high status program on any network). Even though all newscasters claim objectivity, we know that there is always bias. In fact, some news channels are known for their political leanings: for example, MSNBC is generally considered left of center, while FOX news is right of center.

The news is performed by real people, and filmed "live." The show will be heavily branded by the network or station that underwrites it. Programs follow a narrative structure with headlines, hard and soft news stories, reports, and breaking stories. Reports are typically introduced by a newsreader, details are provided by the newsroom reporter or special correspondent, and viewers are given evidence in the form of actuality, interviews, and/or statistics. Another news convention you're probably used to seeing is the 30-second "teaser": "Does shopping on the web put your identity in danger? Find out what you need to know at 10 o'clock." The rhetorical purpose of that one is pretty easy to guess.

On some news programs, banter between anchors and reporters is now customary (not so in the '50s and '60s—back then, it was all formal). News programs are shot in a specially constructed set, where the anchor and newsreaders sit behind a desk or stand with insets behind them. Color, lighting, background sound and camera angles are important to creating the effect of the newsroom. Producers keep news programming interesting to current viewers by adding sophisticated computer graphics and captions to explain stories, and even "tickertape" information running along the bottom of the screen.

C. Reality TV

American Idol is the most watched TV show ever, currently attracting about 24 million viewers each week. The second-most watched show? *Dancing with the Stars*. Unlike other content-specific genres, where the audience members generally have more in common (detective shows, soap operas, sitcoms), people from all walks of life watch reality shows. Your hairstylist, mail carrier, professor, and your mother, if all put in the same room, might very well find they can start a conversation about who received the most votes on the latest installment of *American Idol*.

What is reality TV? Is it "Trash TV"? Shows like this practice the convention of sensationalism, for sure—that's how TV networks procure good ratings—but they also serve to hold certain aspects of human behavior and culture under a magnifying glass. Although they've been around for a long time, mostly in the format of game shows (your parents probably remember *The Dating Game* and *The Newlywed Show*), reality TV programming became much more popular with the networks after strikes by actors and writers. Reality programming doesn't need much of either, and can draw in a huge audience for a much lower budget than scripted shows.

Reality TV includes a range of nonfiction formats: talent contests (*American Idol, So You Think You Can Dance?*), dating shows (*The Bachelor*), docu-soaps (*The Real Housewives of Orange County*), makeover programs (*The Big Loser*), setting-based contests (*Survivor, The Amazing Race*), court programs (*Judge Judy*), tabloid newsmagazine shows (*Entertainment Tonight, TMZ*), job-based dramas (*The Deadliest Catch, Project Runway, America's Next Top Model*), and reality-based talk shows (*The Jerry Springer Show, Oprah*). The format of a reality program emphasizes "the real" and the "unrehearsed" through the use of techniques like hand-held cameras, surveillance video, and on-location environments ranging from actual homes to exotic islands. Some reality shows such as *American Idol* include audience participation.

While reality TV often dwells in the realm of stereotypes, these shows also have the potential to reveal the way in which we, with the help of the entertainment industry, create and maintain these stereotypes that affect our lives in no small way. In addition, reality shows are often concerned with defining the moral boundaries within society.

D. Drama

Episodic TV drama occurs in sub-formats such as anthologies, (single stories with closure after each episode, like *Twilight Zone*), running series (with some continuing themes and also some episodic closure, like *CSI* or *Law and Order*), and serials (which don't focus on closure until the end of the season or series, like *The Sopranos* or *Lost*). Structurally, dramas might progress in four, five or six acts (within an episode or throughout series), and are often marked by cliff-hangers.

Sub-genres of the TV drama are generally identifiable by content- or audience-driven elements; for example, teen dramas (*Gossip Girl*), soap operas (*The Young and the Restless, Desperate Housewives*), costume dramas (Masterpiece theater's *Cranford*), medical/hospital dramas (*House, Grey's Anatomy*), crime/police/legal dramas (*Law & Order*), and family dramas (*Big Love*). Television drama invites viewers into the world and worldview of its characters. In television, it is more often the producer, not the director, who has control over most aspects of the show. The producer's goal is to engage viewers in the heroic or moral struggle of the main character (and to get high ratings).

E. Documentaries

A documentary attempts to tell factually accurate stories about people or events, typically social, political, scientific, economic or historical in subject matter, and narrates the story via interviews, archival photographs and film, and news reports. Primary sources are more important than secondary sources. There are no fictional elements in documentaries; information must be verifiable. The informative appeal of documentaries is sometimes contested; more successful documentaries take the audience places they haven't seen or introduce them to experiences inaccessible or unknown to them. Documentaries are told through a specific point-of-view, which means all documentaries are biased. This doesn't necessarily mean that the information is tainted negatively.

There are several techniques or conventions that filmmakers and directors find useful and effective in creating documentaries. Most utilize archival footage and photographs, such as newsreel footage and old photographs. For example, acclaimed filmmaker Ken Burns uses archival Civil War images in his documentary *The Civil War*. This stock footage is considered the raw material of documentaries, and the narration is key to it becoming a vital part of documentary. Filmmakers also use "talking head" interviews—aptly named because we only see the head of the people who are interviewed to provide commentary or explanation on the subject of the documentary. Interviews can be a major source of material in some documentaries. The technique of the jiggly camera is another convention since often filmmakers are shooting on-location, and keeping the camera steady when following action is somewhat difficult. However, new technology in camera stabilization has mostly eliminated the problem of holding a camera steady.

Usually documentaries use voice-over narration. We hear this voice on a soundtrack, but we cannot see the speaker because he or she is offscreen. Or narrators are seen on-camera, and in effect, may become a character in the story. Re-enactments are another convention in which the filmmaker stages past events. Sometimes re-enactments include the people who originally experienced the events or actors play their roles. Finally, documentaries include real people. Even though documentaries tell real stories, the material is still shaped into dramatic sequences with rising action and a climax, similar to the plotline of fiction.

Reading a Documentary

1. From what other perspectives could this information be told?

2. Does the filmmaker incorporate enough factual material?

3. How does the emotional component of the documentary impact the factual material?

F. Music Videos

A relatively recent genre, music videos are a mix of written, visual, and audio elements. The singer, music, lyrics, and images work together seamlessly or disjunctively to form a distinct genre different from film and television. The director of a music video is the rhetor since he or she is responsible for all aspects of the end product.

Directors tend to have a signature or individual style to their direction of a music video. Record companies and the artists they contract are in the business to sell music. The conventions of music videos include the narrative, camerawork, editing, actors (the performers and extras), setting, props and costumes, lyrics, music, and the way in which connections are made between the music, images and lyrics.

One of the conventions of music videos is to portray the singer (presumably the star) lip-syncing the song in a most flattering way. To read a music video rhetorically, we can use a series of questions beginning with the performer: "Is the singer a character in the narrative? Or does she stand only for herself as the star?" Typically, figures/characters do not speak in music videos, which makes storytelling difficult. Often, music videos do not convey complete narratives. Thus we might ask: Does the story have a beginning, middle, and end? How does the unfolding of the narrative or non-narrative depend on the music and images? As in film, camerawork has an effect on meaning. The movement, angle, and shot distance of the camera all contribute to the depiction of the artist, the performance, and the narrative. Close-ups of the performer especially play a dominant role.

Known as the "Professor of Pop," Andrew Goodwin, author of *Dancing in the Distraction Factory*, contends that, "visuals [in music videos] either illustrate, amplify or contradict the lyrics and music." Questions we can ask related to the visual elements are: What is the purpose of the close-ups of the performer? How do the visual images illustrate, amplify, or contradict the lyrics and music?

Editing of music videos often occurs on the beat in that the tempo of the music drives the editing. Settings have different rhetorical aims. For example, a setting might make social commentary or represent the performer in a particular community. Also, settings are often based on music genre and ethnicity. Two elements crucial to mise-en-scène are props and costumes. Props can carry an excess of meaning in music video, while costumes help identify character type or provide commentary about the world. In music videos, the lyrics create a prevailing mood, feeling, or sense of subject rather than a meaning.

2.11.3   Video Games

Video games have a dodgy reputation. They're for kids, for nerds, for aspiring rock stars, for kicking back and wasting time (or procrastinating from schoolwork). But no one really takes video games seriously (except that guy in your dorm who plays *World of Warcraft* all night), because they're, well, *games*. We *play* games. Anything we *play* can't be serious. Right?

Well. No. Although the word "game" suggests something we do for fun (and indeed, games *are* fun), video games are another form of rhetorically expressive media, with all the elements of the rhetorical triangle present and accounted for. There is, of course, the game itself, which we can read as a text.

Games are often proprietary to a particular medium: the console (PS3, Xbox, Nintendo Wii). There's a game studio and the game designers and programmers (rhetors) who want to make a successful game, which means appealing successfully to a specific gaming audience. There's a message—not to be confused with the objects or goals of the game. And of course there is also a historical and cultural context for any game (all communication is situated).

In learning to critically read a video game, you must first be able to identify its underlying structure. What kind of game is it? What are its goals? What does it expect a player to accomplish? Where does it offer reward or penalty, and what forms do those rewards and penalties take? And finally, what assumptions does it make about its audience's interests and values? In other words, you will need to figure out what the conventions of that particular genre of game are before you can talk about how the game works.

Conventions, of course, will vary by genre, and sometimes vary even within a genre. An **adventure** game, for instance, might prioritize exploration and problem-solving, and award points to a player for finding hidden paths or secret stashes of treasure. They often structure gameplay around a narrative, or underlying story. Players go on quests or missions with specific goals, and have to complete those quests successfully in order to advance levels.

Puzzle games also require a player to problem-solve, but they lack the underlying narrative structure. The emphasis is on the player's ability to solve the puzzles for the puzzles' own sake, rather than to advance a story. Sports games revolve around **simulation**, in which players attempt to create through video gameplay a representation of a real-world experience. **First-person shooters,** like *Halo, Gears of War,* or *Band of Brothers: Hell's Highway* (all from the war genre), offer simulated combat with an underlying narrative. While there might be elements of the adventure game present, the game's objectives will center more around body counts and successful, combat-oriented strategies.

Cooperative play adds another layer to gaming. A **Massively Multi-Player Online Role-Playing Game**, or **MMORPG**, such as *World of Warcraft*, includes elements of both adventure and puzzle games—quests and problem-solving—but here, the context is focused more on the community of the game. Players work with, and against, each other, as well as the game, in order to acquire goods, points, advance in levels, and gain an in-game reputation. A co-op game of the first-person shooter/adventure game, *Gears of War*, will offer a different experience than a single-player version.

Another type of multi-player gaming occurs over networks, such as Xbox Live, which allows players from all over the world to participate in a shared environment and test their skills against each other, These **PVP** (player vs. player) environments bear little resemblance to the actual game-experience itself.

Each game appeals to a slightly different set of audience desires and expectations. Once you've figured out who the audience for a game is, and what the game's purpose is, you then need to think about the game's **message**. This is often distinct from gameplay objectives. What does the game value? Quick wits? Hand-eye coordination? Strategic planning? What social norms or expectations does the game reinforce or challenge?

2.11.4   Advertisements

Like film and TV (and most other multi-media texts), advertising texts are the result of a highly collaborative process, which is something to always keep in mind when you are reading them. Besides all the people who help create the ad itself, ads also go through a process of review and revision between the client and the advertising agency. In the case of big campaigns with millions of dollars spent in distribution, ads might also go through revision based on findings from consumer focus groups and surveys. More than any other text, ads are focused on their audience with a highly specific purpose.

Advertising is applied rhetoric: advertisers employ explicit and consistent use of rhetorical knowledge and theory. The purposes are simple: to persuade an audience to recognize a brand, think positively about a company, or to buy a product or service. Ads are often also a form of "public pedagogy," in that they teach attitudes or habits (they are generally not up-front about this purpose unless it's a public service ad).

Advertising exists in all the media—if there are eyeballs to catch, ads will be there. Large advertising agencies are split into departments based on media: print (magazines, newspapers, billboards, other signage), broadcast (TV and radio), interactive (web-based), and event-based (sponsorships, product placements, and viral marketing). These categories are blurring for advertisers now, just as they are for all of us. For example, it's not unusual to see a broadcast TV ad that works in conjunction with a web site. A popular product (like Coke or McDonald's) will be advertised across many media, and in that case, advertisers work to create consistent messaging throughout.

Advertising generally follows the same conventions as other texts in the same medium: print (still image) ads use written and visual conventions, broadcast ads use TV and film-based conventions, and interactive ads use online conventions. The main difference here to always keep in mind is that ads always have a very specific design on the audience: they are commercial. Here are a few other general practices of advertising texts:

A. Recognizable, Memorable

Because ads saturate our culture, successful advertisers devise some way of marking their text—making it recognizable and setting it apart as a means of connecting with their desensitized and distracted audience. Advertisers make their texts (and the products they represent) recognizable by using a uniform color palette, a repeated design element, a recognizable spokesperson, etc. A company or product logo is also part of making ads recognizable. Large companies employ a "brand manager" for the company itself or for each particular product—the brand manager's job is to keep the representation of the company or product uniform, recognizable, and on target with the goals of the advertising campaign.

Advertising texts must also be memorable because consumers often encounter them when they are not at the place where the product or service is offered. Many different rhetorical devices might be used to make a product memorable; one you're probably familiar is the use of humor. For instance, a consumer may not be at the store when he sees an ad for Orbit Gum. But if she has been exposed to enough kooky Orbit ads on TV, then hopefully she'll think of that product when in the check-out line ("For A Good Clean Feeling, No Matter What").

B. Association, Identification

Advertisements often ask the audience to identify with celebrities, spokespersons, or characters, thereby associating their product with that person. In these cases, the advertisers will choose someone who is particularly relevant for the target audience. Celebrities and other well-known people have something called a "Q Score," a numerical rating established by a marketing research company that is available for a price (the original Q Score company is Marketing Evaluations, Inc.—you can check them out at qscores.com). If the person the advertisers want to use does not yet have a Q Score, then the research company will create one by finding survey participants who fit into the particular target audience and then asking them to indicate whether they have heard of the person and whether they have positive feelings for him.

C. Branding

Products and companies have an ethos, just like people. In advertising-speak, this ethos is a brand. We as consumers develop relationships with brands over the course of our lives that determine our purchasing behaviors. Companies spend millions of dollars to build and maintain reputable brand images. For example, the recent TV campaign that features "PC" (John Hodgman) and "Mac" (Justin Long) is an Apple brand campaign. No one particular Mac product is being sold, but rather, Apple's overall credibility in comparison to PCs.

A credible corporate or product reputation can be very valuable, and in some cases provides incentive for mergers and acquisitions as well as ethical decisions in business strategy. In a famous case in 1982, Johnson and Johnson recalled millions of capsules of its Tylenol product when it found out that several bottles had been tampered with and were contaminated with cyanide. It then introduced a tamper-proof packaging. The resulting public image of the company yielded untold value in the form of public good will.

For example, in one of its most recent European "Is It In You?" campaigns, Gatorade features German soccer star Mikael Forssell (you can view this ad in its print form in your 39B Studio Links). From the context of the ad (a soccer game), we can deduce that it might refer to Forssell's leg strength, his scoring touch, his drive to win, or his general athletic ability. The reader might decide on any one of these (or more than one). By asking the reader to participate in constructing the full message of the ad, the message takes up comparatively more time and cognitive resources from the consumer. As a result, the consumer will be more likely to remember the product.

Mikael Forssell's ethos includes his athletic ability. In the above ad, the substitution of Gatorade for the ambiguous it pronoun implies that some of that athletic ability can be transferred to the consumer, if he buys and drinks Gatorade. The larger campaign enforces this message by associating the product with numerous celebrities from different sports: Michael Jordan, Derek Jeter, Tiger Woods, Venus Williams. By repeating the same basic ad-content with different sports and different stars, they increase the likelihood that the audience will remember the product through repetition. Gatorade also seeks exclusive sponsorship and endorsement deals with national professional sports leagues like the NBA, NFL, and NHL so that its product will frequently be seen in the hands of a pro athlete during the course of a game. When a consumer sees this drink repeatedly associated with professional athletes, she forms subconscious associations between the drink and the high skill and talent of these sports stars. Their ethos—their skill, ability, and professional status—is transferred to the drink, which then transfers that ethos to the consumer.

Notice that this transfer of ethos is largely implied. All advertisements make promises. They identify needs and then claim that a certain product or service will answer those needs. But most consumers would reject out of hand the claim that drinking Gatorade will make a person perform at the level of a professional athlete. If the ad explicitly stated this claim, the ethos or credibility of the company might suffer. By creating subtle and largely subconscious associations in their marketing communications, Gatorade is able to suggest that drinking their product is a pre-requisite for having it in you.

2.11.5 Web Sites

The World Wide Web is, at its heart, a series of networked machines that store and transfer data. But we tend to think of the web as an actual *place* (virtual space) in which we can find just about anything. We talk about surfing and navigating, as if the web is a physical environment that we must negotiate. For our rhetorical purposes, it's better to think of the web as a multi-modal medium, combining written text, visual images, video, and sound to create web pages of many genres for many purposes. As with any act of communication, the structure and conventions of a web site depend on its genre, intended audience, and purpose.

A. Web 1.0

When the web was first being spun, technology limited the creation of web page content; in the days of first-generation browsers, most of the internet consisted of words on a screen. The audience surfed to the site, looked at the content, and surfed away again (not much interaction in those days). Therefore, a web site had to make catching and keep audience attention a high priority. Thus, web conventions were born.

One top-level technique for classifying a web page is to identify its top-level domain, for example .com, .org, .gov, .mil, .edu, or .net. Of those five types, the .com is most common (although the 'com' actually stands for commercial, not common). No matter its type of domain, the balance between image and text, and between information and appearance, is crucial to a web page's success in appealing to its audience. Conversely, critically reading a web page's image, text, and color content is also a good way to discover its target audience, primary purposes, and rhetorical effectiveness.

A storefront site, like Amazon.com, is aimed at persuading a visitor to make a purchase. Everything on the site is placed there in order to fulfill this purpose. The site shows small images of many products to simulate an actual shopping experience. Unlike your basic brick-and-mortar mall store, however, Amazon has to rely on its web page to do the work of a salesperson. The site offers suggestions for other products you may wish to buy, related to something you've already purchased or searched. Amazon was one of the first major web companies to develop personalized content for each shopper so it could forge a connection with its customers.

Contrast Amazon's purpose with that of an .edu web site, like UCI (www.uci.edu). UCI site's purpose is primarily informative, with secondary purposes of projecting UCI's image to anyone who wants to visit the site (including people from other universities, parents, and prospective students). In order to do this, the site uses a lower image-to-text ratio than Amazon. Because visitors will be looking for specific information about academic programs, faculty, student services, enrollment, grades, registration, available jobs, etc., the site offers detailed menus or a search feature on every page. Instead of the storefront clutter of Amazon (rows of images meant to attract our shopperly attention), UCI.edu is constructed with smooth, uniform backgrounds, simple graphics, and images that show pleasant snapshots of campus life.

B. Web 2.0

Web 2.0 refers to web sites that emphasize collaboration, interactivity, and community. While many sites remain the province of a single author or entity, Web 2.0 sites blur the line between audience and author, allowing the audience to participate in the discourse and create the community. Sometimes this participation is limited to leaving comments or feedback, but some Web 2.0 sites even turn the audience *into* the authors.

You're probably familiar with social networking sites like Facebook, MySpace, or LinkedIn. They're all Web 2.0 sites designed to create/reinforce connections among groups of people (discourse communities). Each member maintains a personal page on which basic information is displayed (name, location, age, etc.), as well as a personal icon or image. The audience also depends on the degree to which the member controls her privacy settings. A Facebook account locked to "friends only" is clearly aimed at a limited audience of already-familiar people. This suggests that the user probably isn't that interested in expanding her social network, but would rather maintain the one she has. But someone who creates a MySpace page with minimal privacy options, studded with personal information, video clips, songs, and photographs is trying to attract visitors to her page, and to forge new social connections. Although social networking sites do allow audience participation—you can post to someone's Wall, or leave a comment—the primary control over the page remains with the member-author.

And then there is YouTube, where users can upload video clips of just about anything: Concert footage, music videos, Rhetoric In Practice projects, fan-videos, vintage television commercials—the sky, and copyright protections, are the limit. Users can comment on each other's videos, but only the original poster can remove or alter the video.

Another Web 2.0 killer app is Wikipedia, the well-known and much-maligned online encyclopedia. Like any encyclopedia, Wikipedia strives to provide objective, accurate information, presented in short articles that include images, hyperlinks, sources, and citations. What makes Wikipedia unique is that it allows *anyone* to update it. While in theory this means that everyone contributes accurate information, in practice it means that sometimes the primary purpose of the site—to offer accurate information—is sidelined in favor of interactivity. This is where the site gets its dodgy reputation (and why your teachers will discourage you from using it as a source for research papers). If *anyone* can post or overwrite *anything*, then there is no guarantee of accuracy on Wikipedia's articles.

Chapter 3

PROCESSING COMPOSITION

Writin' Ain't Easy. Often during the first week of classes, we ask, "Do you like writing?" Most students do not raise their hands. Chances are, you don't like writing and you don't consider yourself to be a "good" writer. If you like writing, consider yourself good at it, and look forward to writing assignments, you are very rare. Even professional writers admit that sometimes writing is a painful process. A number of famous writers (Dorothy Parker, Ernest Hemmingway, to name a few) have been quoted as saying, "I hate writing; I love having written." In other words, while the product may be satisfying, the process is often like pulling teeth.

Writing is just another form of communication—we don't usually tie ourselves up in knots when it comes to other forms of communication: we can give opinions to friends about a new restaurant without procrastinating; answer the phone and talk to a family member (usually no pain involved); speak up in class to answer a question (maybe a bit more painful); ask our professor for an extension (sometimes more painful than others). Why is writing so much harder?

Past Experiences. One reason might be the experiences you've had thus far with school writing assignments. If you keep a diary or post a blog, you'd probably say that this kind of writing isn't nearly as painful as a writing assignment for school. In the past, perhaps you had a teacher who wrote a lot of comments everywhere on your paper (in red!) that confused and/or depressed you. Maybe you had a teacher who told you it looked fine but then gave you a poor grade, so you stopped trusting what you thought was good. Or maybe you had a teacher who wasn't very nice about how she commented on your work and wrote things like "Huh?" or "This makes no sense!" on your paper.

If you get a low grade on a multiple-choice test, you're bummed, of course, but you don't take it personally, the way you might with writing. If, for example, you confuse the definition of fission and fusion on your test, you might be a little upset that you didn't study harder, but you probably won't throw your hands up in the air and say, "I'm a bad rememberer!" However, a low grade on an essay often evokes a more personal response: "I've always been a lousy writer!" Writing is more personal because it is connected to identity—we put ourselves into those sentences. Because writing is part of who we are, how we express ourselves or communicate our intentions to the world, we carry all those past bad experiences like hearts on our sleeves.

Past experiences accumulate and can make for some pretty tortured attempts at new writing projects. It's time to turn a corner. You've begun a new journey now—as you progress through the composition series, make it your goal to use what was good from your past writing experiences and forget the bad.

Becoming Better. Many people have the mistaken assumption that good writers are somehow born with the ability; when they sit down to write, perfectly formed sentences and paragraphs flow into a finished product as if by magic. If you think you're "no good" at writing, you might be holding yourself up to this unrealistic ideal.

The truth is, there is nothing magical about the writing process. The only way to improve is to maintain a positive attitude and keep practicing. You learn to become a better writer the same way that you acquired language and learned how to communicate in the first place—through lots of practice, trial and error, and more practice. Ten weeks in a course won't magically make you a perfect writer, but we hope that your composition classes will set you on the path to a life-long pursuit of becoming better.

In the book *Outliers*, Malcolm Gladwell explains the 10,000-hour theory of success: simply put, that success doesn't happen overnight. Find any successful individual, and you'll probably discover that this individual spent at least 10,000 hours practicing, increasing her skills, and perfecting her technique. Michael Phelps, the gold-medal Olympic swimmer, swims 50 miles per week when in training. The Beatles performed more than 1,000 gigs in Germany before they became famous in England. Likewise, writing takes sustained practice. Even though some writers may possess greater natural talent (just as some athletes possess the right physique for a sport), gaining success at writing means spending time writing, and rewriting, and writing some more.

Process and Product. In your composition courses, you'll be asked to write for various purposes and audiences. You will, of course, be writing some academic essays, since this is a genre often assigned to college students. You might think of the academic essay as an Olympic event or the big game—the **product** of much time and work.

But you'll also be asked to compose texts that are more like practice—those 50 miles per week in the pool. We call these practice-like assignments **process** assignments, and though the stakes are a bit lower (you write several smaller assignments and the grades are all averaged together vs. you write one essay and get one big final grade), the importance of this practice cannot be underestimated. This practice writing is not just "busy work." It's a necessary part of the process of becoming an accomplished communicator. Would Michael Phelps have ever won gold if the only time he practiced was the night before the Olympics?

Both the process and the product of composition are important, and that's why we'll focus on both—and you'll be graded on both—throughout the composition series.

3.1   Composing Academic Texts at the University

You're no stranger to writing. You've had to write essays all through high school, and you had to write them to get into college. You may not like writing much, but you know some strategies, and you probably already have something of a process developed: you get the prompt, you come up with a main argument, you pick three ideas to discuss. Then you wait until either inspiration or desperation strikes and you write the essay (usually the night before it's due) and turn it in after a quick proofread for typos. So, you know about essays—big words, long sentences, one paragraph per point that you're trying to prove. So why are we making such a big deal about college writing? How different can it be?

In a word: very. Here at UCI, you will be asked to produce texts in which you attempt to enter the **academic discourse** of a discipline. Academic texts are highly specialized, specific, and researched: this is a type of writing for which you most definitely need a process. An academic essay at the university still requires an interesting and arguable thesis and organized paragraphs, but it is more analytical than the writing you produced in high school, and you are expected to write with an **academic ethos** that illustrates your expertise in the ways of the **discourse community**. Your ideas must be developed and researched, and your writing style must rise to the level of your content.

And that means no more five-paragraph essays, no more repeating and restating your arguments just to eat up space, no more using big words just to sound more knowledgeable—and most importantly, no more putting off your writing until the last possible moment. You're going to need time for revision if you want to succeed at academic writing because no one can write the kind of intellectual and eloquent texts expected of scholars in just one sitting.

3.2   What's Your Process?

Each of us has a unique writing process and good writers learn to recognize and honor what works best for them. Recognizing personal idiosyncrasies, setting goals, and giving yourself breaks and rewards can often make your writing process more efficient.

Perhaps your thoughts are most organized in the morning? Or maybe you're the kind of person who is most focused when everyone else has gone to bed and your house or dorm is quiet? Maybe you need chocolate or strong coffee or soothing music to help you focus your thoughts and feel energized? Perhaps you need to go out and take a brisk walk or run, or go to the gym when the well runs dry?

What's important is that you start thinking about academic writing as needing a process—and start figuring out what works best for you. Experiment and observe to discover what patterns make you most productive. Here are some practices that you will encounter in your composition courses; we recommend that you make them permanent elements of your academic writing process:

Take Time to Think and Talk About It. Even before a thesis or outline becomes clear, spend lots of time reading (or re-reading) background material, or talking to colleagues, friends, or family about the topic. Try letting your topic percolate as you go about your daily routine, while you drive your car, or as you walk through Aldrich Park. The more you think about your topic, the better formed your ideas and writing will be.

Write, Read, and Revise in Chunks. Try writing a small part of an assignment and then go back and reread what you wrote several times, revising as you read. When you feel good about that section, move on to the next one. If you come back for the next chunk after time has passed, start the new session by re-reading what you wrote in the earlier session(s). Like a loop-stitch in sewing, this back and forth process makes the final text that much stronger.

Write to Learn. Sometimes even after you've thought about it a bit, you still don't know what you want to say about the topic. In cases like these, use writing as a tool of discovery. Set yourself a time limit of five or ten minutes and then free-write: put down everything you can think of about the topic—and then write some more. Keep writing. Somewhere in the process of putting it down on paper, you'll discover what's important.

3.3   Rhetorical Composing Methodology (Déjà Vu)

We suggest that you always begin your process for writing academic texts by walking through some questions very like the ones you learned from Chapter 2 for reading rhetorically. In the discussion below, we'll use examples from your composition courses, but these questions can be asked for any writing assignment you receive while at UCI—and knowing the answers to them will guarantee more effective composition.

Composing: A Rhetorical Methodology

Rhetor. Identify your rhetorical situation for creating the text. Why are you writing? What ethos should you adopt?

Audience. For whom are you creating the text? What do they expect of you as rhetor?

Text. What is your primary message? What are your perspectives about the topic, and how will your own bias color the process?

What medium (media) will you use to construct the text? How will this affect your process?

In which genre(s) are you composing? What conventions of form and content are expected of texts in this genre? How will your text follow, play with, or reject these conventions?

Context. How might the specific historical moment in which you write influence your thinking? Are you composing within a particular subculture? What is the disciplinary context for your writing?

3.3.1   What Is Your Purpose?

Why are you being asked to do this assignment? Are you supposed to inform your readers? Respond? Reflect? Entertain? Persuade? Some combination? Understanding the purpose for your writing will not only put you in the right frame of mind, it will give you a place to start and help you figure out how much processing you'll have to do to effectively complete the assignment.

Many "why" questions can be answered with a careful reading of the assignment prompt, whether it's in an email from your professor or a formal paragraph included in the syllabus. You may have to read the prompt more than once to fully understand the purpose. Look for words like *discuss*, *explain* (purpose = informational), *claim* or *argue* (purpose = persuade). If you can't find the answer to why you're composing in the prompt, ask your instructor.

3.3.2   Who Is the Audience? What Are Their Expectations?

Every day in normal conversation, you make (probably unconscious) choices of how to form your words to satisfy audience expectations. If you talk with your mother about the grade you got on your last bio exam, you will most likely package the info differently than if you're telling the same content to your best friend.

The audience to whom you write will determine not only your tone and level of formality, but also help you plan for many other aspects of your writing. Much of this chapter is dedicated to helping you understand what, in general, an academic audience expects. Additionally, in your composition courses, you'll often be asked to write to the audience of your classmates. These assignments are to help you think about audience while you write, and to get into the habit of thinking about what a particular audience expects.

If you are writing a blog or forum to introduce yourself to your classmates, your language and tone will be more informal and you may create only one draft of your work (proofread, of course!). If you are emailing or texting a friend, or writing a comment on Facebook, you might be more informal still, using conventions such as abbreviations, slang, or emoticons. However, if you are writing an essay that you hope will provide entry into a particular academic discourse community, your process should involve several stages of development, drafting, and revision.

3.3.3   What Is Your Message? What Form Will It Take?

In an academic essay, your message is also called the **thesis**. Later in this chapter, we'll go into more detail about what an academic audience expects of a thesis. Beyond the thesis, you must also consider what form your composition will take—will you be writing by hand in an in-class essay or composing a draft at your computer that will undergo peer review? Is it an essay or a web page? A visual text or written? Although these assignments might be the same genre (essay), the medium in which you'll write will make a difference in how you proceed.

If you are composing a particular genre for a type of publication such as an academic journal, a magazine, a newspaper, or a web site, you should begin by researching the conventions of that genre and publication. These factors will determine the length of your article, how you will shape your language and tone to appeal to your readers, whether or not you should incorporate quotations, citations, and a bibliography into your work, and how much historical background you will need to provide.

Throughout the rest of this chapter, we will focus on elements in the process of writing a formal academic essay. Because the form of a book is linear (it has to progress from page to page), the elements of this process will be presented in a linear fashion. However, the writing process is never really linear—instead, it's **iterative**. That means instead of progressing in a straight line, the steps you'll take will be more cyclical and incremental.

3.4   Reading the Prompt

It may sound elementary to say "carefully read the assignment prompt before you begin your composition process," but this is one area where students often try to save time by thinking, "Well, the teacher already explained the assignment in class and I understand everything about it."

However, a prompt is more than just an overview of the assignment. It's a carefully thought-out, step-by-step process based on your instructor's understanding of the information you need to have about an assignment before you begin. It's a tool to help you gather your thoughts, to ask—and answer—the right questions. It clearly outlines the objectives of the assignment—the goals you are expected to accomplish and the skills you will be developing while you compose your text or multi-media project. It also states what your instructor is expecting in terms of length, annotation, and accompanying materials—as well as something about how the assignment will be graded.

Just as you revise your compositions, instructors are always revising prompts based upon their years of experiences with student writing and what students need most to understand a particular assignment. So, a prompt is designed with your success in mind. But first you have to read it—more than once—and ask questions if there is anything you don't understand. Just as you annotate a text, you should highlight or underline key points or steps of the prompt. This kind of critical prompt-reading is necessary not only for big assignments like essays, but also for process assignments like blogs, forums, or wikis.

3.5   Exploration and Discovery

Exploratory writing has a very important purpose—it's not just busy work. In your composition classes, you will be asked to complete exploratory assignments (i.e., a forum to answer study questions on a text, or a blog to reflect on your initial response to a film)—but in your other university classes where writing is assigned, you'll probably have to perform exploratory writing on your own, as part of your process for understanding and developing ideas.

Exploratory writing deepens your understanding of a topic and helps you discover what you think about it. Here are some tried-and-true exploratory methods:

3.5.1   Brainstorming

This classic idea-generating technique is used in the business world as well as at the university. In this technique, the point is to get as many ideas down on a page as possible, without self-censoring—thinking too much about which ideas are "good" and which are "bad." Once you have put some thoughts on the page, you can start to make connections between ideas, and gradually an argument starts to take shape.

3.5.2 Making a List, Grid, or Flowchart

For some topics, it seems logical to start with listing, or even drawing a grid or flowchart. Students who are naturally visual find this an especially helpful tool to explore their ideas. Making a list, grid, or flowchart works best when you don't edit or self-censor too much: just write down every possible idea, and then start to draw the connections between them. Remember, you are exploring to discover, so there is no "right" or "wrong."

3.5.3 Free Writing

This is exactly what it sounds like: writing that doesn't take any particular shape. This is like talking through a problem with a friend: you don't necessarily know how long it will take to find the answer, but you talk and talk until an answer surfaces in the conversation. Free writing is analogous to practicing scales or riffs before you begin to play a musical instrument—it warms up your mind.

If you've never practiced free writing before, the best way to start is to time yourself. Set aside a 5- or 10-minute period and then write everything that comes to mind about a topic or a particular aspect of the topic. Don't stop writing, even if what's coming out doesn't seem to make sense. In the rush of free writing, you will often come up with ideas that you did not know you had! Some instructors will ask you to free write in class, providing focus for your efforts. Keep in mind that only you can determine if you've written enough. If you write for a page and still haven't discovered anything new, then keep going.

3.5.4 Paraphrasing

Frequently in your college classes, you'll be asked to use a demanding nonfiction text as a foundation for your writing assignment. It's very important in cases like this that you fully understand what the text is saying. The best way to make sure that you have critically read the text is to write a paraphrase of it—or at least to find the most important sections and paraphrase those. The process of having to read carefully enough to then rewrite the ideas in your own words will not only bring you a deeper understanding of the text itself, it may give you ideas for how to develop your own arguments about the text. Your instructor may ask you to paraphrase passages of a text in order to help you think more critically about that passage.

3.5.5   Asking Questions

Sometimes the best way to deepen your understanding of a subject is to ask yourself questions—and then, of course, take the time to answer them. You can start with the journalist's classic five questions: Who? What? Where? When? Why? And don't forget to add How? to get a general shape of the problem. Then you can ask more detailed questions.

1. How would I define X?

2. What are all of the parts of X? And what might I name those parts?

3. What has caused X? And what might be consequences of X?

4. What's the significance of X?

5. Have I ever experienced X?

6. What does X remind me of?

7. Who might be on the side of X? Against it?

8. Do I understand the significance of the text or subject I'm writing about?

9. Have I found meaningful connections between one part of the text and another? Do I see meaningful connections between the subject at hand and other sources I've read and experienced?

10. Have I spent enough time looking closely at all of the details of the text or subject at hand?

Asking who, what, where, when, why, and how is an especially important exercise in 39C when you are trying to define the parameters of your research problem. It's also helpful in 39B for determining the rhetorical situation of a text.

3.5.6   Outlining

Once you've worked out some of your preliminary ideas through pre-writing, you may want to create an outline. Outlining can help you to see where some of your ideas overlap and intersect. A good outline provides a clear organization of ideas and helps you to think more logically about the material at hand.

How do you decide the order in which you will present your ideas? There are two basic ways to approach this problem: you can put your most important idea first, or you can put it last. If you start out with the most important idea (or claim), then you are starting out with a bang—which is sometimes just what you want to do. If you save the most important idea for last, it's like the grand finale at the end of a fireworks show—and sometimes this is the effect you wish to have on your reader. Your ultimate decision about the order in which you present your ideas, topics, and claims depends upon finding the most effective way you can come up with to achieve your purpose—to deliver a convincing argument to your chosen audience.

While there are no hard and fast rules for determining the most effective organizational model, there are a few strategic points to consider. First, is the argument you're trying to make fairly straightforward, or does it require a lot of background information to move from point to point along a more complex path? If your argument is pretty simple, starting off with a bang may be a good way to grab your audience's attention. Of course, you run the risk of losing your readers' interest pretty quickly if they have nothing but lesser points and a summary conclusion to look forward to for the rest of the essay. There's a reason why Disneyland saves the biggest fireworks for the finale.

On the other hand, saving the big guns for the end may be a risky rhetorical strategy if you're pressed for time. That's why starting with your most important point and working back from there may be a more effective way to compose an in-class essay.

In most rhetorical situations, however, if you want to hold your readers' interest it makes sense to start slowly and build toward a satisfying, even flashy, conclusion. The more complex your argument is, the more sense this generally makes. Remember that many of the formal assignments you'll be writing ask you to come up with complex, arguable theses that require a great deal of background research or understanding of the problems or texts around which you will be constructing your arguments. Putting the most important idea first may confuse rather than dazzle your readers if they lack the contextual information they need to understand the point you're trying to make.

So where do you start? Simply put, start with your audience.

Who Is Your Audience and What Do They Know? How would you define your audience? Where are they starting from in terms of your argument? What are their assumptions and expectations? How familiar are they with the topic, problem, or text you plan to analyze? Now, list the key contextual points they will need to know to understand your argument. Label these points in your introduction.

Where Do You Want to Take Your Audience? What basic claims do you plan to make? For what reason(s)? What conclusion do you wish your audience to reach as a result? Label these in your thesis.

©Hayden-McNeil, LLC

How Do You Plan to Get Them There? Expanding on the broad frame set up in your thesis, list the specific points your audience will have to consider (in a sequence that makes logistical sense) in order to reach the conclusion you want them to make. Under each point listed, note any specific quotations, statistics, or other evidence you have or think you will need to support it. This is your argument.

If you have trouble determining the order of your points, remember that just as most travelers like to take the most direct route to their destination, so readers prefer the most direct path between points in an argument. When in doubt, ask yourself what came first, or what is closest to your reader's point of reference. Then, what point follows that one most closely in time, space, or proximity of ideas? And so on.

Think of your argument as a journey, your audience as the travelers on that journey, and you as their tour guide. If you think of your outline as the MapQuest directions for that journey, your outline points should correspond to the steps along the road that your audience will need to follow to get from one point to the next.

How many points you outline depends on the number and types of connections you're going to need to draw between your ideas in order for your audience to follow your argument. The more complex your argument, the more detailed steps you'll need to guide your reader from point to point along the way.

Some writers like to create an outline using words or short phrases, while others find it more useful to write complete sentences. However, don't write so much that you can't see the structure and flow of ideas at a glance. Remember, the outline is only the skeleton of the essay. You'll have to write the meat and bones later.

Know too that not all outlines are written *before* the composition process. One extremely useful tool is called **reverse outlining.** This means that you create a new outline by pulling out the thesis, topic sentences, and main ideas from your first draft to troubleshoot the organization and progression of ideas. A reverse outline will immediately show you whether or not your ideas are flowing in a way that makes sense to a reader, and where there might still be weaknesses or holes in your argument and evidence. It will also show you whether or not you've left out any key points and arguments from your original outline.

3.6   Formulating a Thesis

The success of an academic essay depends on the focus and strength of the argument. You have a point to make, and you need to make sure that your reader understands that point early in the essay. While a whole essay is needed to develop your argument and make it convincing to your readers, you should be able to sum up your argument in one or two sentences: the thesis. In your composition courses, your instructor will require you to create a thesis early in the process of development. Since the thesis of an academic essay is the most important sentence in the paper, you should revise it several times—even before you turn in your working draft.

A thesis must do two things well: (1) state the main point of your paper in a sentence or two and (2) provide some direction for how you will develop the thesis in the body of your paper.

Because it's a concentrated form of the whole essay, the thesis sentence should use words precisely— much like a poem boils language down to its essence.

Although you will create the best working thesis you can before beginning the process of composing your paper, you may find—as you write your body paragraphs and develop your arguments—that your ideas change or become clearer. For that reason, it is always best to revisit, rethink, revise, or even rewrite your thesis during or after the first working draft of your paper to reflect any shifts in your thinking that have occurred.

Don't be frustrated if you need to revise your thesis. In fact, most good writers do. After all, your working draft should help you to see what's clear and what's not clear in your argument.

3.7   Drafting

Developing your ideas into an extended essay is the hard part, because it involves actually translating general ideas in your head into concrete words and sentences and staying focused on what you want to say. The bad news is that it takes time. The good news is that writing gets easier with practice, like any other skill. The following steps aren't a guarantee of success or a magic formula, but they are a series of steps and guidelines to help get you through your draft.

Re-Read the Prompt. Take time throughout your process to remind yourself of what the prompt is directing you to do in your paper (your purpose, audience, etc). If you've drifted off the best path in your latest revision, re-reading the prompt will help you get back.

Review Selected Passages (Scenes). Look back at either the text you're analyzing or the sources you are using to help you support your argument throughout the process; this will help you make sure you understand the nuances of the texts you're working with. This will also give you a chance to hone in on tools to strengthen your argument—look for pertinent quotations, strong examples, or ideas that can be paraphrased. If you're writing about a visual text like a film, look for specific lines of dialogue, actor's facial expressions, or other elements of the mise én scene that can be used to help develop your ideas.

Expect Change. As you write, you may realize that the really cool scene or quotation you'd intended to analyze doesn't fit with the shape your argument is taking, and that you're moving away from your outline. That's okay! As long as you're still on track with your purpose, let your ideas change and develop. This is a draft, after all.

Give Yourself Enough Time. This is the key, and something we can't stress enough. You might've written successful papers in high school the night before they were due, but that habit won't work well in college. Please don't try to write a seven-page paper all in one sitting. Writing your paper over three or four days will give you a chance to get some perspective and see things more clearly. Even when you're not writing, your mind is always at work sifting through ideas and coming up with solutions.

Write More than One Draft. And this is why we insist on lots of time for writing an essay. No one ever does his or her best in just one draft. Making time for at least two drafts will exponentially improve your final product. Also, your goal is to create a **working draft**, which is different from a **rough draft**.

The rough draft is the very first attempt(s) you make at writing the paper. A working draft is, however, is a paper that is as complete, organized, and focused as you can make it—the best you can do with what you know about the assignment at the time. Peer reviews and your instructor's input will help you discover your next steps toward a finished essay. In the 39 series, peer editing and drafting are actually part of your final essay grade.

Remember: Complex Composition Requires a Process. Improving your writing takes time. Let your goal be steady improvement with each draft and each assignment. Become aware of what you do well and watch out for common error patterns. In an interview, Ernest Hemmingway reported to have rewritten the ending to *A Farewell to Arms* 39 times. Other accomplished writers readily admit to revising almost obsessively. So, if you find that you need more than two drafts to do well on your papers, then you're in good company.

3.8   Getting Feedback

It's difficult to ever be 100 percent objective about your own writing. That's because you are too close to it after spending so much intensive time composing. Ideas that are quite clear in your head, and which you think are quite clear on paper, are sometimes not so clear to a reader. And sometimes you'll know that there are certain problems with your ideas or structure, but you just won't know how to make your draft better.

Fortunately, there are many places where you can go for help—and experience has shown that students who ask for extra help usually get better grades. At UCI you have three main resources: your instructor, your fellow students as peer reviewers, and free on-campus resources such as LARC and the Peer Tutoring Services.

3.8.1   From Your Instructor

Conferencing

Take advantage of your instructor's office hours! Conferences present a useful opportunity to discuss and clarify any questions you have about your draft or comments you've received on it from your peers or your instructor. She can also help you plan what you need to do next in terms of conceptual and structural revisions of your draft. If you can't make it to a face-to-face conference, your instructor might offer online AIM office hours—or might not mind you sending an email to ask for help. When you email any instructor to ask for help, remember your rhetorical situation: be respectful and detailed in your question, and always sign your name.

Written Comments

Pay close attention to your instructor's comments. These will help you assess how effectively you've responded to the prompt and give you suggestions about how to make your writing stronger. Read these comments carefully and use them to help you create a plan for revising your final draft. If you have questions about what the comments mean, don't be afraid to ask for clarification.

Some of your instructor's comments will address your language. For example, he or she might point out that a verb tense is incorrect or that the syntax in a particular phrase is awkward. If you are not clear about something, ask for clarification. But don't expect your instructor to correct grammar and mechanics for you. Ultimately, you are the one who is responsible for fixing errors in your writing.

Don't feel intimidated or singled out if your teacher writes a lot on your paper. Sometimes instructors provide the most feedback on papers that they believe have the greatest potential. Or they may have written a lot because they find your ideas interesting and want to see you develop them to their fullest extent.

By the same token, don't feel that your paper is perfect if the instructor did not write much on it. Many instructors will spend class time going over generalized grammar or conceptual problems they see on drafts within the class community rather than make the same comment over and over on individual papers. But, again, ask for more help if you need it. Instructors enjoy helping students or they wouldn't be teaching in the first place.

RHETORICAL ASIDE

Consider the rhetorical situation involved when reading your instructor's comments. Your instructors are readers, just like anyone else. They may be more experienced readers, but, like all readers, they might miss something, or read incorrectly, or get the wrong idea about a sentence. Therefore, don't imagine that you can simply correct all the marked areas and have an A paper. Your instructor may choose to comment on only the most pressing problems, or concentrate on a particular type of problem for that particular draft. Or, he may not spot a problem or overreact to something on the first read.

You are responsible for what you create and how you revise. You must develop a voice inside (the editor in your head) until it is strong enough to listen to feedback from as many places as you can get it—and then you must decide how you will proceed as a result of the feedback.

3.8.2   Peer Review

In your composition courses, peer review is actually a part of your grade in the class. There's a reason for this: peer review operates as a learning experience on two levels. First, you will never be 100 percent objective about your own writing, but critically reading the work of others enables you to revisit important elements of the assignment, including creating an arguable and complex thesis, drafting paragraphs with strong topic sentences, effective quoting and paraphrasing, making clear and well-developed arguments, and maintaining an academic tone and ethos throughout.

Second, the more you play the role of the perceptive academic reader, the more familiar it will become to you and the more capable you will be of seeing places to revise in your own work. You won't always have peer reviewers to offer feedback (or instructors), so the more of these skills you can internalize now, the better your writing will be as you advance through the university. You should always have the goal of further developing and refining the editor in your head.

Besides teaching you important self-editing skills, peer review helps to build strong class community. Studies have shown that you learn as much from other students as you do from your instructor. Some instructors opt to conduct this peer review as an in-class workshop. Others extend the workshop environment outside of class by holding group conferences, assigning online exercises, or conducting office hours focused on a particular theme.

Regardless of the types of peer review exercises you take part in during your first-year writing courses, the goal remains the same: to improve your writing by making it a part of a classroom community, where writers and their audiences have real responsibilities. Remember, language is by nature a social entity—language was created for the purpose of communicating between two or more people. Therefore, the only way you can become a better manipulator of language, whether it be reading and interpreting or writing it, is to communicate with others about your ideas.

Sometimes writers are so focused on what they are communicating that they don't see what ideas are still between the lines. Your peers' comments can give you valuable insights about undeveloped parts of your argument, as well as any structural weaknesses. Remember, at this point in the writing process, they have more objectivity than you do.

Ask Specific Questions of Your Reviewer

A lot of students come to peer editing with a rather negative attitude. "I don't ever get any good feedback," they complain. Part of the problem is their approach to peer editing. You can't just hand your paper to a groupmate and expect insightful commentary. Give your peer editors some idea what you're looking for. Instead of asking "Is this okay?" ask a specific question, such as "Do you think I should switch the order of these two points?" or "Does this introduction help you understand the background of my argument, why it's important, and how I'm planning to develop this paper?" Share your concerns with your reviewer to ensure that you get more focused advice.

Try Asking for Help Earlier in Your Writing Process

Don't wait for a complete draft before seeking feedback. Sometimes students are embarrassed to show other people unfinished writing, but that's exactly the point when you can most benefit from feedback. (Do you really want to labor over a paragraph for three hours, only to have your peer editor tell you it doesn't work with your argument?) As you outline or create your first drafts, you can seek help from your teacher, trusted friends, and fellow students.

Just remember that *you* must do the actual writing. *Never* allow anyone to re-write your work for you. That defeats the whole purpose of the composition process, and it is a form of plagiarism that could get you in more trouble than it's worth.

Ask for Clarification

If your reviewer's comments are vague or unclear, ask him or her to explain the comment in a different way. Your reviewers, especially your classmates, are learning about this process just as you are. That means that sometimes you might have to help them to help you. The best way to do this is to not let them get away with pleasant but unhelpful responses such as "This is great! Don't change a thing!" That's great for your ego, but not so great for improving your writing.

Compare and Contrast Comments

If everyone agrees that your introduction is too brief, or that your thesis does not answer the prompt, then you'll need to give this comment serious thought. You may, however, receive some conflicting advice on how to revise your paper. This is not necessarily because your editors are inexperienced. After all, even experts can disagree about writing. Consider all the comments and then decide which are the best ones to focus on as you revise.

Don't Judge the Worth of All Comments Based on One Reviewer

You are bound to get some comments that are not helpful, even when you ask for clarification. Don't let a few unhelpful comments convince you that peer review is not valuable.

Remember the Bottom Line

No matter what anyone says, it's ultimately you who must decide what deserves to be kept, expanded, deleted, or changed, based on what will best serve your paper's purpose. Learn to weigh outside input against your own best instincts.

Make Asking for Feedback Part of Your Composition Process

If you get into the habit of asking other people what they think about your writing, you'll become a better writer as a result. You don't have to only get feedback from your instructor or your classmates—you can ask anyone whose opinion you trust to look at your paper. Talk with friends throughout the writing process. When starting an essay, it might be especially helpful to bounce your ideas off of someone whose opinions you trust.

Asking for feedback reminds you that writing is a social process; you're no longer operating in a vacuum, wondering whether you understand the assignment or whether you are communicating clearly. By seeking feedback, you are taking positive, constructive steps to develop as a writer.

However, because writing is tied to your identity—it is your writing, your thoughts composed—**you** must be the final judge of how to revise. In order to be a successful composer, your inside voice (your internal editor) should drive you to be more of a perfectionist than any teacher or peer could ever be—that voice knows you (it is you); it must expect the best and only the best, and insist that you keep processing until you are proud to sign your name to the text.

3.9   Giving Feedback

So you're looking at one of your group mate's papers, and you're thinking, "How can I comment on this? What do I know about writing? What if I'm wrong?" And while it's true that you may not have the expertise of your writing instructor, your role as a fresh audience to an essay can be just as valuable as the opinion of any expert. Besides, you've been in the same class with your group mate, reading the same texts, listening to the same class discussions. You really are an expert. Tell the writer how well her text plays to a real audience (in this case, to you).

3.9.1   But What Should I Say?

Your instructor will usually provide review questions particular to an assignment. But if your roommate comes to you at midnight and asks you to look over his introduction and first body paragraph, you might need to revert to the basics. For any peer review situation, start with the largest order concerns. Does the draft address the prompt? Is the writer's purpose clear? Are the points arranged logically? Is the writer's ethos sound?

Note that these questions don't begin to address grammar, editing, or proofreading. There's a reason for this. First, at the drafting stage, you're looking at ideas that aren't yet fully formed. Sentences will come and go. If you get bogged down in the dangling participle in the third sentence of paragraph two, you might not notice that paragraph two doesn't have anything to do with the thesis. Your job is to critically analyze the argument and the evidence used to support claims.

3.9.2   Nuts and Bolts

However, it is the job of a peer-reviewer to help a writer recognize **error patterns**, such as consistent misspellings of a word, consistent mistakes in verb tense, using "there" instead of "their," faulty parallel constructions (which often occur in draft thesis statements). Often students who are recent immigrants to this country or speak a second language at home are used to different word patterns and may not even be aware that they are making an error if you don't point it out to them.

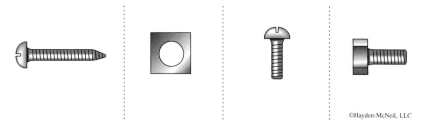

Use your judgment to understand the difference between errors your colleague can catch on his or her own, and errors he simply does not recognize. Also, there's nothing wrong with saying, "This paper needs a good proofreading." Some students are just careless and have not taken sufficient time to read over their writing. If dozens of typos, misspellings, and other errors make it difficult to follow your peer's argument, let her know.

When You Offer Peer Review

1. Avoid giving upbeat but empty comments just to protect your peer's feelings.

2. Show respect for your colleague by being honest yet supportive. Point out the parts of the essay that contribute to its current level of effectiveness, but point out deficiencies as well.

3. Make your advice as specific as possible.

4. If something works, explain why and how. If something does not work, mark specifically what needs revision and explain exactly why it is not working.

5. Focus on the progression of the argument.

6. Look specifically at how the argument unfolds, and honestly assess the writer's effectiveness at persuading you to agree with his or her viewpoint.

7. Remember the big picture.

8. Always consider the goals of the prompt and the particular assignment you are reviewing, and let those considerations shape your comments.

3.10   Revising Rhetorically

Having to revise does not mean that you are bad writer. Good writers write multiple drafts of their stories, poems, essays, or reports. In between each draft, the writer asks for comments from colleagues or editors, and then makes changes to help clarify a point, smooth a bumpy transition, or enhance an example.

Professional writers are not afraid to remove whole paragraphs or sections from an essay or a chapter and start again with a clearer purpose in mind. The good thing about sentences is you can always make more.

The same is true of any medium in which you might compose. A landscape photographer might set up, frame, and shoot dozens or even hundreds of photos before she ends up with one in which the lighting and composition fulfill her intended purpose. And even then she might further enhance or manipulate the color, increase the contrast, crop the photo, or perform any number of small adjustments in Photoshop before she is completely satisfied. Artists might paint over whole sections of their canvas and start again, directors reshoot scenes, musicians lay down multiple tracks until they get the desired result. Revision is part of the composition process.

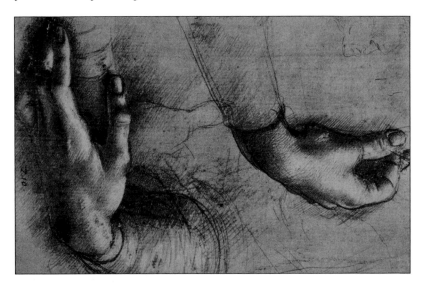

3.10.1   Large-Scale Revision

Think of revision as a two-stage process. The first is the "big picture." In a multi-media project such as a film, that might mean making sure that the scenes are edited together in the proper sequence. In an essay this means revising to enhance or clarify your overall argument—perhaps rewriting the thesis, throwing out or adding whole paragraphs, inserting new examples and analysis, finding an academic source with stronger evidence to back up your argument, or re-thinking your conclusion. Once you know you've got the overall essay on track, move on to small-scale revision, looking for smaller components or elements of the essay that need attention. In other words, it's a good idea to make changes to your argument, development, and organization before you start worrying about word choice or punctuation.

After you've completed your working draft and received comments back from your peer reviewers and your instructor, take some time to categorize these comments and make a plan of action before you start any revision. If you've received detailed comments, revision can feel overwhelming, but the process will feel a lot easier if you try to accomplish only two or three tasks in each revision session. Spreading out your revision over a few days will also give you a chance to percolate ideas and find new solutions. Remember: writing takes time.

A. Revising for Argument and Purpose

If you're writing a thesis-driven essay, you will find that each draft helps you to clarify your argument and purpose (your rhetorical situation). Revisit the prompt, and make sure your essay is fulfilling the assignment requirements. Find your thesis. Does it still describe the argument you made in your essay? Are your ethos and tone appropriate for your audience? Do your arguments or multi-media elements develop and deliver your message in an effective and clear way?

B. Revising for Development

Sometimes revision helps you to see where you've written "short hand" paragraphs. In other words, when writing a draft of an essay, it's common to write brief paragraphs that introduce important topics of discussion, but don't fully develop analysis or explanation of that topic.

Scan through your paper to see if you have balanced paragraphs. If you have several long paragraphs followed by a very short paragraph, that short paragraph might be in the wrong place or need further development. Take a look at your long paragraphs, as well. If any run on for more than a page, you may find there is more than one idea being developed at the same time. Can these paragraphs be broken in two? Look for your topic sentences. Do they match the points you develop in your paragraphs? Are your points supported by with relevant evidence? Make sure that every paragraph offers concrete textual examples or specific, researched data to develop its point.

And finally: don't assume your audience interprets the evidence the same way you do. Look at what you say immediately before and after a passage you quote or information you cite. Does your introduction to that evidence show your reader how or why this quoted text is relevant or credible? Does what you say afterwards explain why it's important for your reader to understand? Do you make clear more than simply what the evidence means, but how it's relevant to the point you are making? If not, you may need to analyze the passage or data further. If any of your reviewers said they didn't understand one of your paragraphs, it probably means that you need more description, explanation, or support.

C. Revising for Organization

The order of paragraphs in an essay is directly tied to your purpose or argument, and each new paragraph should make sense to the reader in light of what came before and what comes next. It may help to think of your argument as a journey, and yourself as your reader's guide on that journey. It's up to you to not only pick the most effective route, but to take your reader by the figurative hand and lead the way, taking care not to go down any blind rhetorical alleys or bounce around in time and space. That's what your instructor generally means when she says your paragraphs should "follow a logical progression."

Unless you're writing a timed essay, it's usually best to start your essay from a fixed point in time and space and move forward chronologically and spatially. If you find you must move backwards or sideways for some reason, be sure to do so only after providing your reader with advance notice of the turn you're about to make. And always be sure your verb tenses clearly indicate where you are in time. This is especially important in 39C, where you are asked to write an historical analysis that examines past events in order to assess a current problem and offer a future solution. Without accurate verb tenses to keep them grounded, your readers can find themselves literally "unstuck in time."

It's usually easier to revise your organization after you've clarified for yourself what your argument or purpose is. This is where reverse outlining can come in handy. Or better yet, find a colleague to reverse outline for you.

One helpful exercise to test the logic of your essay's organization is to reprint your paper so that each paragraph is on a separate page (without page numbers and title). Then, shuffle the paragraphs and give them to a peer to read. Ask them to the put the paragraphs in an order that makes sense. If they are able to reconstruct your original organization, then you probably had it right. If not, take this new organization under consideration. Another advantage of this exercise is that it clearly shows you where you may need to write new transitions between paragraphs to create a better logical flow.

It's important to understand that even the most complex argument has an underlying narrative—or a story—to tell as you guide your readers through the stages of your essay. Like all stories, it's usually best to start with the basics: set the stage, introduce the players, define your terms, lay out the conflict. How much information you need to give your readers at the outset depends a lot on where they're coming from (the rhetorical situation). How familiar are they with the setting, the cast of characters and the situation you're going to lay out? Decide how much information they'll need to get their bearings before you take them out on the open road.

If your audience is starting out in unfamiliar territory, you may need to give detailed instructions to get them from the "hotel" to the "freeway." If they're heading out from "home" they already know how to get to the main road on their own and you start your argument a little farther along the route and build from there.

But, remember that even the most logical progression of paragraphs ever constructed won't convince your reader to follow your argument if he doesn't *believe* you know where you're headed. A lot depends on the little things you do to in the opening paragraphs of your essay to establish your reader's trust. You do this through the strength of your ethos—the steadiness of your voice, the confidence of your tone, and the credibility of your evidence.

D. Revising for Voice, Tone, and Ethos

When you write, you create a particular picture of yourself through voice, tone, and persona. When you work on your final draft, you may wish to change particular words or sentences to create the right impression of you as a writer.

Try not to use absolute terms like *always, never*, or *from the beginning of time*. This leaves you vulnerable to a single exception nullifying your point. And be sure to be precise as possible with numbers and terms. Say *$1.47 million* instead of *a lot of money* or *the California State Assembly* instead of *the government*. Throw words like daggers instead of horseshoes. Show your reader that you've done your homework, you know what you're talking about, and you can cut right to the heart of an issue instead of being satisfied with coming close enough to maybe win a style point or two.

Remember that while style is important, so is substance. And the substance of a strong academic paper is its explanation and "demonstration" of its thesis. Rather than merely *telling* the reader—making claims about a text or an issue— an effective academic essay *shows* the reader how you came to make your claims by including concrete, relevant evidence, quotations, and examples to back up the points of your argument.

E. Revising for Flow: Transitions

Again, think of your paper as an effort to take your readers on an intellectual journey made up of the interesting story you are presenting, or the analytical reading you have crafted, or the position you are taking and defending.

On any trip it's nice to have signs along the way to assure your readers that they're still on the right road, there are only twenty-five miles left, or that the highway is flooded and the bridge is out just ahead. In an essay the road signs you create are the transitions between ideas, sentences, and paragraphs. These transitions clarify the connections between one idea and the next.

If you find that you can rearrange your paragraphs or examples in any order without harming the sense or logic in your paper, you may have well-written paragraphs, but you may not have developed the logical connections between your points. Consequently, your reader is likely to get frustrated with paragraphs that seem, to him, to be random (and readers who are forced to work hard to follow an argument often give up and stop reading entirely).

If you haven't connected the dots between the points in your argument, you have not demonstrated how your ideas work together to support your thesis. Unlike points on a map, even the most direct route seldom travels in a straight line from thesis point A to point D. Especially with a more complex argument, the journey often resembles a trip on the subway, with transfers between different train lines from Manhattan to the Bronx Zoo. Don't leave your reader stranded on the A platform without directions to the D-train.

If you can't figure out the transfer points, go back to your notes and passages from the text or film you are analyzing until you can see how each of your individual points connect to and build upon each other. Sometimes you may find that one of the stops you've been making is really a deadend and that as interesting a side trip as it may be, it bogs down your argument and leads your readers astray. Don't be afraid to cut a paragraph that doesn't move your argument forward.

But remember, once you've determined the best route to take, you still need to create explicit transitions to show your reader how to get from one point to the next. The reader does not have the benefit of all the research and planning you have stored in your head. If you don't provide clear transitions between all the stages of your argument, you just might lose her somewhere along the way.

F. Revising for Flow: Continuity

Coherence is made not only through careful transitions and the logical development of your argument, but also through the consistency with which you use major concepts, metaphors, and idioms, and through careful attention to things like the continuity of your verb tense, voice, and tone. Your goal is to make your writing flow easily and seamlessly.

Key Terms. Avoid quoting the dictionary to define your terms. You can define your terms more powerfully by how you use them rather than by presenting an explicit definition. Be sure you use your key terms consistently throughout your paper. If their meanings shift, explain why and connect your explanation back to your thesis.

Verb Tense, References, and Pronouns. Check for continuity, particularly if you have cut sentences or words or added sentences during revision. If your narrative starts in the present tense, and stays in the present tense, make sure that your verb tense doesn't slip unintentionally into the past tense. Of course, should you turn your attention from present to past events, your verb tenses should indicate this, but it's generally a good idea to start a new paragraph, and provide a clear transitional phrase to your let your reader know you've made a shift in time. And of course the same goes for future events.

However, one of the conventions of some types of academic essays is to write exclusively in the present tense, even when analyzing events in a text that may have occurred in the past. Literary analysis is one such example.

If you refer to the author of a text, make sure you provide a clear introduction to that author using his first and last name on first reference, and last name only on all subsequent mentions. Be sure, too, that you use the correct gender when referring to a particular author or expert you are quoting. If you are unsure, look it up.

3.10.2   Small-Scale Revision

A. Sentence Clarity

Good writers learn to be detail oriented. After all, how you express yourself can make a big difference in how well you analyze a text, express an emotion, or convince an audience to take action. Say what you mean, and mean what you say.

B. Use Transitions Between Sentences

Just as paragraphs flow more easily when they are logically connected to one another, so should individual sentences use effective transitional phrases to link one thought to the next.

C. Avoid Wordiness and Redundancy

You'll find that university instructors are more likely to be impressed with your writing when you are direct and clear. To avoid writing long complicated sentences, sometimes you need to take a closer look and see if you've used six words when two would do just as well, or see if you've inadvertently repeated yourself. (Legal language often does this, as in "cease and desist." In academic writing, that's usually just filler.) Or worse, when you use two similar words or phrases connected by *and*—as in "he was fast *and* quick" or "the student was insecure *and* unsure of himself"—it indicates that you're still unsure of yourself as a writer, and you'd rather your reader make your editing decisions for you.

While it is important to include words and phrases that create essential transitions in your paper, you also want to eliminate words that do not contribute to your argument. If you're unsure what to cut, start with adverbs and all adjectives after the first modifier of every noun. Simply put, less is more.

D. Vary Sentence Construction

Sentence variation is important for making your writing flow and for keeping your reader's attention. A repetitious pattern in your sentence structure or length—such as all long sentences or all short sentences—may distract the reader from your argument. Too much sameness in length or repetitive structure—like beginning each sentence with "The" or "He"—makes for tedious reading.

E. Use Effective Verbs

Generally speaking, strong and active verbs combined with the active voice can make your writing forceful, clear, and concise. You've probably been told since you were in grade school to avoid the passive voice, and for most of the essays you'll be writing in the composition sequence, this is good advice. You're going to be asked to analyze the rhetorical strategy of a particular writer or filmmaker in 39B, and writing in the passive voice runs the risk of losing sight of that rhetor's imprint on her work.

Likewise, it's difficult to ascribe causal responsibility for the kind of public-policy-related problems you may be analyzing in 39C if you make the problem the subject of your sentences, as in the passive-voiced "mistakes were made in the planning of the Iraq War." Using active verbs and putting the cause ahead of the action it precipitates allows you to draw a clear connection: "Relying on faulty intelligence, President Bush launched the ill-conceived war in Iraq."

Of course, there are exceptions to this writing rule of thumb. Some academic disciplines such as biology and social science, for example, use the passive voice to express a sort of grammatical hyper-objectivity in reports and other types of texts within their fields. That's why it's always a good idea to consider your rhetorical situation and respect the conventions of the genre in which you are composing.

F. Choose Precise Words

This can help you create the finely textured coherence that makes your writing flow. Words are not hand grenades—don't keep throwing them at your reader just hoping some will hit the mark. Be precise: close enough is not good enough if you want your reader to trust your academic ethos.

G. Choose Inclusive Language

As an academic writer, it is extremely important that you use language that is appropriate and inclusive. Appropriate language includes language that is non-racist and gender inclusive. Part of the reason that we use this type of language in academic writing is that we want to get our ideas across to as many different types of people as possible. Writers who offend readers with inappropriate language risk losing the trust of their audience, and with it, their ability to persuade.

3.11   Proofreading

Everyone makes typos while writing, even the professionals. For example, many writers are not able to maintain consistent use of plurals and singulars (or agreement), particularly if they are writing long, complex sentences and arguments. This inconsistency is a slip rather than a result of not knowing the rules of English. That's what proofreading is for. Frequent errors will undermine the most brilliant argument, and constant typos will have the audience doubting your ethos.

Therefore, part of learning to write clear academic English is learning how to proofread effectively. After you've worked hard to make a solid argument, you wouldn't want your reader's attention to be interrupted by minor slips in punctuation or grammar, or by occasional lack of clarity in word choice or transitions. In your composition courses, it is particularly important for you to edit carefully, so you and your teacher both have an accurate sense of how much you already know about academic English and how much you can correct on your own.

That being said, it is especially difficult to proofread a paper that you have just finished writing because you're still too close to it to see its flaws. In fact, studies have shown that your eyes just add in the word or skip over the error without even seeing it when you've been looking at something you've written for too long.

Tips for Proofreading

1. Read your paper aloud to a friend or classmate and ask her to tell you to stop reading if any of your sentences don't seem to make sense.

2. Let your paper sit overnight and read it the next day with pen in hand.

3. Try reading your paper backward—last sentence first, then next to the last, etc. This makes it easier to focus on the form and clarity of individual sentences.

3.12   Formatting

Once you have written your final draft, you need to consider the physical presentation of your essay. For the Writing 39 series, a course offered by the School of Humanities, you will be expected to write your papers using the MLA (Modern Language Association) format because MLA is the most often accepted format in the humanities. Here are a few things to remember about MLA formatting:

Font. Standard fonts are Times New Roman or other serif fonts in 12-point type.

Page Numbering. The page number appears in the top right corner of every page as part of a "header." In older versions of Microsoft Word, use the "View" menu and choose "Headers and Footers." In the newest version of Word, use the "Insert" menu and select "Page Numbers."

Page Margins. Maintain a 1-inch margin on the left, right, top, and bottom of the page. The header (page number) should be one-half inch down from the top of the page. Your software may not do this automatically; in fact, newer versions of Word automatically set the margins at 1.25 inches. To set the margins back to 1 inch, choose the "Format" menu and then select "Document."

Remember that in different disciplines, the formatting styles change, so make sure you know what's expected. Getting the correct format for your essay is part of your ethos. After all, you wouldn't show up to a formal wedding in flips-flops and cutoffs, would you? If you don't know what formatting is expected of you, ask your instructor.

3.13   Reflection as an Aid to Learning

Reflection on your work is part of the necessary feedback loop in learning to become a better writer. If you visualize the process assignments and essays in your writing classes as a series of single steps in an upward learning curve, you can see why it is important to stop, evaluate, and digest each new writing experience and the feedback you receive in the form of peer review and grades.

Reflection begins with you. For formal assignments in first-year writing, you'll usually be asked to turn in an Acknowledgements and a Writer's Memo with your final draft. Both the acknowledgements and memo are writing exercises that encourage you to look back over your writing process and to take a moment to think about what you've accomplished. In the acknowledgements, you will stop to thank those who have helped you along the way.

The Writer's Memo gives you a chance to think about what you've learned during the process of writing the assignment and to figure out what you still need to work on. You'll be asked to read the grading rubric for the assignment and then give yourself a grade—and if you are honest with yourself, this self-assessment will help you learn to become a better editor and writer. Here are the questions you will be asked to answer in a typical Writer's Memo.

The Writer's Memo

1. What are the strengths of your essay?

2. What are the weaknesses of your essay?

3. What did you learn about your own writing process while writing and revising this essay?

4. What part of the essay did you work hardest on?

5. According to the rubric for this assignment, what grade do you believe you will receive, and why? Use phrases from the rubric to explain your answer.

6. Are there any particular aspects of your paper on which you would like feedback, for example, transitions, a claim you're not sure you supported convincingly, or a place where you took a risk?

3.14   Getting a Grade for Your Writing

And here's the part we all dread the most, both students and instructors: the grade. As much as we talk about writing as a process, there comes a time when you have to decide that an essay is finished—at least as done as possible under the constraints of the assignment deadline. And there comes a time when you'll get your instructor's assessment of your writing. Although it's tough to think of grades outside the context of your GPA, remember that you're making the transition between high school writing and college writing, and learning new skill sets. The grade is an assessment of your writing skills on a particular assignment—not of you as a person, and not of you as a writer.

Think of your writing grades as saying, "Here's how much you seem to understand about this type of writing at this time." This may be enough to indicate that you have a pretty good handle on what you're doing, or it may indicate that you still need more practice with this particular genre of writing. So try not to think of your grades as labels that say "super-writer" or "loser-writer." Think of them as indicators of where you are on the road and how far you may still need to go.

When you receive your graded paper from your instructor, spend some time reflecting on your grade and your teacher's comments. Be sure you understand what your instructor is telling you about how best to approach your next paper. If you are not sure, ask.

3.14.1 The Process of Reflection

Many of the process assignments in the 39 series are specially designed to help you stop and reflect on your progress. For example, in most classes at the end of Week 5 you will write a self-evaluation blog. This assignment gives you the opportunity to consider how well you are meeting the goals you set for yourself at the beginning of the term, what skills you have acquired or strengthened, what you might do differently to get the maximum benefit from the rest of the term, your experiences with the assigned readings, and how your classmates and your instructor have—or have not—given you the support you feel you need. Most likely you will write a final self-reflection blog at the end of the term, as well.

Commenting on the forums and blogs of your fellow students is also part of the reflection process because it helps you to see your work, progress, and ideas in the context of what others are thinking, learning, and doing. Responding in this way also gives you much-needed perspective on your own work. Often we think we are the only ones facing challenges with certain assignments. The truth is, everyone struggles or feels frustration at times.

3.14.2 Last Words

In this chapter, we've tried to emphasize the fact that academic writing needs a process. No one becomes a better writer over night, or a Shakespeare in a single term. But if you are mindful of the rhetorical context, purpose, and goals of each assignment, and do your best to practice the elements of the process that work best for you, you can expect to make steady progress.

Sometimes everything just seems to "click" and you realize that you've made a quantum leap in your understanding. Other times, not so much—everything seems to be coming slowly and nothing makes sense. In the difficult times, flip back through this chapter, and find a method to help you get to the next step. You never know when the next breakthrough will come.

Chapter 4

DEVELOPMENT

Two **key characteristics** of rhetorically effective communicators are awareness and adaptability. For example, if you get lunch at Wendy's, past experience makes you aware of what to do: you order a #1 with cheese and a Dr Pepper—and although you say "thanks," you don't tip the person who took your order. But if for dinner you're lucky enough to be eating at Pascal's in Newport Beach, you adapt to that very different environment: you're aware that you won't be eating burgers—and even if you haven't been there before, you know you should tip the waiter (and probably the sommelier too). In each case, these are rhetorically informed communicative acts: you are effective because you are aware of the situation and environment (you **know** something about it); consequently, you can decide **how** to communicate effectively. Throughout this book, we've been calling this ability to adapt to different communication situations **rhetorical know-how.** _ability to adapt to different communication situations_

The same kind of awareness and adaptability, rhetorical know-how, is necessary to be a successful college student, especially when it comes to your writing assignments (but also in the more everyday communicative encounters you have with colleagues and professors). For example, with reading: for any given text, your expectations can vary widely and affect your response. When you sit down to read your email, for instance, you expect a completely different set of conventions than you would sitting down to your biology textbook—and a whole new set applies when you go see a movie or read a favorite novel.

Now let's switch from reading to writing. Since you know as a reader you have expectations for certain pieces of writing, it makes sense that when you write, your readers have expectations, too. Part of your job when writing is to make yourself familiar with the different expectations readers of your work will have in the many different writing contexts you will face (including email and biology).

In other words, expectations on the part of the reader translate into the choices you make as a writer. A professor, for instance, will expect a full greeting and closing signature in an email, but your best friend might find that weird. You may have already noticed that a formal academic paper can be very different in a sociology class than it is in a history class, or even between two classes in the same field of study.

Rhetorical know-how and adaptability apply to how to develop your ideas through writing, too. College writing assignments may ask you to summarize, define, analyze, and argue—or to switch from one to the other frequently. Each situation may require quick, complex choices about how to develop your ideas that aren't spelled out in the prompt.

One assignment may direct you to summarize, define, and analyze. Another may expect you to avoid summary and focus on description and classification. It's equally possible that in any one essay, you may need to use all of the tools at your command, moving smoothly from one to the other within the same paragraph, page, or over the course of the entire essay. The situation—each different writing situation—requires that you become aware of its requirements and possibilities, and then adapt accordingly.

4.1   Modes of Development

In order to become a complete communicator—aware, adaptable, and effective—you'll need to feel comfortable with each mode of development individually, just as the first step to playing an instrument is to learn the musical scales. Even though she may be able to play Debussy's "Clair de Lune" flawlessly, a concert pianist will still play scales to warm up during a practice session. The movement of her hands upon the keys has to be familiar to the point of habit.

In the same way, as a college writer, the modes of developing your ideas have to be so familiar to you that you can call upon them instantly when needed. In this chapter, we'll discuss several modes of development that you'll be asked to practice in your composition courses—your scales.

The good news about these modes is that they grow out of the everyday ways that we think about and perceive the world, so you're already familiar with them. We begin to perceive and know as young children learning language; at the same time we learn language, we learn how to use it specifically in different situations—learning what things are called, how we should interact with them, and how they interact with each other.

Definition is a mode of development that you'll call on often in college writing assignments. But it's also a mode of thinking and a way of knowing that you've been practicing (like the musical scales) since you first learned to talk. For example, maybe your family had a dog. Chances are, when you were ready to start verbalizing, your mom or dad pointed to him and said "dog" or "doggie" (or *perro, chien, hund, aso, chó*—whatever word is applicable in the language you first learned).

Eventually, when you put the two things together enough to understand that what they were trying to tell you with all this pointing and noise is that they wanted you to call the big four-legged slobbery thing a "dog," you responded. We learn language and communication through social interaction with others.

So, then, since you were little, you've been practicing definition. You pointed at your furry friend and responded: "goggie!" As you pointed and spoke, in your thoughts you were developing an idea through the mode of development called definition. With time, you came to understand "dogness" by seeing and identifying dogs.

But we can't understand any concept in isolation—language and communication are social acts—we learn them from and through our interactions with others. So we find relationships, and in doing so, we learn more modes of development. We group things together when they seem alike—**classification**.

We also learn to further define concepts by understanding what they are and are not—**compare and contrast**. Your next-door neighbor didn't have a dog, but she did have a pet—he also had four legs but he didn't slobber and you learned to call him "cat." Your friend told you a funny story about the time when her cat chased his tail—**summary, narrative**. We learn how the things we've defined interact: as the dog chased the cat, they broke the flowerpot—**cause and effect**.

4.2   Summary

Summary is a widely used rhetorical tool that isn't limited to book reports and essay exams. Everywhere around us, we can find summary being used to communicate ideas: movie commercials and theater trailers often tease audiences with just enough plot and character information to inspire interest, while the reviewers who critique these films provide synopses that help to illustrate the films' strengths and weaknesses. Episodes of TV dramas often begin with "Previously on…" summaries of previous episodes or seasons. The back cover of a book might include a plot synopsis to catch the attention of potential readers, and academic articles are often preceded by abstracts, outlining the whole argument in a few sentences.

However, effective summaries aren't just a random collection of high points. A good summary can (and often does) serve a greater purpose than simply providing a quick overview of the text. The best summaries arrange information around a specific rhetorical goal, often dictated by the purpose, genre, and audience of the particular text.

4.2.1   Purposeful Summarizing

Summaries usually focus on the most important elements of a text, but what's important is often dependent on what the summary is trying to accomplish. "Previously on..."-style synopses for TV shows don't revisit every character and plot point in the show's history; they usually include only the information and events that are vital to understanding the episode you're about to watch. No matter the genre, effective summaries tend to follow this example, providing a *selective* overview in order to achieve the writer's rhetorical purpose.

Summaries can also function as a kind of storytelling shorthand. For example, **montages** are often used in visual texts to illustrate in a few minutes events that take much longer to develop in the actual film. This kind of summary serves a greater function than simply saying to the audience, "This is what happened." The purpose of a montage is often to intrigue potential viewers with a condensed understanding of the plot, drawing them into the story.

Often the genre of the text will dictate the information that can or should be included in the summary. A film review may give a plot synopsis in order to analyze its good and bad aspects, but will almost never give away its ending, since the purpose of a film review is to help readers decide if they want to see the movie. If a review needs to give away the ending, you'll usually get a "spoiler alert." A critical essay in a film studies journal isn't bound by the same conventions, and may summarize the film's surprise ending in order to support the argument. Academic articles often contain another form of summary called an abstract, a brief paragraph containing the writer's primary argument, along with a brief description of its main supporting points. After reading such an article, 39B and C students may be required to write an annotated bibliography, very briefly summarizing the article's purpose, audience and usefulness in the field.

All of these forms of summary change the information they include based on audience. Movie previews for an action film might spend less time outlining the plot and more time on the shootouts, car chases, and explosions. The audience of a romantic comedy, on the other hand, might be drawn to time spent on the characters and the conflict that keeps them apart.

4.2.2   Summarizing in the Writing 39 Series

Each class in the Writing 39 series will require you to practice using some form of summary in order to develop your ideas. In 39A and 39B, you will need to write focused, brief summaries of elements in a text as a way to introduce evidence in your Rhetorical Analysis essay. You'll also learn evaluative summarizing in the Annotated Bibliography assignment. You'll expand that skill in 39C, writing annotated bibliographies as a way to archive the ideas you've found in your sources. You'll also summarize the arguments of others in your essays to support your own claim, or as grounds to refute another writer's claim.

When composing a summary for your own work, keep in mind not only what your readers *need* to know, but also what they might *want* to know. If your reader is unfamiliar with the text you're analyzing, your summary may need to be more comprehensive. Or your instructor may direct you to assume the reader is familiar with the text, so you need only to summarize in order to situate the reader in your argument, or so you can support and develop your point. In the following example, the student's purpose was to provide an example within her glossary definition of the term **imagery** for the audience of her fellow 39B students.

The student uses a text from the class, so she knows her readers are familiar with it. Her summary is light-handed because of this: she's using quotation in her summary just to orient the reader in the text so she can make her real point about one type of imagery. This is a common purpose of summary: using it as a setup for your own analysis.

 SAMPLE SUMMARY

An example of *auditory* imagery can be seen in *Sandman: The Dream Hunters* when "the fox strained to hear another word, but there was nothing." She wants to hear a more human sound, but "all she could hear was the whisper of the wind as it stirred the fallen leaves, the sighing of the trees as they breathed and swayed in the wind, and the distinct *ting ting* of the wind chimes in the little temple." The peace of the sounds the fox hears after eavesdropping on the conversation of the creatures she comes across signifies the finality of the monk's fate. Instead of hearing what she wants to hear, the fox hears only the peace of the countryside, which serves to worsen, rather than alleviate, her anxiety. The auditory imagery makes the moment more vivid.

Questions to Ask When Writing Summaries

1. Why am I summarizing?

2. Which details should I select for inclusion?

3. Is the summary accurate? Comprehensive enough for my purpose?

4.2.3 Annotated Bibliography

The basic purpose of the annotated bibliography assignment, like all Critical Reading assignments, is to help you learn to read more carefully and critically by identifying how a text is situated and constructed.

In addition to practicing effective summarizing and paraphrasing skills, creating an annotated bibliography requires careful assessment of an author's qualifications, thesis, evidence, medium or genre, purpose, and audience, so you also gain good practice in identifying a text's rhetorical situation, thus laying the groundwork for a more detailed analysis.

The language of an annotated bibliography must be precise and concise, and therefore you will also learn how to write with an economy of style. Your instructor may even ask you to write, peer review, and revise your annotated bibliographies.

Furthermore, in researched arguments, which you will construct in 39B and even more so in 39C, annotated bibliographies can help you to evaluate the usefulness and relevance of your sources, and also help you to remember information from them when you are actually writing your paper.

The Four-Sentence Pattern for Annotated Bibliographies

For the purposes of your composition courses, you will be expected to follow a specific pattern when you construct your ABs—a highly structured, four-sentence paragraph adapted from the format first advocated by Margaret K. Woodworth in her article "The Rhetorical Precis." The pattern is based on the rhetorical triangle; it requires you to identify particular rhetorical elements of the text that start from the "angle" or perspective of the rhetor.

Bibliographic Citation. Begin your annotation by identifying the source being annotated as you would in an entry to a Works Cited page in correct MLA style. If you found your source online, even if it was originally published in print, be sure to indicate which database you used, and when you accessed it, according to MLA guidelines. *(handwritten)* Annotated Bibliography Format:

  SAMPLE ANNOTATED BIBLIOGRAPHY: THE CITATION

Sánchez-Escalonilla, Antonio. "The Hero as a Visitor in Hell: The Descent into Death in Film Structure." *Journal of Popular Film & Television* 32 (2005): 149–56. Winter 2005. Print.

After the bibliographic citation, write the following four sentences formatted into a single paragraph. Remember to double-space your paragraph, just as you would any formal academic writing assignment.

Sentence #1 establishes the rhetor's **credentials** and **thesis**. Introduce the rhetor using biographic information that establishes the rhetor's credibility and provides a brief summary of the rhetor's thesis or message. Be sure to use the rhetor's full name, synthesize the most impressive, relevant details of his or her biography into a brief phrase, and follow this by a that clause and an accurate signal verb, such as argues, asserts, challenges, or contends, to introduce your thesis summary.

Avoid phrases that simply lead to identification of the rhetor's topic such as "the author writes about" or "the author says that." To give more significance to your claim, you should also include the rationale behind the author's thesis. You can do so by adding a *because* clause; for example, "the author argues that x because y."

 SENTENCE #1: CREDENTIALS AND THESIS

    Antonio Sánchez-Escalonilla, a noted Film and Cinema Professor and Spanish language scholar, argues that following classical conventions, the hero or hero-ine of current films often undergoes either a figurative or literal journey into hell in order to achieve his or her full potential as a hero and to complete a substan-tial amount of growth essential to his or her character.

Peer Editing Practice

1. How effectively does the writer establish Sánchez-Escalonilla's credibility? What specific information is most relevant to establishing particular exper-tise for the subject of the article? (Look at the title to remind yourself about the subject.)

2. Assuming the information is correct, how clearly is the thesis summarized?

3. How effectively does the writer use economy of language? Is there anything that could be cut?

Sentence #2 identifies the **medium** and **genre**. Classify the text according to medium—a film, a book, a general circulation news magazine, a scholarly jour-nal, the internet—and by genre—gothic novel, Japanese anime, film review, academic criticism, YouTube video—and note whether the text challenges the conventions of the genre in any significant way.

The information in this sentence can help you figure out the intended audience and by extension, the message of the text. Media critic Marshall McLuhan is famous for saying, "The medium is the message." In essence, this means that what we communicate is fundamentally shaped by how and to whom it is conveyed by the rhetorical constraints of the medium.

 SENTENCE #2: MEDIUM AND GENRE

Escalonilla constructs a thesis-driven academic argument for a scholarly journal in the field of popular media criticism.

Peer Editing Practice

1. Is there anything else about the medium or genre of the text that should be added, corrected, or revised?

2. How might you revise the language to make it more concise and precise?

Sentence #3 lists the **types of evidence** the rhetor uses and explains how the evidence is used to support the thesis or convey the message. Notice that you are not asked to quote any evidence directly. The point here is not to parrot what's been said, but to summarize what kinds of evidence are used. Examples of evidence include: statistics and data, analysis (logical, rhetorical, cultural, historical, etc.), quotes from authorities, references to other scholars in the field, narratives (anecdotes) that are used as examples, lists, definitions, and more.

Often, the genre or intended audience will dictate the kinds of evidence that a rhetor uses. Scholarly journals require more rigorous standards of evidence and consequently appeal to their audiences differently than newspaper articles or novels. For example, an anecdote aims for a different kind of appeal (pathos) than raw data from a scientific study (logos). If you're unsure of genre or audience, try working backwards from the type of evidence the rhetor uses and its particular rhetorical appeal to help you determine the genre and audience.

 SENTENCE #3: TYPES OF EVIDENCE

In order to prove the importance of the journey, Escalonilla cites numerous stories of heroes in his work, beginning with ancient Greek myths to modern literature such as the cinematic journeys of *The Lord of the Rings*, *E.T.*, and *Groundhog Day*.

Peer Editing Practice

1. How well does this sentence convey the types of evidence the writer uses? Could it be more specific in word choice?

2. How might you revise this sentence to make it more concise and precise?

Sentence #4 identifies both the **audience** and **purpose** of the article. Decide which particular audience, group, or groups the rhetor is attempting to reach and for what purpose(s). Be as specific as possible. It's not enough to say the text is aimed at the general public. Consider what you've established in the first three sentences: What clues can you find in the thesis, the genre and medium, and the evidence that would help you determine the particular age, race, class, gender, religion, occupational field, educational background, academic discipline, interest group, or political party the rhetor is targeting? When considering purpose, ask yourself whether the text is designed primarily to inform, to entertain, to persuade, or to prompt the audience to act (or a combination of these).

For this concluding sentence, it's not enough to simply say the text is aimed at anyone who's interested in the text's message. Don't get caught in the kind of circular reasoning that mistakes *what* the rhetor is saying for *who* he's saying it to and *why*.

 SENTENCE #4: AUDIENCE AND PURPOSE

Escalonilla's audience can be narrowed down to those studying or otherwise interested in the film industry, and also to the casual reader with an affinity for cinema. His central purpose is to explain the importance of the common formula of the hero's descent to hell and to educate his audience on why it is so often used in media and literature.

Peer Editing Practice

1. How specifically is the text's audience identified?

2. Are there clues in other parts of the AB that could help specify the audience even more accurately?

3. What about purpose? Is it logically connected to the message, medium, and evidence identified in the previous sentences?

4. Are there any unnecessary words or awkward phrases? How might you further clarify this sentence?

You may find the AB's four-sentence format confining at first: for example, it may seem much easier to describe the author's thesis in three or four sentences *rather* than just one (and usually it is easier to do this). The *value* of sticking to the format, however, is that you'll learn to provide a concise summary of the most important parts of a text—this is an essential tool for writing both analytical and researched arguments, where it is often necessary to provide "snapshots" of texts for your readers (such as when you first introduce a text) rather than engaging in drawn-out summary.

If you have trouble writing just one sentence for each category, practice writing longer and more complex sentences, rather than giving up and straying from the format. Once you have the content down, work on cutting out unnecessary words and combining ideas to streamline your sentences.

Annotated Bibliography Rubric

- Does each sentence accurately represent the text being annotated?

- Are the sentences comprehensive in their coverage? (i.e., is the full thesis described in sentence 1; are all the major types of evidence cited in sentence 3?)

- Are the sentences written clearly, with precise diction?

- Are the sentences succinct and well-focused on the appropriate subject?

- Is the bibliographic citation presented in accurate MLA format?

4.3   Description

Description is a bit like summary, because in both, you are attempting to capture the essence of the thing being summarized. However, description is more specifically about sharing how something looks, smells, sounds, feels, or tastes—using the senses. In your experiences as a writing student, you may have seen the phrase "show, don't tell" jotted in the margins of your paper. This is a favorite comment with writing teachers not only because description makes for a lively reading experience, but also because it informs the purpose of your text and refines your address to a particular audience.

4.3.1   Purposeful Description

Descriptive writing may seem like a straightforward reporting of your observations, but well-crafted description, like all writing, involves a series of choices in service of producing your desired effect. In order to describe effectively, you need to choose a perspective, decide what to focus on, and determine exactly who will be reading it.

Take, for example, the following description from the menu of Wolfgang Puck's celebrity-popular restaurant, Spago:

> Sautéed veal sweetbreads with chanterelle mushrooms, tangerine gastrique, confit bacon, orange kohlrabi puree and micro-peppercress salad.

Compare that to the online menu for KFC:

> Bite-sized pieces of all-white meat chicken, marinated for a tender inside and breaded for a flavorful, fun crunch on the outside. A great snack for adults, and a fun way to please picky kids.

Both menu writers chose words that paint a precise picture of the food, but they also meet the expectations and desires of each audience—and to some extent define the audience in the process. "Tangerine gastrique" sounds appealing to a totally different set of diners than does a "fun crunch"; the descriptive language in both cases implies something about the purpose, image-consciousness, and tastes of the diners—even how fast they want to eat!

4.3.2   Description at the University

One of the first steps in descriptive writing is careful observation. Or from the alternate perspective, if you're recording an observation, description is a necessity. Observation is familiar to those of you who have written lab reports in the sciences and have tracked the results during an experiment.

The decisions you make about how to frame your description not only inform what is displayed for or concealed from your audience, they also reveal your interpretation of the thing you are describing. The interpretive potential of description has been the topic of much discussion in the social sciences. A **thick description** is when an anthropologist describes not only a particular human behavior, but also describes the context in which that behavior was enacted. In *The Interpretation of Cultures*, Clifford Geertz, who coined the term, argues that it is the context in which the behavior occurs that allows an outsider (like an anthropologist) to interpret meaning in the behavior. His example is a wink: with no context or relationship, no foreknowledge of the winker, a wink is difficult to read. To assign meaning to a wink, you have to know more than just a description of how someone's eye moved in a particular way.

Thick description in anthropology is a lot like **rhetorical analysis** of a text; it's not enough to just know what happens in the text and to describe the plot— that's just describing the wink. To understand the text rhetorically, and to have an easier time ascribing meaning (interpretation), you have to also be able to describe the context in which the text was first enacted. If that context was different than your own current context, then you'll also need to consider how your own context colors your perceptions of the text and its context.

History is another discipline for which description is an important mode of development. In the following example, historian William Cronon's description of our own Aldrich Park reveals the way in which descriptive choices are inevitably linked to interpretive ones:

> Like so many other features of Irvine, it is a carefully planned and constructed place. Its symbolic role on the campus is to offer a representation of nature— pastoral, parklike, Edenic—at the heart of the university.... The paths in the park have been carefully laid out to prevent people from traveling straight across it. They do so quite cleverly, inviting the walker in by means of a well-crafted optical illusion that makes it look as if they do go straight across; only after one is already committed to one's route is one permitted to see that the lines that at first seemed straight are in fact curved and broken.

As Cronon shares his observations about what the park *looks* like, he simultaneously reveals what it is he thinks the park *means*. Cronon's comparison of the park to the city of Irvine as a whole reinforces his larger argument that the park, despite its apparent naturalness, is actually a human-designed place intended to have a particular effect on its visitors.

Fiction and poetry often use description as a vital part of their own "arguments" and become objects of interpretation themselves; sometimes, the description itself is the point, as in "The Red Wheelbarrow" by William Carlos Williams:

so much depends

upon

a red wheel
barrow

glazed with rain
water

beside the white
chickens.

The simplicity of the description defies the expectations of the reader, and brings visual and tactile detail so present to the reader's imagination that it makes the lines come true. Fiction writers often use description to set the mood of a scene, or to direct the reader's attention to details the protagonist may not be aware of, complicating the plot. The selection of detail can do all these things, as in this description of the title character at the start of Jorge Luis Borges' story, "Funes the Memorius":

I remember him with a dark passionflower in his hand, looking at it as no one has ever looked at such a flower, though they might look from the twilight of day until the twilight of night, for a whole life long. I remember him, his face immobile and Indian-like, and singularly remote, behind his cigarette.

4.3.3   Description in the 39 Series

In all the WR 39 courses, you'll practice writing rich, thick descriptions in order to support and develop your ideas. Description figures prominently in the first half of 39A: first you learn to describe, then you learn to analyze. Careful description of detail, whether visual or textual, will help you define the artist's purpose, and in turn allow you to develop your own claim. You'll work with thick description in 39B in the Rhetorical Analysis essay. In 39C, you might be asked to locate and describe the nature of a problem, or you might be asked to define the community out of which a successful individual emerged.

During the early phases of the writing process, try to cast a wide net with your observation: observe and write description, then observe and write some more. In other words, whether it is a visual text, a short story, or a government policy, return to your object of study multiple times and describe anything that might be significant. As you develop a stronger sense of the overall purpose of your text, you'll be able to pay special attention to the way you frame your description and how much of its context you should also describe.

In the following example from a 39A class, the student describes the content and some of the context for a Schick razor ad to both get the attention of his reader and to develop his point about the ad's methodology, so he frames the description to do both.

SAMPLE DESCRIPTION

On either side of the ad, two serious-looking men, clad in standard lab attire (white coats, black ties, pocket protectors), are each rubbing a babies' butt against his face. The babies are identical and based on facial expression, both seem to be enjoying this. This "lab test" is a literal acting-out of the cliché that babies have extremely smooth butts. Using this well-known cliché in an exaggerated and direct way allows for the ad to use humor to reach the reader. Humor can be a powerful means of grabbing the attention of a consumer, especially if it is shockingly weird as this.

Questions to Ask When Writing Description

1. What is my purpose? To report? Explain? Persuade? Entertain?

2. How should my language choices reflect that purpose?

3. Can I assist my reader in non-verbal ways? Is there a visual image I can include? If so, what portions of my description become redundant?

4. What is the shared frame of reference for my audience? How is the object I'm describing similar to or different from objects with which the audience is already familiar?

4.4   Definition

Another close cousin to summary and description, **definition** is also a way of thinking about and developing a concept or object more deeply. Definition is most concerned with setting boundaries: what characteristics does it have and what characteristics is it lacking?

Earlier in this chapter, we discussed how definition could be thought of as one of the first ways we learn how to understand language and the world around us. This is definition at its simplest—a means to use language to label simple objects. However, definition can also be an extremely complex philosophical undertaking. It was a frequent subject for the classical philosopher Plato, who in many of his dialogues describes Socrates' attempts to answer the question "What is _____?"

Aristotle, Plato's student, was a great cataloger of philosophical ideals, rhetoric, drama, and poetics. Aristotle's writing has had an unparalleled influence on the history of Western thought; in a nutshell, he provided a basic formula for defining that is still used today. First, place the object within its primary category (Aristotle used the Greek word *génos*, from which we get the words genus and genre). Next, describe how the object differs from others within the primary category (in Greek, *diáphora*, from which we get the words different and differentiation). For example (this is one of Aristotle's examples), a human is an animal (primary category), who, unlike other animals, has the capacity to use reason (differentiation).

This is, of course, a fairly simplistic definition of a human, but it sets the basic boundary lines, and is thus a good place from which to start. From here, we could expand the definition to include other characteristics of humanity and some of the more intangible concepts created by humanity, like love, honor, or justice. Sit down for five minutes and try to write a definition for something like love, and you'll realize that definition is an important practice that is necessary to expanding your capacity for complex thinking and writing—this is definitely a mode of development that you want to have in your arsenal.

4.4.1 Purposeful Definition

As with other modes of development, the length and detail of a definition depends on its purpose and rhetorical situation. Let's say you're in a grocery store and you ask a fellow shopper, "What does 'organic' mean?" The shopper points to a display of organic apples and says "organic means healthier." The shopper's casual definition may be enough to convince you to buy an organic apple, but it is a highly evaluative and narrow definition.

At home, you may wish to expand the definition of your fellow shopper and find out why it's healthier. You look at the sticker on the apple: "USDA Organic." On the USDA web site, you discover that the government defines organic as involving "cultural, biological, and mechanical practices that foster recycling of resources, promote ecological balance, and conserve biodiversity." This definition focuses on farming and its relationship to the environment. You still don't know why it's healthier, but you now realize that definitions can change depending on who is doing the defining.

On the *New York Times* web site, you find Mark Bittner's definition of organic, written for a popular audience: "generally free of synthetic substances; contains no antibiotics and hormones; has not been irradiated or fertilized with sewage sludge; was raised without the use of most conventional pesticides; and contains no genetically modified ingredients." Now you know what makes your apple healthier—and how definitions can vary depending on rhetorical situation.

Dictionary definitions can help you understand what a word means, but like our Aristotelian definition of human, a dictionary definition provides only a most basic meaning. The dictionary will tell you that "organic" means "of, relating to, or derived from animal matter." In this case the dictionary definition describes the word in the broad context of the sciences, or its general use. Dictionary definitions will not necessarily be specific to your particular rhetorical situation.

In the same way, dictionary definitions in your writing may not be the most useful definition for your reader. By providing a more developed definition of a concept or issue, you can demonstrate how you understand and interpret a concept or issue within a specific rhetorical situation.

Many debates in academic writing often occur over conflicting definitions of a concept or issue. You can use a definition to establish your understanding of a concept or issue, although keep in mind that not everyone may agree with it.

4.4.2   Definition in Everyday Contexts

Because of the way it establishes understanding, definition is a common tool for writers of all kinds. Advertisements provide suggestive definitions to encourage you to buy the products. For example, an ad campaign for the Chevy Silverado truck defines the Silverado as "America's Best Truck"; In-N-Out's motto identifies its burgers as having "Quality You Can Taste"; and the Dallas Cowboys are billed as "America's Team." Not everyone agrees on these definitions, but advertisers hope you will remember them the next time you think about their products.

Scientific reports require precise definitions of the object of study, as in this basic description from an "Examination of Protozoan Cultures to Determine Cellular Structure and Motion Pattern":

> Unicellular eukaryotes belong to the kingdom Protista, and are often referred to as "protists" or "protozoans." The name "protozoan" means "first animal," but eukaryotes may display either plant or animal-like characteristics, or a combination of both.

You will find this type of formal definition prevalent in many of your science classes—in fact, you may find yourself memorizing many similar definitions. These are the basic groundwork of the field that you need to master in order to analyze, contextualize, and make conclusions.

Historians use definition to mark specific actions or events. A defining moment provides the reader with your interpretation of an event as a significant moment in a historical context. For example, Barack Obama's election to the presidency can be considered a defining moment in the history of U.S. race relations, or as a personally defining moment in Obama's life story. When Facebook reached over 200 million active users in April 2008, it was considered a defining moment for the social networking site, changing the way people communicated. Identifying a defining moment requires you to consider the fact of an event within the broader context of its history.

4.4.3   Developing a Definition: Find the Boundaries

When you're at the first stages of developing a definition, remember Aristotle. Start by thinking about the general category of the concept or issue you are defining. How much should you describe the concept, object, or issue in its broader context? Then consider what makes the concept, object, or issue distinct from other things in the same general category. What are the distinguishing features? You must also consider what purpose you hope to achieve in your definition, how you'll be using the term, and who will be reading it. The grocery store context first narrowed the definition of "organic" for your apple, but understanding the farming/environmental context of the apple led you a useful source for your purpose: understanding why the apple is healthier.

Another approach is to use synonyms to think through the definition. For example, we all have experienced the emotion of happiness. But happiness is not always the same. How is the happiness of seeing friends different from the glee of opening presents, the satisfaction of finishing a research assignment or the contentment of summer vacation? Using synonyms can clarify what defines happiness at a specific moment for your rhetorical purpose.

You might also ask yourself what the object of definition is *not*. This is a useful strategy to identify what lies outside the boundaries as you wish to define them. "True happiness is not attained through self-gratification, but through fidelity to a worthy purpose." In this definition, Helen Keller provides a negative definition—what happiness is not—before asserting what she believes happiness is.

4.4.4   Definition in the 39 Series

All the writing courses at UCI will ask you to practice developing your ideas through definition. In 39B, you might need to look up key terms that are specific to a particular genre or type of media. Understanding literary terms and knowing how these terms are used will help you apply what you're learning about reading texts to your work on the Rhetorical Analysis essay. In 39C, you'll use research from several sources to help you develop important definitions.

In 39C, you'll work with many different types of definition as you develop your ideas—you may define a politically-contested term, a policy, a moment in history, a problem, or the control group in a research study. What kinds of definition is this student using in a paragraph from her historical analysis of the rise of the consumer flower industry?

 SAMPLE DEFINITION

The most important event prompting the use of pesticides in the cut-flower industry is the discovery of dichlorodiphenyl trichloroethane (DDT). DDT was synthesized in 1874 by a German chemistry student, but it wasn't until 1939 that a Swiss chemist, Paul Miller, discovered it as a potent pesticide. DDT was first used as a pesticide in 1942 or 1943 in Europe, then North America, then elsewhere (McGinn 67). It was first recognized for its ability to kill off the cotton boll weevil which destroyed many crops and cost farmers millions of dollars. Years later, it was found that DDT could fight off other agricultural pests, even those that affected the cut-flower industry. Pesticides became the new answer for farmers' crop loss and were used without precautions. The "prodigious pesticide [was] use[d] in gigantic greenhouses, where they process tons of flowers each year." However, the discovery of DDT and its subsequent broad use has shaped the problem that "threatens worker health and safety, jeopardizes the environment and [impacts] consumer health" (Anderson).

Questions to Ask about Developing with Definition

1. What is the general category of this object or idea? What are its distinguishing characteristics?

2. Who is my audience for this definition? What do they need to know in order to understand it?

3. What is my purpose for defining this concept? How will that shape what is included in the definition?

4.5   Narration

You might think of narration as occurring only in fiction, but we use narratives to understand our world, through both imagined stories and real-life ones. Narratives are a way to share experiences with the audience. Sometimes we create narratives of what happened to us to understand our past; for example, history textbooks are narratives written by people with specific, research-driven opinions about how things came to be. Other times, we use narratives to make sense of contemporary life and the important events—political, social, and cultural—that comprise it. Such narratives often take the form of news stories or reporting. Other narratives focus on the writer himself/herself and can occur as blogs or tweets. In all these cases, the type of the narrative—the purpose and intended audience and subject matter—affects the style and structure.

4.5.1　Examples of Narrative in Everyday Texts

When people get into car accidents, they typically file reports with their insurance companies and/or the police: narrative accounts of **who** was involved in the accident, **when** it occurred, **where** it occurred, and most importantly, **how** it occurred. Such pieces of information form the basic foundation of narratives that are then used to assess liability. Because of the potential legal and financial penalties, each driver in an accident will likely compose the narrative in a way that minimizes his or her own fault. Both parties will consider the intended audience (the police, the insurance companies) and the purpose (to appear as blameless as possible), and this will affect the way each report is written.

When an incident is recreated or imagined outright, whether for the purpose of determining legal liability or producing entertainment, it is a narrative. It can be a report of a laboratory experiment, the detectives on *CSI* piecing together the story of a murder using the evidence, or a news story that presents the basic facts (who, when, where, why, how) along with the details that make for a gripping story. In all these cases, it's the selection and presentation of detail that makes the story happen.

Take for instance, a story entitled, "An Athlete on the Rise, A Man Struggling," which ran in the *Orange County Register*:

> Their lives were going in opposite directions: the baseball rookie who had just pitched his best major league game and the convicted drunken driver struggling with an inability to take orders.
>
> But the rising star and fallen rebel were on a collision course.
>
> Their paths crossed on a night that began in celebration and ended with Angels pitcher Nick Adenhart, 22, dead on a surgeon's table and minivan driver Andrew Thomas Gallo, 22, behind bars another time.

It's the reporters' arrangement of detail at the start of the story that sets the tone for the drama that follows, so that the description of the accident as the loss of the promising pitcher can do more for the reader than just present the facts. The writers provide the traditional pieces of news information (who, what, when, where, why, how), but not in a straightforward order.

The story begins by telling us about two people with two very different lives who suddenly collide (which sounds like the premise for the movie *Crash*). The names are revealed in the third paragraph. As the story progresses, it will follow a similar pattern, withholding certain factual details (such as the speed of Gallo's car and the time of the accident) until the very end. This emphasizes the central figures in the story, and it's the dramatic—and dramatically presented—collision of these two lives, literally, that is at the heart of the story.

4.5.2 Developing with Narrative

In a conventional narrative—say, a personal essay, an autobiography, or a horror novel—a number of different devices and strategies are used to grab the reader's attention. The writer presents an engaging narrator (a character with a distinct voice), ensures smooth transitions, builds conflict and suspense, and keeps the reader involved in the story by either implicitly or explicitly presenting the stakes, the central concern of what's being recounted.

A narrative can proceed linearly from start to finish or it can occur out of order, depending on the writer's purpose and what he wants to emphasize. In the movie *Memento*, the story of a man's search for his wife's murderer occurs in reverse order, a narrative choice by writers John and Christopher Nolan that heightens the suspense and helps us identify with the main character's disorientation. In the example above, the passage begins with the crash and comes full circle, returning to the crash at the end.

Many nonfiction narratives function like fictional dramas by building suspense and tension and keeping the reader engaged. In *The Art of Fiction*, John Gardner uses the Fichtean curve to illustrate the path of a protagonist's journey in a traditional story:

The Fichtean Curve

Climax

Complication

(Choices—conflict leads to climax)

Resolution

Character's "normal" path
©Hayden-McNeil, LLC

Every step along the way, the protagonist is faced with challenges, external or internal, and acts to overcome them. The protagonist struggles toward the climax, which leads to the resolution.

In a traditional story, vivid descriptions, memorable details, an intriguing plot or idea, an appealing theme, a lively structure, and engaging language (use of the active voice, along with the use of an *interesting* voice) are necessary to keep it interesting and moving.

However, note that not all narratives function like stories. Both audience and purpose affect the actual text itself. In most lab reports and news stories, the purpose isn't for the writer to establish an interesting voice, but to describe a process in detail. In fact, many science and news reports are written in the passive voice in order to highlight objectivity and neutrality. As you craft your narrative, make your choices based on purpose and audience, pay attention to the use of detail, and create a timeline that you hold together with transitions.

4.5.3   Narrative in the 39 Series

Although you might not be asked to write a full-length essay narrative, you will be practicing developing your ideas with narrative throughout your composition courses. No matter the topic, you, as the writer, will need to find a way to keep the reader interested. In that sense, your nonfiction writing may follow many of the conventions of a typical narrative—a vivid theme or point, smooth structural flow, and gripping, detailed descriptions. You may use personal experience in some assignments when you draw on yourself as an expert in the field, perhaps in the form of a blog or film review. Using personal narrative can make your argument more convincing. You may even write a short story or create a fictional blog or film for your final project in 39B. In 39C, the research you do may involve reconstructing events based on your research in the same way a historian might.

Here's an excerpt from a blog for 39B in which the writer describes how she got her name. Note the writer's approach—her voice, her tone—and how she uses the subject to introduce other aspects of her background.

 SAMPLE NARRATIVE

> At the very moment when I was born, my grandmother gave me a name that sounded almost exactly like her own name just because she hated the person who "stole away" her youngest daughter, my father. However, my father did not want to be defeated and tried to change the name. Interestingly, they had another family war in the hospital. Of course, my grandma won the victory and that was how I got my name.

> ## Questions to Ask about Developing with Narrative
>
> 1. What is the central theme, idea, or subject?
>
> 2. Who is the narrator?
>
> 3. Who is the audience?
>
> 4. What ethos is necessary for the author or purpose? Will you be using other appeals (pathos, logos) to connect with your audience?
>
> 5. What should the tone of the writing be like given the audience and the type of narrative? And what about the voice of the narrator?
>
> 6. What is your point-of-view/perspective? What is your reason for choosing it, and will it help with your purpose?
>
> 7. What is the structure of the narrative, and how does it serve the purpose or theme?

4.6   Cause and/or Effect

Describing cause and/or effect is a means of development where you create conceptual relationships between events or ideas. An important part of recognizing conceptual relationships in your own writing involves exploring potential **causes** and **effects,** and then being able to see the relationship(s) between them. Cause and effect can be tricky, because what you may have initially thought was a causal relationship might not be one.

Sometimes your search for relationships may begin with the effect, sometimes the cause. You may pull over on the freeway because your car is wobbling and then you see that there's a nail in the tire and it's a bit low. You get towed all the way to the gas station, where they repair your tire, but as soon as that's complete and you get back up to speed on the road, there's the wobble again. You had an alignment problem, and have to head back to the gas station. It will be up to the mechanic to decide if this effect (the wobble) is related to the nail, or has a completely unrelated cause (uneven tire wear because you're not keeping the tires properly inflated). Finding the true nature of cause and effect means to first avoid jumping to conclusions.

The conclusions we're so swift to get to are often the result of bias. For example, our political inclinations may lead us to dismiss ideas that may point to a more likely answer. We may discover that what we thought was the cause of a problem, a situation, or an outcome, is actually only a corollary, or another *effect*. Being conscientious writers in 39A, active readers in 39B, and thorough researchers in 39C will help lead us to more accurate explanations of causes and effects.

Likewise, we may find ourselves attributing particular effects *to* causes that are really unrelated. This can happen when our biases or insufficient information leads us to see faulty lines of connection, like "because there's a nail in my tire, my car is wobbling." It's important to constantly re-visit our own assertions and assumptions, making sure we have provided the most accurate assessment we can.

It's also important to investigate others' claims of cause and effect. Remember that rhetorical claims are being made all around you, all of the time, and that these claims are sometimes flawed or inaccurate. Most advertisements base their claims in a flawed cause-and-effect relationship that is actually a kind of **logical fallacy** called a *non sequitur* (Latin for "it does not follow"). Axe Body Spray Deodorant runs attention-getting commercials in which an average-look-ing guy is suddenly attacked by swarms of gorgeous women right after spraying himself with Axe. We are invited to believe that Axe is the *cause* of this erotic *effect*. Although we may dismiss this as ridiculous, think about how often ads use this strategy: it must work on someone, and that person isn't taking a critical look at the cause/effect relationship.

4.6.1   Cause and Effect in the 39 Series

Each course in the 39 series will deal to some extent with cause and effect; 39A introduces issues of narrative chronology, and you'll be asked to look for the causes and effects related to the class theme; 39B discusses the ways in which particular texts use the cause and effect relationship for particular rhetorical effects (and how we, as critical readers, can interpret those ways). In some 39C classes, you are asked to conduct your own research on the causes of particular problems in the world, to plot the effects those causes are generating, and to propose your own solutions; in other 39C classes, you're asked to consider what contributed to (or caused) an individual's success, or how that individual's success can be seen as an effect of a particular set of influences.

> ## Questions to Ask when Writing about Cause and Effect
>
> 1. Do I present a clear description of both elements?
>
> 2. Is there a logical relationship between the cause and the effect?
>
> 3. Is the cause/effect relationship contextualized clearly?
>
> 4. What purpose am I trying to achieve with my analysis?

4.7   Examples

The concept of "learning by example" isn't new to you. Such learning begins when we are children and continues throughout our lives. We make use of examples every day—in conversations, in emails, in class—and our understanding is enhanced by the practical use of examples. Say, for instance you wish to rent a room in a hotel; you might go to the web site and view a *sample* room so as to get a better idea of the amenities. Similarly, when it comes to your writing, appropriate examples can help your audience's understanding of the message or concept that you wish to convey. Your choice of example should reflect your awareness of your audience and purpose.

4.7.1   Purposeful Examples

Aristotle defined rhetoric as the ability, in each particular case, to see the available means of persuasion. Successful rhetoric, then, will require you to choose and use the right example at the right time. Examples can take many forms, but whatever form they take, their success or failure as support depends upon their suitability to a given rhetorical situation. In your classes at UCI, you will encounter a wide range of rhetorical situations; in each instance it will be up to you, as rhetor, to determine which examples will resonate most effectively with your context, purpose, and audience.

When choosing examples for a given argument you must always ask yourself *why* you feel that example will be beneficial to your argument and *how* it will enhance your audience's understanding. If the idea you are discussing is complex, perhaps a simple, expository example would be most beneficial. For example, "America is like a salad bowl: individual ethnic groups come together in one place, yet maintain their cultural uniqueness."

On the other hand, perhaps you wish to complicate your audience's understanding of an idea or challenge biases; an example may do that as well. For instance:

> While we tend to think of pre-1960s Hollywood films as very conservative in their portrayals of women, before the censorship guidelines of the Hays Code were put into effect in 1934, women were frequently portrayed on-camera, in films such as *The Divorcee* and *Blonde Venus*, as assertive, street-smart and sexually uninhibited individuals.

4.7.2   Developing with Examples

An example can be anything that increases understanding of an idea. In academic arguments, supporting evidence can come in the form of images, graphics, quotations, summaries, or paraphrases from the text you are analyzing. This means that assertions in academic writing need to be *supported*, *illustrated*, and *developed* through the use and subsequent analysis of specific examples. You may need to use visuals, including a film clip, a photograph, or other image that can help you support and illustrate your idea. When you choose to include a visual example in a given assignment, the same rules of *kairos* apply: they must be suitable for the rhetorical situation at hand. As with quotations, you must interpret the significance of the visual example for your audience.

It's important to remember that no example, however excellent and appropriate, is self-explanatory. The relationship between the example and the idea it supports must always be made clear. We mustn't forget that both authors and audiences have biases, and therefore, we cannot assume that interpretation is self-evident. After presenting an example, you should explain how your example supports your assertion, how it is relevant to the controlling idea of your paragraph, and thus, why it is significant to your argument as a whole. The longer and more complex the quote or paraphrase, the more in-depth and detailed your analysis must be.

4.7.3   Examples in the 39 Series

In 39A, you are asked to analyze a wide variety of texts; your writing will require you to support your claims with examples from those texts. Likewise, in 39B, you'll be analyzing texts from many different media, genres, and historical periods, looking particularly at the variety of rhetorical strategies rhetors use to achieve their desired purposes with a variety of audiences. Again, you will need to wisely choose examples from the texts themselves to develop your ideas: a quotation from a novel or short story, a certain aspect of a scene in a film, or a particular element of a print image. In 39C, you may be asked to write a formal advocacy essay; in this case, your examples are more likely to be comparative: in order to argue that one given policy will work, you might offer an example of a similar policy that has worked.

Like choosing which elements to focus on for a summary, choosing which examples will best illustrate an idea is a complex and important decision—one you can only get better at making with time and practice.

When choosing examples for a given argument you must always ask yourself *why* you feel that example will be beneficial to your argument and *how* it will enhance your audience's understanding.

Consider the following example, from a Rhetorical Analysis essay on the great Hindu poem, *The Bhagavad Gita*:

 SAMPLE EXAMPLE

> The omission of conjunctions provides Krishna with authority and control of his message. Through this technique, the translator is capable of reformulating the appeal of Krishna's message through the direct style of Krishna's voice.

To support her point, the student must choose the best possible example, one that not only supports her point, but the point of the poem as well. The lines are simple, but the student's point is both illustrated and supported by it:

> Knowing the Self, sustaining
>
> the self by the Self, Arjuna,
>
> kill the difficult-to-conquer
>
> enemy called desire.

Questions to Ask when Using Examples

1. What kinds of examples would be appropriate for my point?

2. How many examples should I use? Do I show the variety of examples that may support my point?

3. Am I choosing the best possible examples from the text?

4. Do I adequately set up and analyze the example in light of my point?

4.8   Classification

Classification is a way of organizing based on relationships, and as you learned from the section of this chapter on definition, it is closely tied to that practice, as well. We can begin classifying something by asking if there are other things with similar characteristics, and then categorizing them into groups. You are probably already familiar with classification practices in the field of biological science: it's how we sort living things into categories (taxonomy is the formal word).

For example, we might divide animals by creating three groups according to whether they walk, fly, or swim. But if you stop to think about it, those three categories aren't watertight. How would you classify alligators, for example, or ducks, or the duck-billed platypus? The single-trait mode of categorization is one way to organize, but its "leakiness" asks us to be more specific in defining those categories. We have to define the level of detail and the criteria we need in order to most effectively classify for our purpose.

4.8.1   Purposeful Classification

Like other modes of writing, the degree of detail in classification is dependent on purpose and audience. If you go to a sushi restaurant, you'll see the menu organized by type: nigiri, sashimi, or hand rolls rather than by types of fish (as you might see at, say, a seafood market). When you scroll through the TV schedule, you see shows categorized as comedy, drama, reality, talk show, etc. Within those genres, they can also be sitcoms, movies, news shows, documentaries. Sometimes one show can fall into multiple categories.

If you've read Chapter 2, "Methods for Reading," you'll remember that most of that chapter is one big classification system: we suggest that when you want to read a text critically and rhetorically, the first step is to identify what categories the text fits into and what conventions you should expect from that type of text.

4.8.2   Developing with Classification

Definition is related to classification because each category within the classification must be well-defined; you need to know its boundaries in order to know what fits in the group and how the group functions. Here is how poet William Blake saw it: "To the eyes of a miser a guinea is more beautiful than the sun, and a bag worn with the use of money has more beautiful proportions than a vine filled with grapes. The tree which moves some to tears of joy is in the eyes of others only a green thing that stands in the way... As a man is, so he sees."

Let's use Blake's trees, for example: to classify them we might start with the leaves. They may all be lovely, flat and many shades of green as Blake might see them (emerald, chartreuse, celadon, or viridian), but a botanist would classify them as compound or simple, lobed or pinnated, serrated or smooth.

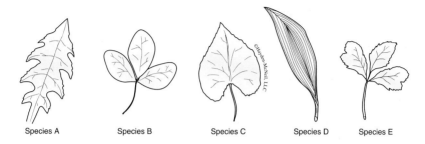

Species A   Species B   Species C   Species D   Species E

These sub-categories will indicate what genus the tree is (oak, elm or sumac), but there are other ways to categorize according to purpose.

Say you want to plant a tree in your front yard, and you're thinking about an oak. Would you like a fast-growing tree? Then oak is a bad choice—a sumac would be better. But a sumac won't be very tall; maybe you should go with an elm. But that may not work if you'd like a spreading tree to provide lots of shade: you're back to your original oak. So you may classify trees according to shape, speed of growth, or by full height. It all depends on your purpose.

As a result, when you're called upon to develop your ideas through classification, you have to develop a system or be very familiar with the one required in the field. You have to decide how many categories you'll need, and define the basis for your classification. For any given item, you have to decide how close it is to its ultimate destination in the system. You might think of each category and sub-category as a box, and sorting can mean deciding how to deal with things that are outside of the boxes or could convincingly go in more than one box.

4.8.3   Classification in the 39 Series

All the 39 series courses will ask you to classify, both in your writing and in class discussion. Part of 39A is identifying the characteristics of writing genres (narrative, academic, analytical essay, etc.) in order to learn what's required of you as a rhetor and communicator. The same is true of an even wider range of possibilities in 39B: you could be watching films, TV shows, commercials or shorts and also reading academic articles, short stories, and nonfiction. All require an understanding of genre classification. But as we've seen, 39B also asks that you learn the vocabulary of rhetoric, so that you can understand the uses of rhetorical devices, and identify, classify, and analyze them in the texts. In 39C, in order to address the opposition in your advocacy of a solution to a particular problem, you must be able to classify kinds of arguments in order to refute them.

Take for instance the movie *Pan's Labyrinth*. Since the film involves a lot of historical detail involving Spain under the fascist regime of Francisco Franco, you might think about categorizing it as historical drama. In the narrative, there are rebels fighting the regime, so you could also classify it as a war film. But the movie also involves a faun, fairies, and a child-eating monster. Is it a fantasy film instead? This places it in the same category as *Lord of the Rings*, something that might seem misleading. When artists break new ground in their genre, classification becomes strained. You might be tempted to compare it to a literary genre, like magical realism. This category may actually help you in your analysis of the film.

You also must classify the terms of your analysis itself, deciding what definitions apply to any given example. Say you're getting ready to write the Rhetorical Analysis essay for 39B on Hayao Miyazaki's film *Princess Mononoke*. You might decide to write about ethos, logos, and pathos and to put all your analysis into those three categories. But you may soon come to realize that you need more detailed terminology. Turning to the glossary entry for figures of speech, you discover that your analysis of Ashitaka's cape and mask seem to be operating metaphorically, as this student did in her analysis:

⬤ SAMPLE CLASSIFICATION

> By wearing these fierce-looking coverings, Ashitaka is able to form an emotional barrier between himself and the other characters. This distance does not allow Ashitaka to let his emotions cloud his judgment, thus making him unbiased and neutral. In political terms, he is a moderate who sees the pros and cons on either side of the debate.

The student *uses* a metaphor to *describe* the metaphor in the film. But does this use of the mask and cape fall into the ethos, logos, or pathos box? Will putting the rhetorical purpose of the metaphorical function of the cape and mask into one of those categories help develop your point?

Questions to Ask when Classifying

1. Are the categories too "leaky"? Have I defined the categories with enough precision?

2. Are there sub-categories within these categories that I need to address?

3. What are the characteristics or conventions of all the items in the category?

4. What is the relationship among all the categories and sub-categories?

4.9   Comparison and Contrast

> In order for the light to shine so brightly, the darkness must be present.
>
> — Francis Bacon, Sr.

We often compare things in our everyday lives to come to a more informed decision. You've probably noticed how many advertisements establish a brand's superiority by comparing a product to another "leading national brand." You may have done a similar comparative analysis when deciding something as big as what university to attend or something as small as where to eat lunch: A is better than B because it does X, Y, and Z.

You'll see this comparative analysis in the texts you'll read in the 39 series. In literary texts, writers use similes, metaphors, conceits, or analogies to establish a figurative relationship between two distinct objects to express wonder, love, sadness, etc. Thus, we can know what *is* by clarifying what it *is not*. In an academic argument, a writer does this comparison more formally and purposefully and in the process cites logical reasons for the comparison and contrast.

4.9.1   Purposeful Comparative Analysis

As with all the other means of shaping your ideas discussed in this chapter, the purpose, context, and audience should guide your development. Your purpose could be *informative*: you may want to merely inform your audience about the pros and cons of A and B in a side-by-side analysis (Bing vs. Google; owning vs. leasing or renting). Or your purpose could be *evaluative* or *argumentative*: based on the merits and demerits of the two you could argue that B is superior to A.

This method of exposition may often use elements of definition, description, and classification to establish a relationship between two similar or contrary topics under analysis. Juxtaposing the two categories allows for a detailed breakdown of their distinctive features that leads to an in-depth analysis and a more meaningful awareness of relationships between disparate ideas and subjects.

In some classes your instructor may ask you to write an essay comparing two texts, theories, scientific processes, historical events, eras, or figures. In other assignments, you may have to use comparison and contrast as supplementary proof of a larger argumentative claim. Even when not an assignment requirement, this process can help generate ideas during the pre-writing or drafting stages to help you go beyond basic summary or simplistic analysis. Whether organizing an entire essay, or a part of it, here are two ways to frame your analysis:

- A "classic" comparative analysis framework asks you to give the two ideas, texts, or issues equal weight in your discussion. This may be more informational or expository as you objectively describe two similar things with crucial differences or two seemingly opposing things with surprising similarities. For instance, you could demonstrate the resemblance between Disney's *The Lion King* and Shakespeare's *Hamlet* by comparing important characters and themes from both texts.

- A "keyhole" or "lens" framework allows you to see one weighted category through the filter or lens of another (explaining an unknown subject through the familiarity of a known subject). The "lens" method is useful for a more argumentative and critical perspective as it allows you to investigate a subject through the medium of time, differing disciplines, or competing theories. For instance, examining Shakespeare's *Macbeth* (1606) through the lens of Charles I's execution (1649) illuminates one period of history through another, or the present through the lens of the past and vice versa.

4.9.2   Organizing Your Comparative Analysis

Depending on purpose and assignment requirements, there are several ways of organizing comparison and contrast in your essay:

- For **pre-writing**. Venn diagramming to discern similarities and distinctions can lead to an organization scheme or outline.

- A **whole-to-whole** or alternating comparative analysis (also called block-by-block or text-by-text arrangement). Discussing all of the main points of A first and then all those of B, is a good way to demonstrate which category is superior or more extensive for a big picture understanding.

- A **part-to-part** or divided comparative analysis (also known as point-by-point arrangement). Discussing one critical concept from A and alternating it with one from B and following it up with your interpretation and commentary allows for a more in-depth look at similarities or differences, and works best to emphasize contrasts. Be careful though: this process depends on writing effective transitions between each point.

4.9.3   Tips on Good Comparison/Contrast

Be fair. Any piece of evidence can be tainted due to bias or inaccurate representation. Don't commit the fallacy of *stacking the cards* where one side is too heavily weighted against the other, and the superiority is therefore misrepresented. Another fallacy to avoid is *straw man argument* in which the writer has already made up his mind and conducts a pseudo comparison and contrast that misrepresents B in order to make A look better. Infomercials on TV are often guilty of such comparative fallacies where all alternatives are portrayed as laughable or ridiculous.

Establish context. For an argument to work logically the two things being compared cannot be absurdly dissimilar or unequal. To repeat a cliché, you can't compare oranges and apples. Be careful to ground your comparative analysis within a relevant and specific context if your prompt does not already do so.

The context or *unifying frame of reference* relates to the purpose or content of the assignment and could be an idea, theme, process, theory, or historical or cultural background. Get cues from reliable research sources that often suggest a frame of reference (and remember to credit your sources).

Determine your criteria for comparison: Once you have established context you will need to lay out a list of common referents against which you will judge both categories. When comparing which car to buy, for instance, your criteria could be cost, mileage, power, brand name, looks, safety features, financing options, consumer reports or reviews, etc.

Other variations could be the journalistic questions: who, what, where, when, why, and how.

You can even organize your paragraphs on the order of importance based on these criteria that could become key terms for each topic sentence.

Specify word choice. While revising, tighten and condense your language and word choice in order to cue the direction of your comparative analysis. Your thesis and/or your topic sentences should have already set up sign posts, but some transitional words or phrases could further alert your readers about your purpose and strengthen your overall ethos. Some words helpful in signaling intent for comparisons would be: like, similar to, also, in addition, similarly, in the same way, likewise, again, compared to, in like manner, at the same time, etc.

Connectors to cue contrast could be: unlike, in contrast, contrasted with, on the contrary, however, although, yet, even though, still, but, nevertheless, conversely, whereas, regardless, despite, while, on the one hand/on the other hand.

4.9.4   Examples from the 39 Series
Here a student from 39B is comparing the use of rhetorical devices in the TV show *Heroes* and the graphic novel *The Watchmen* in a part-to-part arrangement. While the analysis could be stronger, and the word choice more specific, the student still is able to competently transition between the two texts. Hint:

Just by looking at the number of times the writer refers to the two texts should tell you which one they are highlighting in their keyhole analysis:

> *Heroes* also refers to its main episodes with the word "chapter," much like a comic book would. *The Watchmen* is similarly divided into twelve chapters, each with it's own title, such as "Chapter I: At Midnight, All The Agents…" first introduced on page six. The chapter titles are placed a small ways into the chapter, not just on the first page. Similarly, Kring displays the chapter titles of *Heroes* on screen a few minutes after the episode has begun. By presenting the titles a couple pages into the chapter, Moore creates anticipation and curiosity in his reader; Kring also utilizes this technique in *Heroes* to draw the same response in his viewers.

Here is another student from the 39C series advocating the advantage of Integrated Pest Management (IPM) techniques as an effective deterrent to herbicide overuse. Note how detailed and fair and balanced the research needs to be in order to prove the comparative claim. In this paragraph they are comparing IPM to a British bill (EDM 1267) to show IPM's superiority using a variety of transitional words and phrases to cue the reader:

> Due to decades of herbicide dependence, farmers have become too comfortable with the herbicide "treadmill;" companies, such as Monsanto, continue to develop more toxic herbicides in response to resistant pests and weeds resulting in a never ending vicious cycle of stronger herbicides and the evolution of newer herbicide resistant traits. According to Peter Rosset, co-coordinator of the Land Research Action Network focused on agrarian reform, this is especially true with low income farmers, who would rather spend $7 per liter of cheap, toxic herbicide rather than $150 per liter of Javelin, a safer and more environmentally friendly herbicide (6). A somewhat different approach to eliminate toxic pesticides is proposed by the United Kingdom House of Common's EDM 1267. This Early Day Motion, proposed by Martin Caton on January 13, 2011, requires all products with neonicotinoids, including herbicides to be banned due to environmental damages (Early Day Motion 1267 1). In theory, banning pesticides from the agricultural industry would certainly eliminate the problem of herbicide overuse, but for smaller farmers this may come at too high a price. This plan may force farmers to rely on overusing approved alternatives or experiment with even stronger ones being developed by the chemical industry. In addition, EDM 1267 focuses only on the banning of neonicotinoids thus still allowing herbicides without neonicotinoids, such as Monsanto's RoundUp, to continue and ramp up its production to fill in the gap left by the removal of neonicotinoids. This proposal then, does not switch off the pesticide treadmill; it just puts us on

another one. In contrast to EDM 1267's inflexibility, IPM's diverse techniques adjust to the farmer's needs making it feasible to practice. Instead of abandoning herbicide use all at once, farmers could slowly mix in herbicide use along with biotechnological controls as a solution. For example, according to Lisa Tewksbury, an entomology research associate at the University of Rhode Island, purple loosestrife, an invasive plant accidently introduced to the United States from Europe, had been successfully controlled by the introducing Galerucella pusilla and Galerucella calmariensis beetles ("Beetles v. Purple Loosestrife" 1). Farmers worried about the infectivity of the beetles would still have the option of reverting back to herbicidal method, if the invasion gets out of hand. In addition, since the beetles feed specifically on purple loosestrife, farmers do not have to worry about the beetles becoming an added pest. Once the farmer becomes more accustomed to IPM, farmers may begin integrating more and more of IPM's methods as opposed to relying on herbicides.

Questions to Ask when Comparing/Contrasting

1. Am I being fair to the texts I'm comparing?

2. Have I established adequate context for the text involved, so that my comparison will be on equal ground?

3. Have I established the criteria for judging the text involved?

4. What claim (thesis) does the comparison/contrast allow me to make?

4.10   Using Sources: Appealing to Authority

When we speak with authority, it means that our listeners or readers will respect and give credence to what we say. When we don't have sufficient authority to convince our audience directly, we have to appeal to other authorities to give power to our ideas and increase the likelihood that our audience will agree. Authority (your ethos) depends very much on the context in which you exercise it. A judge has authority in the courtroom, but she has no grounds to order people around at a basketball game. A referee can't sentence a criminal in the courtroom, but he can eject a player when he's on the court.

In a non-academic context, authority comes from the facility a speaker or creator has in the medium at hand. ESPN hires analysts from the ranks of former players and coaches, and chooses those who can speak confidently (and sometimes loudly) about the game. The responsible and credible stockbroker, like the sports analyst, has experience and keeps up to date with the regulations and news of the securities trading industry. A director like Guillermo del Toro achieves his authority on film with research, awareness of his audience, a willingness to act boldly and take chances, and a proven track record making films that are successful. Your own ability to speak authoritatively in class comes from familiarity with the material and a willingness to take a chance.

In an academic context, authority comes from formal credentials like a relevant Ph.D., and from using commonly accepted standards of argumentation and presentation. In order to achieve authority in a field of study, we conduct research and experiments and report our findings to the wider community.

When a college writer produces an essay, article, lab report, or any other type of text, that writer enters into an ongoing conversation. Often, that conversation has been going on for a long time before the occasion of the writer's intervention, and it will continue long after. With this in mind, when we write we must take into account both what has been said before and what has not been said. We must exercise what the legal and business fields call "due diligence"—exploring the current state of research and discourse in the discipline, evaluating the accepted knowledge in that field, and making a good faith effort to ensure that what we say will make a significant contribution to the conversation.

Once we have performed this research for own benefit, we need to demonstrate this competence and knowledge to our readers. It lets them know that they can trust us. If properly done, our readers will accept our specific claim and begin to consider us as an authority in our own right.

The way in which we deal with sources in our writing varies with context. Most often, the genre of the text you want to create will determine the appropriate ratio between research and original analysis. Sometimes your use of authority will be as a summary of what others have thought, and sometimes it will be an analysis of what they thought in order to arrive at a new conclusion. At all times, you should consider what effect you want to produce in your reader. What are the conventions for research in the genre in which you are writing? Will including another source dilute or bolster your own analysis?

Additionally, you must evaluate the credibility of your sources. The venue or medium of your source will affect its believability in the eyes of your readers. For an academic audience, an anthropological journal carries more weight than a documentary on the History Channel, which in turn has far more credibility than the *National Enquirer*. So you must spend a good deal of time evaluating the credibility of your source. Wikipedia may be a good place to go to get an informal point-of-view, but its lack of rigorous oversight keeps it from being a credible academic source (*see Chapter 7: Using Wikipedia Wisely, for more detail*).

When marshalling sources to your cause, keep in mind that knowledge and information are power. By effectively citing sources and treating them in an ethically responsible manner, you will better persuade and/or inform your reader. By accruing a credible ethos, you establish a relationship of power with respect to your reader. You have the power to sway your reader this way or that. To misuse sources—to unethically appropriate their data without credit, quote them out of context, or to misrepresent their conclusions—constitutes an abuse of that power.

4.10.1   Modes of Citation and Integrating Sources

Authority and credibility (**academic ethos**) come in large part from the writer's ability to demonstrate his or her knowledge of and fluency with the conversation or discourse within a given subject or discipline. You achieve this in writing by distinguishing your sources from your own original material, and this is done with citation. Since composition classes are offered by the School of Humanities, we use the Humanities-preferred method of documenting and formatting—MLA. Other disciplines have their own style and formatting guides. When you begin writing in a particular academic discipline, always find out which formatting style is preferred. Connect Composition Plus (CCP) includes instructions for how to use all the various styles used in academia.

Four Ways to Integrate a Quote

1. *Signal phrase* set off by a comma.

   According to Michael Levin, professor of philosophy at CUNY, "There are situations in which torture is not merely permissible but morally mandatory" (298).

2. *Signal verb* with a "that" clause.

   Michael Levin, professor of philosophy at CUNY, *argues that* sometimes "torture is not merely permissible but morally mandatory" (298).

3. *Signal clause* or full sentence set off by a colon.

   Michael Levin, a professor of philosophy at CUNY, argues for state-sanctioned violence against certain criminals: "There are situations in which torture is not merely permissible but morally mandatory" (298).

4. Quotation is integrated into the grammar of the sentence.

   According to Michael Levin, sometimes "torture is not merely permissible but morally mandatory" (298).

4.10.2   The Three-Step Method for Integration

Step 1: Introduction

Start by introducing the source with a phrase or sentence that lets the reader know that you are about to quote, summarize, or paraphrase. If you are quoting passages from an assigned text in class, then you probably don't have to establish credibility before you use the source, but you do still need to introduce it.

If you're working with outside sources and the author's qualifications are not generally known to your audience, establish credibility when quoting from or even paraphrasing the author for the first time, using an introductory phrase that indicates what makes her a significant and reliable source. If you're quoting from a source that is already credible and doesn't need credibility established (because it is a news report, it has no author, or for some other reason the author himself is not important), then don't waste words.

For example, if you are using a quote from the *L.A. Times* to help establish background and context, you don't need to introduce it with something like this: "Joe Potato, who graduated from UCLA cum laude and was a star football player in high school, is now a reporter for the *L.A. Times*. He argues that..." In a case like this, you don't need any of that information to establish credibility with an academic audience. Just tell your readers that your information was reported in the *L.A. Times*.

Perhaps the trickiest part of integrating quotations is making the quotation match the grammar of its surroundings. All pronouns used should be clear, the verb tenses should match, and the sentence in general should make sense grammatically. Here's a quotation that goes awry:

⬤ **CONFUSING INTEGRATION**

Hardin argues that "since we all share life on this planet, they argue, no single person or institution has the right to destroy, waste, or use more than a fair share of its resources" (452).

This is not only a grammatically incorrect run-on and a mixed construction, but it is confusing to the reader. Who are the "they" referred to in the quotation? To solve this problem, use the introduction to the quotation to clarify who "they" refers to, and use less of the quote:

⬤ **BETTER INTEGRATION**

According to Hardin, environmentalists believe that since everyone "share[s] life on this planet...no single person or institution has the right to destroy, waste, or use more than a fair share of its resources" (452).

When editing, make sure you have not overused signal verbs such as "states" and "argues." Think about what the verbs mean; for example, don't use "says" unless the author was actually speaking, and use a more specific verb like "writes" instead. Vary the mix and choose your verbs for their precise meaning. Signal verbs are not exactly interchangeable: your choice depends on the context of the quotation and the point you are making in quoting it. Signal verbs such as "states" or "reports," for example, let the reader know that what will follow is a fairly neutral statement of facts or data. Signal verbs such as "argues" or "claims," however, suggest a more debatable point, while "concedes" or "acknowledges," strike a more conciliatory note.

You need to be aware of the verb's **connotation** in order to use it correctly. If you're unsure, the best way to find out quickly is to enter it into your word processing software's thesaurus function, or to look it up in an online thesaurus. Of course, there's always the old book-style thesaurus, as well. If you aren't entirely certain how to use a particular verb, don't use it, and pick one that you do know, instead.

Step 2: Citation

Include an MLA style "in-text citation" in parentheses after a quotation, paraphrase, or summary. The purpose of the parenthetical citation is to show the readers which entry in your Works Cited you're including material from, in case they want to look at your sources. By using citations, you're letting other scholars follow your research tracks—that's why you need to include the citation after paraphrase and summary as well as direct quotation—you are showing your reader that the ideas included here are not your own.

If you're only quoting from assigned texts in your essay, ask your instructor whether she wants you to use parenthetical citations and a Works Cited. The answer will probably vary depending on the assignment.

What goes in the parenthetical? Whether you're quoting from assigned texts or using outside authorities, there is one simple rule to follow about what goes into the parenthetical. If you have included the author's name in your introductory remarks, then include only the page number in the parentheses. If the author's name is not included in the introductory clause, it must be included in the final parentheses. If there is no author name for your source, then include the first few words of the title from the bibliographic entry in the Works Cited and the page number.

Variations on page numbers. If the source uses paragraph numbers instead of page numbers, then include the paragraph number in the parentheses: (par. 4). If there are no page numbers or paragraphs (as will be the case with many internet sources), then no page number is necessary. However, always make sure that you have given your readers tracks to follow so that they can turn to your Works Cited and figure out what you've quoted from.

Block quotations. Finally, if you are using a quotation longer than four lines of text (or more than 40 words), follow the format for a block quotation. However, please be aware that in shorter essays, a block quotation is probably too long to include. You should consider paraphrasing or summarizing some of it, and quoting only the words and phrases that are necessary to your argument in their original form.

Step 3: Commentary

Provide your reader with commentary of your own that refers to, explains, and clarifies your use of the source. In other words, after providing the quotation, paraphrase, or summary from the source, take some time to make the significance of the material clear. Don't just repeat what the quoted material already states—enhance it, add your own ideas to it. Consider the following two interpretations of the same passage:

 LOGICAL ANALYSIS

With reference to a study by the U.S. Labor Department, William A. Henry reports that "about 20% of all college graduates toil in fields not requiring a degree" (353). Henry cites this statistic to reinforce his argument that a college degree is less valuable today than some might think. In presenting this information, however, he fails to make his case convincing because, aside from the fact that 20% is a relatively low percentage, he relies on a false assumption, namely that the value of a college education depends upon whether or not graduates apply their degree toward their occupation.

LANGUAGE ANALYSIS

With reference to a study by the U.S. Labor Department, William A. Henry reports that "about 20% of all college graduates toil in fields not requiring a degree" (353). Henry colors this statistic with a description that corresponds with his ideas about the degradation of higher education in recent years. While the findings of the U.S. Labor Department simply indicate that about one in five graduates goes on to choose a job that does not call for a degree, Henry makes the situation sound particularly negative by describing such people as having to "toil in fields." His choice of words makes it seem as if all those people must endure exhausting manual labor.

Both of these examples choose different elements of the quote to emphasize and interpret. If you're having trouble writing your commentary, think about why you chose that quote in the first place. What is it that you want your reader to understand about the quote? Why did you choose to include it? What's important to your argument? If you can't answer these questions, maybe you don't need the quotation.

4.10.3   Appealing to Authority in the 39 Series

You will be asked to use outside sources for essays in all the 39 courses. Evaluating and using authoritative sources will play a large role in 39C, where you will use them to support your own argument. But you will also spend a great deal of time in 39B analyzing the rhetorical strategies that grant authority to a text (which may include graphic novels, films, videos, or poems) so you can then use those strategies yourself. You will also use source texts to support your ideas in 39A. All of the courses in the series ask you to cite and analyze the texts you read, watch, and examine in order to grant authority to your own work.

> ### Questions to Ask when Appealing to Authority
>
> 1. What is my purpose, and what kinds of sources would be appropriate?
>
> 2. What kinds of texts will I need to draw on to understand the problem, and will I use these in my own argument?
>
> 3. Do I fairly present the authority, or am I taking ideas out of context?
>
> 4. Have I clearly integrated and cited the authority?

4.11   Analysis

The next two sections, analysis and argument, represent the majority of your writing in college, and often require a combination of all the other modes.

Analysis is one of the most important modes of composition for college. The word "analysis" generally means dividing something into components, carefully scrutinizing each one, and then seeing how the parts relate to the whole. Analytical writing uses many of the other modes in its process. In an analysis you break the object of analysis into parts (classification); you closely look at each part (definition, description, summary); you synthesize this information to say something about how the parts work together to produce the whole (cause/effect). Analysis is about describing the relationship between the parts of something and the whole.

Analysis isn't easy, and it takes practice to do it well. The good news is that you've been practicing for a good portion of your life. If you've ever predicted the ending to a movie or a television show, you've practiced critical analysis. What you are picking up on is not so much the content of the story (what the story is about), but its formal aspects (how the story is presented). By the time you are experienced enough to be able to figure out how a story line will end, your analysis tends to be so quick that you are not aware of it as a process at all.

Say you're going to see the latest *Transformers* movie. Based on the genre (action/adventure, with a dash of sci-fi and superhero for flavor), you can already guess that there will be a clear-cut divide between good and bad guys, and that the movie will spend its plot developing a conflict between those two sides that will be resolved by the end of the film, probably with cool CGI and an epic battle. In addition to the giant transforming robots, there will be a human male hero and a female love interest; they will both survive the conflict and the film, because the movie is supposed to reinforce the message that good triumphs over evil, and since it's meant to be a box office blockbuster, a happy ending is pretty much guaranteed. You know all of this before you ever set foot in the theater, because you've analyzed the genre conventions and audience expectations of *Transformers* movies, based on your prior knowledge of the genre and the first film. Not bad for a little casual analysis.

Lest you think you will leave all analysis behind when you get out of college, there are whole professions dedicated to nothing but analysis. Systems analysts determine the computer systems and software for a business's particular needs. A business analyst figures out what a client needs, and how best to meet those needs. An industry analyst sifts through data and predicts market trends. And of course, a psychoanalyst investigates the underlying, unconscious causes for human behavior and formulates treatment and therapy based on those causes.

4.11.1   Developing Analysis

Academic analysis is a more deliberate version of the same analytical process you use every day. Like all the modes of development discussed in this chapter, it's a way to develop your topic in order to make a critically informed argument about it. Academic analysis can take many different forms. The process you use to craft your analysis will depend, in large part, on your focus and purpose. No matter what the object of your analysis, there are certain steps you must take before you even begin.

The Four Steps to Analysis

1. Understand the "big picture."

2. Break down and select parts of the text you want to examine.

3. Describe your selections carefully.

4. Describe how those parts interrelate with each other, the "big picture" and your argument.

4.11.2   Analysis in the 39 Series

As we've seen, analysis is an important mode of development for academic writing. In 39A, you'll write a Rhetorical Analysis of a Visual Text; in 39B, you'll write texts in several genres that employ analysis, and also compose a Rhetorical Analysis of a text and its context. In WR 39C, you will not only be asked to analyze texts, but you will also have to become an expert on the history of a particular problem or person and then write an Historical Analysis; instead of breaking a text into pieces, you will select moments from history to research, dissect, and discuss, and show how those moments contribute to the current problem in an academic argument or show how the history of a community shaped a particular individual. You will demonstrate not only the insights or results of your analysis, but also how you got there. In other words, you have to show your work.

Rhetorical Analysis

In both 39A and B, you'll be asked to write a Rhetorical Analysis essay about a text you've covered in your class. In both cases, your class will spend a lot of time critically and rhetorically reading a variety of texts from different genres and media. The focus of this analysis is "rhetoric"—a study of how a text communicates. You'll be analyzing not *what* a text means, but *how* it communicates its meaning.

As an example of rhetorical analysis, let's consider the famous 1984 Mac commercial that made waves when it was shown during the Super Bowl. If you haven't seen it, go to YouTube and search "1984 Mac ad."

In the ad, a narrative, we see a blue-grey, industrial environment populated by bald men in shapeless, colorless uniforms. The men march through corridors to a central assembly point, where they sit on benches and stare at a large screen on which an older white man wearing glasses is speaking. These scenes are intercut by a woman wearing a bright red tank top and white shorts, carrying a hammer, pursued by masked and faceless guards. In the final scene, she bursts into the assembly room, rushes past the bald men and hurls the hammer at the screen and shatters it. Then these words appear on the screen: "On January 24th, Apple Computer will introduce the Macintosh. And you'll see why 1984 won't be like 1984."

So what do we need to know about this ad in order to construct a successful rhetorical analysis? The message of the ad is obvious: buy a Macintosh. The purpose is clear as well: to persuade an audience to purchase a personal computer. The genre is video (television) advertisement, and the director is Ridley Scott. You probably also noticed the allusion to George Orwell's famous dystopian novel, 1984. The audience and context, however, is where things get interesting. The ad first aired during the Super Bowl in 1984. That suggests a largely male demographic in the audience. Second, prior to Mac's introduction in 1984, the only personal computers on the market were versions of the PC. Once you pay attention to the context, the rhetoric of the ad gets a lot more complex.

Now comes the hard part: you have to decide which elements of the ad you want to analyze. You could talk about the ad's color usage, the setting, the camera angles, the gender and appearance of the actors, the visual representation of the PC and the Macintosh, etc. Say you decide to focus your rhetorical analysis on the ways in which that allusion to Orwell's novel works on the (Super Bowl-watching, mostly male) audience to persuade them to buy a (totally new kind of personal computer) Mac. You would first need to describe the ways in which the ad alludes to Orwell's text. What in the ad makes you think of 1984? That is your evidence. The analysis part comes when you describe how that evidence contributes to the ad's purpose and message.

SAMPLE RHETORICAL ANALYSIS

The Mac ad aired during the 1984 Super Bowl in which half of America sits down to watch and cheer. Along with such overflow of emotions and excitement during the Super Bowl, Scott also understood Americans' strong anti-sentiment against communist. The Mac commercial was able to utilize pathos as a means to evoke a sense of urgency to buy the Mac computer. Promoting change in society was the underlying message of the ad by using the allusion to 1984. In 1984 the government was able to manipulate technology to control and monitor every aspect of people's lives. With the same idea, Scott tried to convince the audience that the evil PC was trying to control the market and in effect dominate people's choice of personal computer. The statement at the end of the ad allows Mac to be viewed as a crusader for truth and individuality, similar to how Americans believed themselves to be against the perversion of communism.

Historical or Cultural Analysis

In 39C, you may be asked to focus your analytic powers on either the historical or cultural context of your topic. You'll choose important events, trends, people, inventions, or moments in history and put them under an analytic microscope. You may even develop a cause and effect relationship between the historical events you describe or the culture in which they took place.

Let's say you're writing an historical analysis about illegal digital copying and distribution of music. Obviously, your historical story must start sometime after copying music became easy for the average consumer. But do you really need to begin with the creation of the cassette tape? Sure, the whole problem of music pirating may have started with people ripping cassette tapes at home, but those copies were of notoriously poor quality. The files found on compact disk were also too big to replicate easily. The creation of the MP3 file format in 1991 made digital copies both small enough, and of high enough quality, to make digital piracy feasible. Since your argument is focusing on the legal ramifications of digital piracy, you want to include a piece of legal history as well: The Digital Millennium Copyright Act of 1996. And finally, since you are examining the conflict between copyright infringement and fair use, you choose the founding of Napster in 1999.

Now that you've chosen your historical events, you have to prove to your readership a) the significance of your evidence in relation to the larger problem, b) that you have chosen the most relevant, important evidence. You must also show how your evidence all fits together. Why is the MP3 more important than the cassette tape? How did it change the way in which music was packaged and distributed in the early 1990s? How do the Digital Millennium Copyright Act and Napster add to the issues engendered by the MP3's creation? How does each piece fit together into the larger narrative of digital piracy? You must draw connections between the evidence and the larger shape of your argument.

Questions to Ask when Performing Analysis

1. What is the text's primary message? Is there a scene, sentence, or passage that sums up that primary or controlling idea? How do titles or headings hint at or sum up the message?

2. What seem to be the text's primary and secondary purposes? Persuasive? Expressive? Stylistic? Informative?

3. Who is the target audience of the text? What textual evidence and other clues suggest that this is the primary target audience? Are there any secondary or additional audiences to consider?

4. Has an editor provided introductory notes to the text, and if so, what further information do the notes offer about the text's thesis, audience, and purpose? What research could I do to better understand the author's rhetorical situation?

4.12   Argument

You may think that the goal of argument is to persuade. While this may sometimes be true, in most cases, *argument* is the intelligent presentation of a point-of-view supported with evidence. You may fail to persuade someone to see your perspective but succeed in presenting an argument. In your classes at UCI, you are entering into the great dialogue that is academia, a place where many points of view can be carefully considered. This can be intimidating, since it may seem as if it's all been said before; or you may feel that your instructor should be directing your work more specifically. Many beginning writers feel anxiety when they are first asked to present their arguments in class, thinking this is "just my opinion." But presenting an informed opinion—an argument—on the topic is the most common work of academic writing, and is essential in any field.

You already have plenty of experience presenting an argument. You convinced UCI that you would be a good addition to the student body. You have no doubt presented your point-of-view to your parents many times. But argument can be much more complex and subtle: over time, your informed point-of-view has gained you friendship, interesting conversations, or convinced the family cat to come out from under the bed. You may have changed your mind on what to have for lunch today because of the argument presented to you on the menu (the colors, the arrangement of items, pictures of the food) or by the waiter (pick one of today's specials? or would you like an order of fries with that?). Argument is everywhere.

While you are learning to do Rhetorical Analysis in 39A or 39B—that is, learning to read critically in order to identify a text's method and persuasive appeals—you are learning to evaluate the effectiveness of a given text's *argument*. Since you've discovered that persuasive acts take many forms (ads, music, film, graphic novels, poems, and essays), you have also discovered that the argument can be both complex and multifaceted. They can be aural, visual, or written. There may be no one way to see the argument. And you are also learning that the ability to break it down into its parts in turn leads to your own ability to present a complex and multifaceted claim in your own work.

You may also notice that, like analysis, argument requires using multiple modes of development in harmony. In order to effectively argue, you may need to present a seamless mix of the different modes covered in this chapter. Your argument may involve summary, analysis, use of example and an appeal to authority all at the same time. You will need to learn to balance description with analysis, for instance. In his paper on the graphic novel, *Watchmen*, this 39B student uses analysis of a visual motif to support his argument.

● **SAMPLE ARGUMENT #1**

By depicting the Doomsday Clock at the beginning and end of every chapter, Gibbons provides social commentary on the inevitability associated with a nuclear war; regardless of the Watchmen's attempts to stop the deaths of millions of people, the clock always moves its position toward midnight by one minute. The clock's methodical countdown represents a sense of the inevitability of nuclear war, suggesting that the protection of a hero is ultimately useless: "Simply given the mathematics of the situation, sooner or later conflict would have been inevitable!"

The student is claiming in his paper that the despair caused by nuclear escalation in the 1980s is the main contributing factor to the more humanized and realistic heroes in the text.

4.12.1   Analyze the Problem

In order to arrive at his thesis, this student had to spend time thinking about both the text and the prompt. The skills you learn in critical reading will help you construct a complex argument and present evidence in the most effective way. When you begin, you should first try to understand all possible approaches to the topic, the different ways you might answer the prompt. Understanding the point-of-view of the question is part of academic ethos. It helps, in other words, if you can see the goal of the assignment. You may be asked to make a claim based on scientific evidence, or you may be asked to apply an abstract concept and present an original claim—these are different purposes and require different approaches to argument.

You will also need to break the object of your analysis into parts, carefully discussing the role of each part and its relationship to other parts and to the whole. In your analysis, you may need to relate the cinematography of *Pan's Labyrinth* to director Guillermo del Toro's thematic goals, and to use that information to form a claim about the movie's rhetorical appeals to its audience. That requires an awareness that a film (or a painting, ad, or other visual text) can itself be making an argument using strictly visual components.

It makes sense, then, that there are multiple ways to construct your *own* argument, and that it could take form beyond an analytical paper. Choose the best possible approach to achieve your goal, including choices of medium. Perhaps the construction of a wiki or web page will be the most effective presentation of your argument. These would allow easy access to links, video, audio, and images that you can use to present evidence. You may need to generate charts or graphs, or change the elements of your style. The prompt may confine you to a short analytical essay, or you may need longer, sustained research.

Make a Claim

Academic argument requires that you formulate a complex claim about your topic, but that doesn't happen instantaneously. In the 39 series, you are being the given the tools you need to formulate complex claims, from the early steps in class discussion, forums and blogs, to the drafting and peer editing of the revision process. Eventually, you arrive at a complex claim that requires the entire paper to fully support and develop.

You may go down many dead ends before you find something worth developing, and you may require a lot of feedback from your peers and your instructor. However you get there, you must have an *arguable point*.

This means that your claim needs to avoid the obvious, and even avoid statements of fact to some extent, since these are really evidence that should be used as support. Your claim should be a conclusion *drawn* from your analysis of the evidence.

Anticipate Counterarguments

Understanding that there is a different way to view the problem can help you to "check your work" so to speak. If you can see another way to view the problem, you probably have a complex claim. In some cases, you may wish to include counterarguments. This gives you an opportunity to present more evidence of your own. Remember, however, that you are a member of the academic community. Argument is one way that our thinking advances, and so it involves understanding as much as it does persuasion. You may at first think the Harry Potter films are for kids, for instance, but after careful review of the relationship between genre, purpose, and audience you may decide they play a larger cultural role. Remembering your own early counterargument—that they're "just for kids"—can help you strengthen your own later analysis.

Remember Your Audience

Since all your work occurs in its own rhetorical context, you must be aware of the reader of your work. As with all of the other modes of writing, argument requires that you present your point-of-view in a way that specifically considers the expectations of the reader. Usually, in an academic context your reader is very familiar with the material. This frees you from summary, so that you need only to situate the reader in order to make your point. Your argument can be paced out over time, with points building and connecting, using careful specific analysis of evidence to reach an equally arguable conclusion. Your audience will expect a kind of conversation, where you present your ideas in a manner appropriate to the rhetorical situation. Remember, the order of your ideas isn't self-evident or shouldn't be formulaic. It's your job as the writer to compose with full awareness of the relationship between your purpose and your audience.

Questions to Guide Development Using Argument

1. Have I defined the issue clearly as I present my points?

2. What is the context of the issue, and does my argument seem aware of it?

3. Is the point-of-view worthwhile; that is, is it worth arguing?

4. What are the other points-of-view on this topic? Do I anticipate them?

Chapter 5

WR 39A, INTRODUCTION TO WRITING AND RHETORIC

Writing 39A is designed with two things in mind: where you've been and where you're going. We begin with a certain awareness that you have to make up for some lost ground, and that you need to re-build your knowledge of what writing is, especially academic writing. This class will give you a new, strong foundation—strong enough to carry you though 39B, 39C, and beyond. You'll learn how it's done in 39A, and gain a new appreciation for the labor-intensive aspects of writing that lead to bold, complex thinking and interesting writing.

We start with the elements of analysis, specifically rhetorical analysis, adding complexity as we go until we arrive at producing a convincing, original argument.

Why rhetorical analysis? In case you haven't already, you should review the sections of Chapter 1 that discuss the definition of rhetoric (sections 1.1–1.4). Assuming you and your instructor have started this conversation, 39A teaches rhetorical analysis with your writing in mind. As you become aware of the dynamic relationship among the styles, purposes, and audiences of the things you'll be reading and watching, you'll become more aware of the effect your

own rhetorical choices have on your intended audience. In turn, you'll gain
the ability to make improvements in your writing that will allow you more control over your purpose, gaining complexity and the interest of the reader as you
improve.

RHETORICAL ASIDE

You've certainly noticed how varied the approaches to learning are
in all your classes. You may be asked within the course of two days
to jump from the large-lecture biology class to a smaller psych discussion section to this small writing class. Every instructor seems
to have a different set of expectations. One may ask for a short essay, another
may be giving you a clicker quiz. You've no doubt already noticed your writing
instructor expects you to participate actively in class discussion. Awareness of
the *rhetoric* of each class can help you get oriented quickly, improve your performance, and even fend off boredom (since you'd have a better understanding
of what you're supposed to *do*). Do a little rhetorical analysis on the situation,
pinpoint the purpose of the class, and you'll gain confidence and control as you
maneuver through your daily routine.

5.1   The Elements of 39A

5.1.1   The "Theme Text"

Each instructor for 39A chooses a theme text as a basis for the class. Because our
focus is rhetoric and the analysis of rhetorical approaches, choosing a single text
that's been treated a wide variety of ways across time, in different media, genres,
and cultures, should help you see how rhetorical choices affect purpose and
the intended audience. The themes for 39A all have an original source text that
through repetition and retelling has achieved cultural significance. Your job is
to carefully examine the different ways the story is told to different audiences in
order to discover the real power of rhetorical awareness, and perhaps begin to
understand why these stories have become so iconic.

A classic example of this (and one of the 39A themes) is Mary Shelley's novel *Frankenstein, or, The Modern Prometheus*. Since its publication in 1818,
Shelley's story of a scientist who creates a new human from scratch has been
translated, painted, animated, filmed, staged, and put to music. The story began
mutating almost immediately after its publication—it was made into a stage play
very quickly, a play that changed Shelley's book into a melodrama that now
seems almost funny. The earliest films marked a strange shift: "Frankenstein"
became the name of the monster, but in the novel, the "monster" has no name.
Rhetorical analysis not only asks the question, "Why?" but also "How?"—where
are the most important manifestations of change in the story's telling? How did

this affect the audience? What were the cultural influences that led to these changes? All the different forms of the story are products of their time, and all have different meanings to their intended audiences. By looking at the stylistic choices of the theme text, you can discover the connection with purpose and audience.

Depending on the text, you may be asked to compare each version of the story to the original. You may be asked to educate yourself in the history of this text, to become aware of the cultural context of its original creation. Did you know, for instance, that Mary Shelley wrote her novel in Switzerland after a gigantic volcano eruption made the summer weather miserable and ruined her vacation? You'll learn to trace the threads of context through its effect on the creation of the text, and in turn its often surprising effect on the audience.

5.1.2   The Class Trajectory

39A is a fast-moving class. Your grade for the course will be based on three major assignments along with your continuing participation in the class community. Each assignment adds a new skill set that you use to complete the next task. You'll begin with a short rhetorical analysis of a visual text, and then do an extended rhetorical analysis of a more complex subject: one of the major versions of the theme. You'll then apply what you learned in an independent argument project, designed by your instructor to teach you how your own rhetorical choices can create convincing and interesting texts.

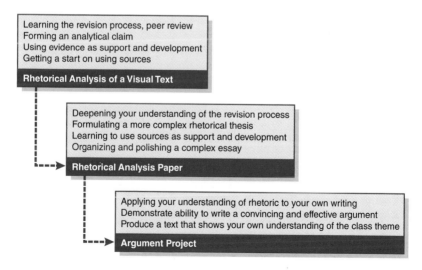

Learning the revision process, peer review
Forming an analytical claim
Using evidence as support and development
Getting a start on using sources

Rhetorical Analysis of a Visual Text

Deepening your understanding of the revision process
Formulating a more complex rhetorical thesis
Learning to use sources as support and development
Organizing and polishing a complex essay

Rhetorical Analysis Paper

Applying your understanding of rhetoric to your own writing
Demonstrate ability to write a convincing and effective argument
Produce a text that shows your own understanding of the class theme

Argument Project

Along the way, you'll be participating in online and in-class discussions of the theme and your writing. Your instructor may also supplement the assignments with in-class writing, such as short-writes or quizzes.

You'll be writing right away, and working in different rhetorical contexts yourself, from forums and blogs to formal essays. All the work you do is designed to help you relearn the writing process. Our chief emphasis in 39A is on drafting, revision, and preparing the final draft. Each of the three major assignments will go through three required drafts and required peer review. You'll need to prepare yourself for drafting by reading, note taking, and prewriting. Your work will be supported by in-class discussion, questions in forums, your blog, peer review, and all-important conferences with your instructor.

Although conferencing is not technically a "required" portion of the class, you should start thinking of it as a regular component of your writing. All the courses in the 39 sequence encourage individual writing conferences. It's really up to you to decide when you need (or are even ready) to discuss your work, but you can talk to your instructor at any point during the writing process (including *after* the assignment has been graded—it's just as important to know *why* you got the grade as knowing the grade itself).

5.1.3   The Class Community
Because 39A is such a small class, perhaps the smallest class you'll have at UCI, it makes sense to take advantage of that and seek the help and advice of your fellow students. It's also true that most of the work done at the University is cooperative, so learning to navigate an academic community is good practice for your later work. You'll be working in 39A with two different tools to help you establish community: blogs and forums (you'll use both of these again in 39B and 39C).

Although your instructor will have his/her own way of using these tools, we can make a general distinction between them. The word "blog" is short for "web log," an online, public journal. Some instructors propose problems or questions to guide your journaling, while others take a more free-form approach. Either way, you should use blogs as an opportunity to get to know the people around you, and what they're thinking about the class theme and about writing. After all, you'll be reading their work, listening to their contributions in class, and learning right alongside them. These free-form blogs will help you practice writing informal transactional texts between you and your colleagues. Here's an example of a short blog exchange between Teresa Lou and Stefanie Farmand:

Teresa: Today is the last class we have before turning in our first final draft for this course. Although I have developed my essay a lot from the first draft, it still feels like I need more time. I'm quite nervous about turning it in on Thursday. As of now, I have a clear thesis but I need to pull the body paragraphs together and begin my conclusion. AH! I am running out of time!

Stefanie: Don't worry—you will get it all together by tomorrow. Just take your time and don't stress out about it or else that makes it worse. Good luck!

Blogs not only help you get to know your fellow students, but they help your instructor take the temperature of the class. They can be very effective and fast ways to provide feedback.

Forums are an opportunity to perform specific tasks in a public way. Your instructor will make a forum assignment, and you will be asked to not only perform the task yourself, but look over the answers of your fellow students. Many instructors use forums to help guide class discussion, provide questions to prompt drafting, or as a peer review tool. (For more on blogs and forums as you'll use them in 39B, see Chapter 6.) Here's an example forum question and response by Ainaria Johnson. The class theme text was *Beauty and the Beast*, and Ainaria was writing on a 1947 poster for a film version by French director Jean Cocteau:

List VERY SPECIFIC DETAILS that you think convey this message to the reader. You should focus on at least three, and describe why you think the designer made the poster look this way.

In the French poster, the Beast is in a vampire-like position, like he is ready to strike. His face, however, tells a different story. The expression on his face makes it look loving more than menacing. I think the artist made this particular pose to show the inner struggle the beast is having.

Conversing with your fellow students in blogs and reading their thoughts in forums also helps you understand their perspective when you read your fellow students' drafts. Peer review is another part of the class community. You'll be expected to provide responsible feedback to your fellow students for all of the assignments you do in 39A. (For more on how you'll be using forums and blogs in 39B, see Chapter 6.)

There are many good reasons for the practice of peer review, but perhaps the best is simple practice with editing skills. The idea is to take the skills you gain looking at others' work and apply them to your own. The more practice you get, the more effective you are and the easier it becomes. Eventually, editing your work should be second-nature. It's not that peer review makes you a better writer (although it can); it would be more accurate to say that it makes you a better critical reader. That skill will help you improve your own writing. (For more on peer review, see the section entitled "Getting Feedback" in Chapter 3.)

5.1.4   Learning (or Re-Learning) the Revision Process

Peer review is just one of the new methods you'll be learning as part of the revision process. You may have been thinking of "revision" as a once-over and a spell-check with some formatting thrown in; or you may see it as a series of steps, with you waiting at each one for the instructor's feedback. Writing, in fact, is more like a never-ending river, with each bend (each draft) providing a new and better perspective on the source. You'll need to shift your perspective rapidly and take possession of the composing process. Once you're given the assignment, you're not "waiting" anymore; you need to get started and not stop until you run out of time.

Writing an academic essay is a whirlwind experience. You'll have roughly three weeks to complete each assignment. You'll begin by gathering information, doing some preliminary research into the topic, re-reading or re-watching the text, and taking notes. As you begin to write the first draft, you may or may not have a preliminary thesis. You focus instead on early description and analysis of detail, carefully drawing conclusions as you go.

These conclusions should lead to a tentative thesis that you'll continue to develop in the next stages. Once you have a clearer idea of your thesis (although this may not be fully crystallized yet—your thesis can change over drafts), you can begin to organize the paragraphs around the thesis, providing and analyzing evidence (including sources you may have found). This leads to a fuller, more complex version that will be more tightly organized. In the end, you'll have a complex thesis that emerges from the entire process, one that grows and develops as you provide support and analysis. You'll draw a strong (non-repetitive) conclusion at the end. When you've got yourself in this position, you'll carefully proofread and check your sources in the final polish.

"How do I get all that?" you may be asking. The answer is "drafting, drafting, and more drafting." It's likely that you've been taught what's often called the "five-paragraph theme" at some point. That model will not work in complex academic writing. It takes time and labor to develop a complex claim, often following ideas down blind alleys. It also takes motivation: although your instructor will only officially call for three drafts (two drafts and a final version that will be graded), you're encouraged to do as many drafts as you can, and to bring them with you to conference with your instructor.

As you might imagine, your instructor plays a key role as you develop your ideas. You can expect short, general comments from your instructor on the first (and usually very rough) draft. Once you have a more substantial draft, you'll get more extensive written comments, along with peer review, on your required second draft. Your instructor will then ask for a third and final draft, which he/she will grade. But remember, those are just the three required drafts. This is a river. You can revise and/or conference as many times as you can during the time allowed.

The process begins as soon as you know the assignment. You can begin the work of writing at that moment, and work on the assignment continuously until you run out of time. Revision ("re-seeing") is a continuous process of improvement, running from early thoughts, notes, and pre-writing to early drafts and working drafts, all the way through to the final polish and source checks. Chapters 3 and 4 of this book cover the whole process. It might at first seem overwhelming—you can expect to experience an adjustment period while you learn these new skills and begin to shake off old habits.

A word about language: many 39A students experience difficulty with proofreading and language errors. It's not the purpose of this class to teach you the rules of style, of grammar, punctuation, spelling, diction, and syntax. But it is the purpose of this class to give you the opportunity to learn to apply rules you already know. We spend extra time teaching you how to teach yourself to be so proud of your writing, you'll want it to be as close to perfect as you can get it. Surface issues will negatively affect your grade; but more importantly, they get in the way of your message. Your instructor will direct individual attention to this aspect of your work, as needed. Now, let's talk about the assignments.

5.2   Rhetorical Analysis of a Visual Text

You've glanced at maybe thousands of movie posters in your lifetime. You've been choosing movies based on DVD covers since you were little. Because posters and DVD covers are carefully constructed "texts" with a specific purpose in mind, it's a good place to begin to learn rhetorical analysis. You instructor will choose the individual images for your essay, but you can expect to be spending a lot of time on the small details of a still image.

You can look at this assignment as a way of discovering the precise purpose a designer may have had when constructing a still image. In order to do this, you don't necessarily need to have seen the film or read the book (something you'll just be starting to do in the first few weeks of class), since part of the purpose of the designer is to get you to do so. You can also learn how the ability to achieve the purpose means limiting or focusing on a particular kind of audience. No movie poster can be all things to all people; movie posters will often have several different versions, each designed to appeal to a particular person, one part of the film's potential audience.

Understanding the context of the image is key, which is one of the reasons you are required to use one outside source for the essay. You're encouraged to discover more about the image, and to use what you learn to help you situate the image in its time and understand the mind-set of its potential viewer.

Eventually, your essay should have a strong claim about the rhetoric of the image: its intended audience, the elements of design that are aimed at the audience and analysis of how they operate, the social/historical context that affects the audience's interest, and the nature of the message the image conveys. (See Chapter 2 for more on reading a visual text.)

5.3   The Rhetorical Analysis Essay

The Rhetorical Analysis Essay is where you'll apply all of the skills you've learned so far (preliminary rhetorical analysis, note taking, revision, and peer review) to a more extended, formal academic essay. (Chapter 1 can also help you with this.)

The Early Stages. Your instructor may offer you a choice about which text to write about—avoid choosing the easy path. Sometimes, choosing what you perceive to be the easier text to discuss actually translates into having very little to say. In an extended analysis, that's a problem. Instead, choose a text that generates lots of questions. Answering those questions can form the basis of your analysis.

Once you've chosen your text, begin by educating yourself about its historical/ cultural context. Many student perspectives have changed once they've gotten their facts right on the topic. It's also important to learn about the medium of the text, and these two aspects can work together. For instance, if you're in a class studying *Beauty and the Beast*, it helps to know that the author of the French fairy tale (Jeanne Marie Le Prince de Beaumont) was a governess, and was using the story to teach little girls how to behave. But it complicates the issue when you find out that she was also a divorced woman attempting to make a living in publishing at a time when this was very difficult for women. She immigrated to America to find work as a writer, where she published the first English version of the story. Knowing this helps you understand some mysterious aspects of the fairy tale: things that can seem annoying can suddenly have purpose (things like Belle's extreme goodness and sense of duty—a good example for eight-year-old girls).

It makes sense, since you'll be learning about the social/historical context of your theme text, to support your essay with sources. In addition to preparing you for 39B and 39C, using source material is a crucial aspect of all analysis, providing both you and your reading with crucial information you need to understand its rhetorical appeal (see also Chapter 7). Begin to gather your sources as soon as you begin your research, and apply your newfound knowledge of context early, since understanding context can operate as troubleshooting, saving you time.

Taking good notes on your text is crucial. Your notes will provide you with evidence as you begin to formulate claims about the text. You should also read/watch the text again, supplementing things you missed in your notes, or adding things you now understand a little bit better.

Drafting the Rhetorical Analysis. Your early drafts will be a bit chaotic. It can take a while to feel like you have a structure. You begin by pulling examples of strong moments out of the text and analyzing their rhetorical purposes. The more examples you have, the more opportunity for strong conclusions. The more conclusions, the closer you get to formulating a claim to hold them all together. You have to start by analyzing enough examples. Center your paragraphs around *claims about* the text, rather then just *observations of* the text. Once you do that, you'll have enough to begin serious revision.

The Working Drafts. In between the first stages and the final polish, you'll often find yourself writing a series of drafts as you try out different organizational principles and different lines of development. You'll also be getting feedback from your peers and your instructor, applying the helpful ideas, discarding the irrelevant ones. You'll have a lot of balls in the air. But soon, you should have a complex thesis that will allow you to organize the essay.

Getting there can be frustrating. There are a number of writing tools that can help. You can do what's called a "reverse outline," which means creating an outline *after* the essay is written. Once you have what may seem like an unorganized mess, you can go back through and list your main ideas. If you take a look at this outline it may suggest a better order. That order may even suggest a common thread that can add to your claim. It may even suggest ways to fashion transitions between the paragraphs.

You can also list your main points of evidence. Very often students are having difficulty reaching the next level of complexity simply because they haven't analyzed enough evidence. If you force yourself to go back into the draft and pull out all your quotes and specific examples, you may find you don't have very many. That means going back to the drawing board, so to speak. Read/watch the text again, looking for specific examples to provide more analysis.

You should also read your work out loud. As your working draft inches closer to the final stages, reading out loud can provide you with a much stronger awareness of your own stylistic choices, forcing you to acknowledge your own sensitivity to the audience since you have to listen to yourself. It's never a good sign if you find your own essay boring. Reading out loud can spark some much-needed energy.

The Final Draft. The final version of your RA should have a complex claim that gets started in the first paragraph(s) of the essay. Each paragraph should be carefully placed in order to develop that claim, with *well-chosen* and *carefully analyzed* evidence. The paragraphs should be going someplace, and ideas should be knitted together with hard-working transitions. The essay should show your expertise with the text being discussed and address the audience (your instructor and your peers) with authority, using outside sources and evidence from the text effectively. You should conclude in an interesting and original way, and hold the reader's attention from start to finish. It should shine with control, with no distracting errors.

In the end, the main goal of 39A is to teach you rhetorical control over your writing. The final draft should leave no doubt in the reader's mind that your position is valid (and interesting). In other words, by the time you're done, you should have learned how to produce a convincing argument, which leads us to the last assignment. (To see what you'll be doing in the Rhetorical Analysis assignment for 39B, see Chapter 6.)

5.4   The Argument Project

39A has a two-prong focus: to teach you awareness of rhetorical methods of persuasion, and to teach you to use rhetorical methods to make your writing more effective. The final project allows you the opportunity to demonstrate how much you've learned. You will now be the "rhetor" in the rhetorical triangle. You will be asked to write a convincing, persuasive essay for a specific audience: the class itself.

Your study of the class theme text has no doubt revealed a number of interesting issues: *Frankenstein* raises issues of the responsibility of the creator to the creation, of science and technology, of our notions of humanity. If you are in a class studying "Pygmalion," you may have discussed questions of beauty and love, of class, the nature of education, of art and the artist. Your final project will be to choose a specific, real-world issue related to one of the class themes, take a stand on that issue, and argue your position convincingly.

A student in a *Frankenstein* class may write for or against genetically modified food. A student in a *Beauty and the Beast* class may write about the role our views of manhood may play in relationships. A student in a "Pygmalion" class might write about the role advanced placement has in education. Whatever subject you choose, you should choose one that is both specific and relevant to you: write about something you care about and you're much more likely to write effectively. And remember this is a direct address to the class. Your peers are your chief readers. They know what you know about the class theme.

The emphasis in this essay is on formulating an argument. This means that you will need to specifically define the problem or issue, present an *arguable position* that takes into account and answers contradictory points of view, and support your ideas with appropriate sources. You should also demonstrate your understanding of the theme text in your argument by using it to support and illustrate your argument. You should also aim your argument specifically at your peers in the class. This will allow you to use rhetoric yourself, with a specific purpose aimed at a very familiar audience.

Your specific purpose is to persuade. This means you will need to make all kinds of different appeals in your essay, building on your understanding of what other rhetors have done to make their point of view believable.

Your instructor will specifically define the topic for you. He/she will also require additional supplemental materials to support it, but you will also be required to demonstrate your awareness in the form of a proposal or cover letter. Your instructor will let you know which one you will be required to complete.

The Proposal. Your instructor will ask you to decide immediately what you want to do for your project. You may be asked to select from a number of options, and to provide more specifics in a proposed topic. She/he may ask you to do that in a formal document, in a class presentation, in groups, or in forums or in your blog. This is to get you thinking and talking about what rhetorical choices you're going to make: Who is your audience? What is your purpose? What stylistic approach will you be taking and why?

The Cover Letter. You'll also be asked to produce self-analysis on your project in the form of a cover letter (so called because it's the introduction to your project: the letter *covers* it). This will help you demonstrate rhetorical awareness. Your cover letter is a direct address to your instructor (your audience) indicating your awareness of your *rhetorical* reasons for designing your project in this way. You'll discuss your purpose, your audience—your choices—rhetorically analyzing your own style and design.

The first version of the cover letter will happen simultaneously with your first version of your project. The cover letter needs to be updated and revised as you revise the actual project. If you change your mind about some major aspect of the assignment, the cover letter should reflect that change. Think of it this way: At any given time while the class is working on the assignment, your instructor or peer editor should be able to look at your cover letter and understand what you're doing for your project and why you're doing it that way.

The Final Result. The Argument Project should above all things be convincing, so that you show an awareness of the conventions of your chosen rhetorical situation. Your project should also add to the class knowledge of the text, which means that your project should have a strong sense of purpose, granting a new perspective on the class theme to the reader. This means your project should also demonstrate your understanding of the class theme, and your role in the class community.

It's important not to overshoot the limitations of time and experience. Although you will have three weeks to complete your project, you're still required to take it through at least three drafts (this includes both the project itself and the cover letter). Pace yourself, and begin thinking and writing as early as possible. There will be dead ends, and aspects of the assignment that will require reading and watching the texts again, multiple revisions, gathering feedback—you may even change your mind and switch to a different option. Factor that in as you begin to plan your strategy. Remember that part of the assignment is demonstrating control and awareness of the work of revision. If you wait until the last stages to take on the complex aspect of your project, you'll run out of time to revise right where the project will need it most.

5.6   Beyond 39A

You'll see all of the elements of 39A in 39B and 39C. Aside from the use of Writing Studio, 39B and 39C both use a similar "theme" structure. You'll be writing a longer, more complex rhetorical analysis essay in 39B, using more sources as support. You'll also be doing a Rhetoric in Practice project that shares some common elements with the Argument Project (like demonstration of awareness of the rhetorical situation). 39C will also ask you to use your growing analysis skills to pursue an extended argument and research project. Part of that project will be making yourself aware of the context of the problem you're researching—something you started in the first assignment in 39A.

39A also has other commonalities with the rest of the sequence. Your classes will be small, encouraging participation. Class community will be play a large role, and you'll be encouraged to conference with your instructor. Of course, throughout the 39 sequence you'll be expected to work hard on revision. These courses may be your only opportunity to get extensive feedback on your writing, but you should take the skill of revision with you for the rest of your writing life.

Chapter 6

WR 39B, CRITICAL READING AND RHETORIC

Ever found yourself cheering enthusiastically in a movie theater as an unlikely hero slices and dices his way through a horde of oncoming enemies? Throwing a crumpled In-N-Out wrapper at your dashboard when a talk show host pontificates against your political grain? Flushing with embarrassment when a stand-up comedian lets loose with the F-bomb on Comedy Central while your grandmother is visiting?

Although at first it might not seem so, these are all moments in which rhetoric is at play. Considering even moments like these rhetorically is part of the plan in 39B. We'll study all different kinds of communication situations through the lens of rhetoric.

The curriculum is designed to teach you the basic vocabulary and analytical tools you'll need to rhetorically read, write about, and construct texts in a variety of situations. The first half of the course will introduce you to some foundational methods for reading and composing rhetorically; you'll examine a range of texts from several genres and media and synthesize what you've learned in a series of assignments. You'll learn to analyze and interpret not only what's being said, but how and why, to whom, where, when, and for what effect. During the second half of the course you'll use these foundational principles to write a formal rhetorical analysis of one of the course texts, and finally to put everything you've learned about rhetoric into practice by constructing a rhetorically savvy text of your own.

6.1   There's a Rhetor in All of Us

For most of your time in 39B, you'll be focusing on rhetorical analysis. If you haven't already read Chapter 1, "Rhetoric," and the introductory pages of Chapter 2, "Methods for Reading," it would be to your benefit to read them now—they'll provide foundational information that you'll need in order to get the most out of this chapter. In Chapter 2, we outlined some steps for approaching a text rhetorically:

Critical Reading: A Rhetorical Methodology

1. Identify **your rhetorical situation** for reading. Why are you reading this text, what do you expect from it, and how will your own bias color your reading?

2. Identify the **rhetorical situation of the text**. Where does it stand within history and culture? Who constructed it, why, and for whom?

3. As part of understanding the text's construction, identify the **medium** (media) by which the text is communicated; how are the medium, rhetorical situation, and message related?

4. Identify the **genre**(s) in which the text has been composed; what conventions of form and content are expected of texts in this genre? How does the text follow, play with, or reject these conventions?

The Next Step: Break the text into parts for closer analysis—for more, see Chapters 4 (on analysis), 6 (on rhetorical analysis), and 7 (on historical analysis).

Call of Duty: Black Ops, "There's a Soldier in All of Us"

Please go to YouTube and type in this search string: "there's a soldier in all of us." In the results, you'll find a broadcast commercial for the video game *Call of Duty: Black Ops.* The name of the commercial is "There's a Soldier in All of Us." Please watch this video before you read the rest of this section.

6.1.1   Your Rhetorical Situation for Reading

If you're a gamer, you may have noticed this broadcast commercial for the popular *Black Ops* installment in the *Call of Duty* video game series. If you saw
the commercial on television or the internet when it was being broadcast, your
rhetorical situation for viewing it then is different than your situation for viewing it now.

If you experienced it as a consumer viewing an advertisement for a product,
your response to it depended largely on your previous experience with video
games, video game commercials, and the culture of gamers in general. Now,
your situation for viewing this text is as a scholar, interested in how the rhetoric of the text functioned for its target audience(s) and within the cultural and
historical context in which it was constructed. No doubt your reading of and
responses to the text will vary based on these two different situations.

6.1.2   Rhetorical Situation of the Text

Where Does the Text Stand in History and Culture?

"There's a Soldier in All of Us" first appeared October 31, 2010 during the network television broadcast of an NFL game between the Saints and the Steelers.
Although primarily a text for an American audience, and therefore embedded
within American culture, it can also be viewed by anyone in the world who
has an internet connection and who can visit YouTube (or countless other sites
where you can now view the video). Since it first aired during a primary sporting
event (this is a convention of TV ads—think about all the new ads released during the Super Bowl each year) and since one of the players in the ad is a famous
basketball player, we can deduce that the text is also somehow embedded within
the sub-culture of American sports fans as well as gamers.

The mise-en-scène of the video itself features a "war zone" that looks Middle-
Eastern; this resonates with American culture in 2010, since we were at war in
both Iraq and Afghanistan at the time, and also suggests another culture from
which (and to which) the text communicates—soldiers at war (or at least those
interested in playing at war). The military sub-culture is also suggested by the
song playing in the background—the Rolling Stones' "Gimme Shelter" is a classic Vietnam-era war anthem.

There are no immediate signals in the video that betray a desire to attract "gamer" subculture, or that even suggest the product being sold is a video game,
but this too reveals something important about its intended audience. While
pre-rendered game footage and direct references to titles and franchises can

excite an audience of gamers, the fact that this advertisement has the potential to reach a much wider audience means it might not necessarily want to employ conventions that could disinterest or potentially alienate the new fans it is attempting to attract.

Call of Duty fans in the audience may take note of the wide array of weaponry and military hardware used in the commercial, or the fact that weapons can apparently be customized by their wielders, but these features are hardly trumpeted in the manner common to most video game commercials. Instead, these elements take a backseat while the video focuses on the broad range of people actually playing the game, who seem to vary greatly in gender, age, ethnicity, and socioeconomic background, suggesting that this experience is not intended exclusively for the gaming community, but for everyone.

Who Constructed the Text?

This text was created by the advertising agency TBWA/Chiat Day (located in Venice Beach) for game creator Activision-Blizzard (located in Santa Monica). A trip to the web site for TBWA/Chiat Day will give you a pretty good idea of who they are: one of the top-ten agencies in the world, they were recognized in 2010 as the "Best International Network of the Decade." Even if you've never heard of them before, you've surely seen some of their work—their clients include Pepsi, Gatorade, Visa, and Apple (Google "TBWA/Chiat Day" if you'd like to find out more).

Although advertising agencies create advertising texts, they always do so in collaboration with the client, who in this case was Activision-Blizzard. The result of a merger in 2008 between Activision (creator of *Guitar Hero* as well as *Call of Duty*) and Blizzard (creator of *World of Warcraft*), on its web site the company describes itself as a "worldwide pure-play online and console game publisher with leading market positions across all categories of the rapidly growing interactive entertainment software industry" (activisonblizzard.com).

Why Was the Text Constructed?

Advertisements are persuasive in nature, and "There's a Soldier in All of Us" has specific designs upon its target viewers. The primary rhetorical appeal is to pathos—in other words, it aims to create some sort of emotional response within the audience that will cause a desired reaction: viewers will want to buy the product and play the game. At the very least, the text aims to leave the viewer thinking, "Wow, that looks like a cool game."

For Whom Was the Text Constructed?

Analyzing the audience for any text requires a little bit of research and a lot of imagination. You can deduce many characteristics of an audience by looking within the text itself. Let's start with the name of the text: "There's a Solider in All of Us." This title ("all of us") coupled with the players featured (a business-woman, hotel concierge, Best Buy worker, fast-food employee, and two celebrities, NBA star Kobe Bryant and talk-show host Jimmy Kimmel) tells us whom the text hopes to reach: everyone—people from all walks of life. The suggestion is that women executives as well as fast-food chefs and professional basketball stars will all enjoy playing *Black Ops*—and to an extent, this is true. According to an *Advertising Age* article written shortly after its release, all the actors featured in the commercial were real-life players of earlier *Call of Duty* games (adage.com).

Typically, a commercial will try to forge a connection with an audience, either by showing members of its target demographic interacting with the product (a mom driving a minivan, a man using a razor), or by showing an idealized image that its audience secretly wishes to be. This commercial does both. First, we see normal people from a variety of professions, ethnicities, and genders—except children and teenagers, because they are under the acceptable level for the ESRB rating. Even celebrities, with their more-exciting-than-normal lives, want to play *Black Ops*. We see Kobe Bryant, smiling to himself as he skillfully handles an RPG emblazoned with the moniker "Black Mamba" (a reference to his NBA nickname, but also an exhibition of one of the weapon customization options in the game). Clearly he's got the moves, even in the game. But we also see Jimmy Kimmel, a comedian, skulking around, blown back by his own rocket launcher. The words "Proud Noob" are written on its side, employing gamer vernacular to punctuate the joke: Kimmel's not very good at this game, but he's still out there blowing things up.

In support of the idea that this text targets "all of us," Grace Chan of the *Bruin Business Review* reveals some interesting demographics about gamers that may surprise you:

> When we think of video and computer gamers we usually picture young adolescent males, but a good 40% of gamers are female, and the average age of gamers is 35 years old. In fact, there are more women players over the age of 18 (33% of the game-playing population) than there are male players under the age of 18 (18%). (bruinbusinessreview.com)

We could stop here and make some assumptions about the audience for this text, but you know what happens when you "assume." We know that the rhetors hoped to reach an extremely wide audience demographically—but in reality, did they?

Make a trip back to YouTube and view the "video statistics" for "There's a Soldier in All of Us." You can find this information by clicking on the icon under the video on the right-hand side (this is a very useful feature of YouTube that you should remember when you're writing your own rhetorical analysis). Notice that over 4 million viewers have watched this video via YouTube and that the viewers for whom it is most popular are males from the age of 13 to 35. Also notice it's most popular for American, Canadian, Australian, and British viewers and that about 1 million watched it via a mobile telephone or via Facebook. These statistics tell us a different story than the text itself about the audience—or at least for which viewers the commercial was most rhetorically effective.

If you were writing about this text and wanted to dig deeper into an analysis of audience, you could browse through popular sites where players chat in forums, or search for other demographic statistics at the Playstation or Xbox networks (the two most popular platforms for the game). Another avenue to explore when analyzing audience is to do a bit of research on audience reception—usually easiest to find by reading what critics have said about the text (this goes for books, TV shows, and films, as well). For example, if you go to a web site for advertisers like adage.com, you can find articles and reviews by other professionals in the business. Or, if you browse the Wikipedia entry on *Call of Duty: Black Ops*, you'll find a breakdown of the scores given to the game by the various video game web sites, as well as links to the reviews (this is more about the audience for the game rather than the audience for the video, so we won't address it further here).

What Are the Form and Content of the Text?

To describe the basic form and content of the text, start with genre and medium. The basic genre is broadcast commercial (or video game trailer). However, we could further catalog the commercial by the type of game, which is a first-person shooter set during a time of war. The medium first used to broadcast this text was television, but that was quickly followed by broadcast via the internet, as well.

As to the basic content, we begin inside a gutted building, looking up at a military helicopter. In the background plays The Rolling Stones' rock classic, "Gimme Shelter." Cut, and we follow that same chopper moving over a blasted urban setting—gutted buildings, a pitiless blue sky, dust. We're somewhere in a desert, and we're at war. Next, we follow a pair of high heels crunching through the rubble, and the cut to a frontal shot of the face of a well-dressed African American woman carrying a rifle, walking alone and confidently down the middle of the ruined street as things explode behind her. She appears unfazed by the explosions, looks up and fires. Two men, one wearing a business suit and the other a white doctor's coat, drop out of the helicopter, combat rigged. A small team busts into a hovel. A Rubenesque woman in business casual clothing fires a shotgun into a door. We see a close-up as she leans back against the wall and smiles. Her teammate, a woman in a broomstick skirt, kicks the door open, and a man in surgeon's scrubs tosses a grenade inside. The action continues as more players appear, dressed in suits or ties or casual jeans and jerseys, behaving like soldiers dropped into combat. The camera shifts from a distant third person to close-ups of the weapons and vehicles to first-person shots that mimic the HUD a player gets during gameplay. Finally, we see a portly man in the white uniform of a fast-food worker; he is strapped with two rifles and wields a pistol in each hand. His body makes the form of a cross as he walks straight toward us with the whole landscape behind him being blown to smithereens. Text flashes onto the screen: "There's a soldier in all of us."

Commercials conventionally display a product, or name it, or otherwise show it in use. This text doesn't do any of that; instead, it sells the experience of being a soldier/player (pathos) and relies heavily on its own cultural context to connect to its audience. The commercial trades on the popular conception of soldiers as heroes, contrasting intense (exciting) military action against the familiar (boring) normality of the "soldiers" whose real-world lives don't involve a lot of action. We see explosions, incoming missiles, gunfire, ducking and weaving and bashing in doors—all action, meant to draw in the gamer and non-gamer alike. We see a variety of weapons and vehicles, suggesting that there will be many destructive options in the game. However, there are no bodies (because that would be depressing), and no actual soldiers shown (because that would remind us that the wars are real, and depress us). There are also no shots of actual gameplay—unusual for a video game trailer, where graphics and gameplay are the primary appeals to a gamer audience.

6.1.3   Next Steps: Break the Text into Parts for Analysis

So far, in sections 6.1.1–6.1.2, the kind of analysis being done is the kind you'll be doing when you work on your Headnotes wiki project in 39B. The basic goal of the headnotes is to provide ample information about the rhetorical situation of a text being studied by your class. But you might also go on to write a rhetorical analysis essay of a text like "There's a Soldier in All of Us," and for that, you'll need to decide on what approach you'd like to take in order to begin your analysis of its rhetoric. Whenever you perform analysis, you'll be breaking the thing you're analyzing into parts and then closely looking at each part and then also at how the parts work together to create the whole. In the first two sections, we offered a short analysis of the rhetorical situation for this text (we broke the situation into its parts—context, rhetors, audience, form, and content).

In a rhetorical analysis you would break the text itself into parts and then begin to look more closely at each one. For example, for "There's a Soldier in All of Us," you could look at the variation of camera shots, the make-up of the players featured, the types of weapons used, the special effects to re-create the war zone, the music and other sounds, the editing style, lighting, or costumes. There's really no limit to the elements you can break a text into in order to analyze them—but the choices you make should be relevant to the overall idea you want to explore and show your insight into the text and how it was constructed.

6.2   The Four Elements of 39B

You may notice that your roommates and friends who take 39B may have a different reading list than you. That's because while all 39B classes share a common syllabus and a common set of objectives, requirements, and formal graded assignments, individual class sections are built around a particular theme such as Beauty, Heroes & Superheroes, Comedy, or Adventure. Even similarly themed classes may differ in reading lists, discussion topics, classroom exercises, and homework assignments.

The four constant elements of 39B are: **Class Community, Critical Reading, Rhetorical Analysis,** and **Rhetoric in Practice.** Each of these four assignment categories counts for 25% of the total grade for the class. The first two elements, **Class Community** and **Critical Reading**, are comprised of many discrete analytical exercises, writing assignments, and quizzes, as well as a variety of ongoing individual and collaborative projects that you will add to, comment on, and revise over the course of several weeks.

The rhetorical and analytical skills you'll be learning through the Class Community and Critical Reading assignments will form a foundational framework, or scaffolding, for the **Rhetorical Analysis Essay** and **Rhetoric in Practice** project: the texts you'll construct during the second half of the quarter.

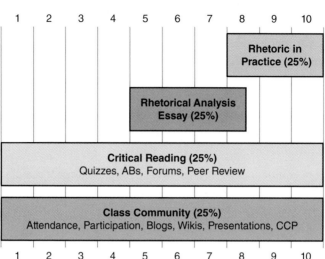

The WR 39B Assignment Sequence

6.3   Class Community Assignments

6.3.1   Communication Is a Social Activity

It is impossible to become a better speaker, listener, reader, or writer in a vacuum—these are all inherently social practices, and so to develop them, you must practice them in the society of others. That's why **attendance** in composition courses is so important: your participation is necessary to your development as a rhetor.

In fact, we think the social aspect of learning rhetorical skills is so important that we've made Class Community assignments count for 25% of your overall grade in the course.

This doesn't mean that perfect attendance guarantees a good Class Community grade—you have to not only attend, but also participate. Your composition classes may be the only small classes that you have in your first year here at UCI, so take advantage of that small audience to practice speaking up in class, participating when asked to work with peers, and responding to your colleagues during classroom discussion. Participation will also help develop a sense of community among class members, making it easier to work together for the rest of the quarter.

6.3.2   Targeting an Audience

Some assignments will be designed to help you practice writing to a specific, knowable audience: the members of your class. You'll be asked to write blogs to the class, participate in online forum discussions with other class members, and write your Headnotes Wiki project to inform your classmates about the rhetorical situation of a text being covered. Taking time to think about the audience of your class in these assignments should help you get into the habit of always thinking about the audience for which you are writing. In fact, we hope you'll start to think of how you can best target your audience in any communication situation you encounter.

Focusing on a specific audience will help you gain rhetorical flexibility, or rhetorical know-how, and you'll start by learning to modulate your written and spoken voice to respond to a range of individual and collaborative exercises. The rhetorical situation of the Class Community assignments calls for a level of diction and structure that is far less formal than a thesis-driven analytical essay, but still considerably more formal than a text message between you and your roommate.

By learning to distinguish between your voice and diction, you can develop both more deliberately. Voice refers to the stylistic language, sentence structure patterns, and verbal tics that distinguish a Hemingway from a Faulkner, while diction refers more to the specific words and level of formality we choose in response to a particular rhetorical situation.

6.3.3   Connect Composition Plus (CCP)

Another contributor to your Class Community grade will be weekly work you do in Connect Composition Plus (CCP), an online, interactive grammar and language textbook. Students come to 39B with varying experiences in high school regarding language and grammar instruction; you may have taken several SAT study tests where you were drilled in grammar, or you may have been in a high school where these topics were never mentioned. The weekly CCP work makes sure that all 39B students are "on the same page" when it comes to the mechanics of language and grammar. Each week, you'll have a chance to review some pages of content about a particular grammar concept like agreement, mixed constructions, punctuation, or wordiness; then you'll take a PostTest of multiple-choice questions about that topic. You're not required to do the reading—if you already feel you know enough about the topic, you can go straight to the PostTest.

It may seem strange that work you do concerning grammar and language would be considered a part of a "Community" grade—if you have problems with grammar or correct usage of words, isn't that your problem? Actually, no—it's also a problem for your readers (your community). Being able to use grammar and language correctly is necessary to be considered part of the academic discourse community. If you write with multiple errors, even if they're small errors like too many or not enough commas, you are showing your scholarly readers that you do not fully understand the language of their community. Your weekly work in CCP will reinforce what you already know about using language correctly and eloquently and maybe teach you a few new concepts, as well.

6.3.4 Blogs

Blogs are a type of ongoing assignment that you compile in the Writing Studio throughout the quarter. Blog prompts are most typically designed as reflective writing assignments that ask you to examine something about yourself, your writing or learning process, or your response to a particular text. There are generally no "correct" answers to the prompts expected. You will, however, be expected to meet a minimum word requirement (generally around 250 words for a C grade) and to not wander too far afield from the prompt. In order to reinforce the online class community, you will be expected to read (and sometimes respond to) several of your classmates' blog entries each week, as well. The idea is to get to know one another and how to think and write in an informal, low-stakes environment that helps you interact less tentatively with your peers and your instructor in class.

6.3.5 The Headnotes Project

Objectives of the Headnotes Assignment

1. To give you practice with collaborative writing and research

2. To give you practice with summarizing the most important points about a topic

3. To give you practice with finding internet sources and synthesizing them into your writing

4. To remind you that understanding the rhetorical situation of a text is part of critical reading

5. To offer information to your classmates about the texts you'll write about in your rhetorical analysis essay later in the quarter

Snapshot View of the Project

To put the Headnote in more practical terms, imagine that you have a photo on your desk that shows you a few years ago in a school gym standing in front of a semi-circle of students your age, all casually dressed, with an older woman in a blue business outfit shaking your hand and smiling with you at the camera. It's easy to imagine somebody picking up that photo and asking "Why do you have this picture on your desk? Who's that woman? What are you so happy about? Were you on a sports team?"

In effect, that person wants to know what makes that photo meaningful. She wants to know its rhetorical situation and what message she should receive from it. You would then have to explain that it's a copy of a picture that appeared on *The L.A Times* web site of you receiving congratulations from the state's senior senator in Washington for organizing a recycling drive at your high school that funded computer upgrades at local schools. By doing so you would help that person understand why the photo is personally important to you as a memento (a message to yourself). More importantly, from a rhetorical point-of-view, you would also help that person understand how the photo is situated in the context of public service and the public media, where it gains meaning and a rhetorical purpose as a message to the newspaper's readers, promoting the kind of civic participation that our public officials want others to admire and imitate. In short, the photo becomes meaningful, both personally and publicly, when placed in its rhetorical situation.

The example of rhetoric that you are addressing in your Headnote is more complex than the hypothetical example of the photo. You will need to do research on the various components that form its rhetorical situation to help the people in your class understand its significance.

Whether you are addressing a poem from a century ago or a TV show from last month, your Headnote will have to provide your audience with similar types of information. To do this, you need to know what kinds of information to look for and where to find it.

Getting Down to Brass Tacks

Before you begin searching for information, it's important that you have defined the purpose and message of your text. In other words, what holds the text together? It's helpful to start by determining whether the text has a primarily persuasive, informative, expressive, or stylistic purpose. Most examples of rhetoric combine these purposes to greater or lesser degrees, but there is usually a dominant purpose. Once you have determined that dominant purpose it will be easier to define the message or point of view that the text is communicating to its audience and who that primary audience is.

It may be argued, for example, that Beethoven and Jimi Hendrix revolutionized the music of their respective eras. They used the rhetoric of music for stylistic and expressive purposes that sent messages in the form of new musical points of view to listeners of their times. A Headnote on the music of either would require a definition of the musical conventions that formed the stylistic context in which the art of one or the other demonstrated such revolutionary musical qualities. Otherwise, readers would not understand what "revolutionary" means.

What's It All About?

The types of information you need for the Headnote may be divided into four general categories: information about the rhetor, information about the audience, the purpose of the text, and its context. Not surprisingly, these categories correspond directly to the rhetorical triangle.

These categories and the kinds of information that may be placed in them do not represent an exhaustive list of the great variety of elements contributing to a rhetorical situation. They do, however, provide general starting points that you will refine as you reach a better understanding of how the rhetorical situation has influenced the text for your Headnote project. (They also make logical dividing points for the division of labor between yourself and your groupmates if you're having trouble getting organized. More about that later.) Of course, like all rhetorical situations, there are no hard and fast rules.

Constructing Your Headnote

In many cases, it makes sense to start the Headnote by providing information about the rhetor and the particular example of his or her work that you are addressing. After that, it's a matter of finding an organization that allows you to give your presentation/essay a sequence of topics (paragraphs) that your audience can easily understand and that makes logical transitions from beginning to end. You don't want a set of observations that abruptly change from one topic to another with no apparent connection or development between them. Your audience will have a difficult time putting the pieces together and determining exactly what it is you're claiming about rhetorical situation and purpose.

It may make sense to divide the segments of your Headnote according to the rhetorical elements mentioned above that you find relevant to your project. These include: rhetor, ethos, audience (and audience reception), historical context, purpose, style, genre, and medium. Or you may find it more effective to combine some of these or use some other principle of organization entirely. Use the conventions of the genre and medium you are working in (an online Wiki), your audience (the class), and purpose (informational) to guide your composing process.

Questions to Ask as You Begin Your Headnotes

About the Rhetor

1. Who is the rhetor?

2. What about this rhetor's biography would help make this text more understandable to members of the class?

3. Is the rhetor considered a pioneer, or an expert practitioner in his or her field?

4. Are there any recurrent themes or motifs that run through this rhetor's work?

5. Is there anything notable or even revolutionary in the way the rhetor used the medium or genre?

6. What did the rhetor say about this text when it was made, or reflecting back on it at a later date?

About the Audience(s)

1. Who is the primary audience for this text? What about the text provides clues to determining the audience?

2. What about this audience is important for the class to understand?

3. Is there a significant secondary audience? How can you tell?

4. If this is a text from a time, place, or cultural perspective different than you own, how does its primary audience differ from you?

5. How did the primary audience respond to the text where and when it was released? What did critics say? Did it upset or confound audience expectations in any way? How and why?

6. Is it looked upon differently by audiences or critics here and now?

About Form and Purpose

1. In what medium, genre, and style is the text constructed? How does it fit into the larger body of work in its particular medium and genre?

2. What are the standard conventions or expectations that mark each of these?

3. Does the text follow these conventions?

4. Is there anything unconventional or even groundbreaking about the rhetor's uses of medium, genre, or style that should be noted? What purpose do these divergences serve?

(continued)

About Context

1. When and where was this text constructed?

2. What is important for the class to know about the cultural conditions and concerns in the historical time and place that the text alludes to or explicitly addresses or that you can infer had an influence on how and why it was made?

All For One, and One For All

Since the Headnote project is a collaborative assignment, each member of your group will receive the same final grade for the project. Therefore it behooves you all to work together as cooperatively and productively as you can to construct a well-researched, well-written, well-designed, rhetorically focused Headnote. From an organizational standpoint, it's probably a good idea to make each group member responsible for researching and writing particular segments of your Headnote; you may also want to assign each group member additional specific "mechanical" tasks such as proofreading, text input, web layout, and design continuity that play to each of your particular strengths and talents.

In evaluating your Headnote, your instructor will look to see how well you were able to research, evaluate, and synthesize the relevant information you selected to help your classmates better understand your assigned text. You will also be asked to rate the contributions of each of your group members.

Presenting Your Headnote Material to an Audience

To give you practice with oral rhetoric and presentational skills, each group will be asked to create a PowerPoint of their Headnote and make a presentation to the class about what they learned about their text and its rhetorical situation. Generally these presentations are about 5 to 8 minutes long, and you'll need to collaborate with your group to decide what should be included in the PowerPoint and how it will be presented. In the Studio File Folders, subfolder Classroom Presentations, you'll find a very helpful PowerPoint called "How to Make a Great Powerpoint."

As your primary audience, your classmates will also grade your presentation. The average of this grade will be recorded alongside your Headnote score.

The Headnotes Rubric

For each element of the Headnote below, 10 indicates the highest level of accomplishment and 1 indicates the lowest. Each element is worth 10 points for a total of 100 points.

1. **Credible research** (from several different sources) was performed by the group and presented in an interesting way to inform the audience about the rhetorical situation of the text, its author, and its original audience.

    1□ 2□ 3□ 4□ 5□ 6□ 7□ 8□ 9□ 10□

2. Headnote provides pertinent and specific **contextual information** that describes the culture and historical situation in which the text was created, published, and received.

    1□ 2□ 3□ 4□ 5□ 6□ 7□ 8□ 9□ 10□

3. Headnote provides pertinent and specific **information about the author/ director/actors/artists** involved with creating the text.

    1□ 2□ 3□ 4□ 5□ 6□ 7□ 8□ 9□ 10□

4. Headnote provides pertinent and specific **information about the text's primary message(s) and purpose,** including some of the **rhetorical devices** used to communicate the message/purpose.

    1□ 2□ 3□ 4□ 5□ 6□ 7□ 8□ 9□ 10□

5. The Headnote provides pertinent and specific **information about the genre and medium** of the text, including noteworthy conventions of this specific genre and medium.

    1□ 2□ 3□ 4□ 5□ 6□ 7□ 8□ 9□ 10□

6. The Headnote provides pertinent and specific **information about the audience** intended for this text, both the original audience and other audience groups of note.

   1 □   2 □   3 □   4 □   5 □   6 □   7 □   8 □   9 □   10 □

7. The Headnote demonstrates a **synthesis** of information. In other words, it is evident that the group collaborated to present a unified text.

   1 □   2 □   3 □   4 □   5 □   6 □   7 □   8 □   9 □   10 □

8. The Headnote has been written and formatted appropriately following the conventions of an **online web text**, including uniform design formatting (color, font, layout), appropriate images, and links related to the topics discussed.

   1 □   2 □   3 □   4 □   5 □   6 □   7 □   8 □   9 □   10 □

9. The Headnote is **written clearly and precisely with few errors** in grammar, punctuation, or spelling.

   1 □   2 □   3 □   4 □   5 □   6 □   7 □   8 □   9 □   10 □

10. The Headnote includes **appropriate citations** for all summaries, paraphrases, and direct quotations (in the genre of a web page, citations are usually done as **hyperlinks**); a **Works Cited** is included that properly lists all sources used in MLA format.

    1 □   2 □   3 □   4 □   5 □   6 □   7 □   8 □   9 □   10 □

6.4   Critical Reading Assignments

6.4.1   Language, Knowledge, and Power

Being able to critically read all different kinds of texts is an important ability for every college student to have. By "critically reading," we mean understanding the rhetorical context and purpose an author has for constructing a text, and then analyzing how and for whom the text has been constructed in order to achieve that purpose. The Critical Reading component of 39B is designed to enhance your understanding of the assigned texts for the course. You'll practice critical and rhetorical reading not only of the thematic texts chosen by your instructor for your particular section (novels, short stories, poems, scholarly essays, nonfiction articles, textbooks, graphic novels, films, TV commercials, YouTube videos, web sites, etc.), but also of the writing produced by your colleagues.

The objectives of the Critical Reading assignments are twofold. Individually, your Critical Reading assignments are intended, on the most basic level, to demonstrate to you and your instructor how carefully and purposefully you've read the assigned texts. But collectively, they are intended to give you the practice and knowledge you'll need to construct the more complex Rhetorical Analysis and Rhetoric in Practice projects you'll be completing toward the end of the course.

Put another way, critical reading is a vital part of the writing process. In fact, reading and writing processes are alike. In both, you make meaning by actively engaging a text. As a reader, you are not a passive participant, but an active constructor of meaning. Exhibiting an inquisitive, "critical" attitude towards what you read will make anything you read richer and more useful to you in your classes and your life.

Critical Reading assignments come in many flavors: study questions to be answered in a blog/forum; in-class multiple choice or short answer quizzes; take-at-home electronic quizzes; short in-class essays; take-home practice essays; annotated bibliographies; and others that are specific to your section. Like the Class Community, your Critical Reading assignments will add up to 25% of your total grade.

6.4.2   The 10,000-Hour Rule and Kobe

Learning to become a better communicator is similar to learning how to become a better athlete—it's all about time spent in practice. In *Outliers*, a study of what makes people successful, Malcolm Gladwell posits the "10,000 Hour Rule": most experts in their fields have spent at least 10,000 hours honing their specialized skills. Class Community and Critical Reading assignments won't require 10,000 hours (phew!), but they will give you vital everyday practice in thinking like a rhetorician.

Living near LA, you've probably heard stories about Kobe Bryant's work ethic, that is, when he's not playing *Black Ops*! He spends hours upon hours in practice—probably way more than 10,000 hours. Sometimes he works alone—studying the playbook, watching old game films, or working alone in the gym. But a lot of the time he is working with his coach and teammates—practicing footwork, dribbling, passing, defending, and firing shot after shot at the hoop from all over the court—so he'll be ready for whatever situation arises come game time. The Class Community and Critical Reading assignments are like Kobe's practice: there's no game on the line, so you get to work a bit on your own, and a bit with your classmates, developing your basic skills, your voice, and a sense of how to use them in particular rhetorical situations.

6.4.3   Adapting to the Situation

While some instructors like to place Blog assignments exclusively in the Class Community category and Forum assignments in Critical Reading, others may use one of these online tools exclusively and/or place individual assignments in one or the other category, depending on the learning emphasis of each. From a rhetorical standpoint, the purpose, rather than the Studio tool, determines which category the assignment falls into. In other words, an assignment that asks you to introduce yourself to the class by explaining the meaning behind your name would likely fall into the Class Community category, while a Blog or Forum that asks you to discuss the rhetorical significance of names in a text your class is reading would likely fall into the Critical Reading category.

6.4.4   Forums

Forums are typically designed as "write-to-learn" assignments that help you practice the sort of critical reading and writing skills you'll need to develop for your Rhetorical Analysis essay later in the quarter. Like the Blog Assignments, the Forums are conducted online at the Studio, and allow you to not only read, but comment on your classmates' posts. Since the Forums can be conducted in a continuous discussion thread, they are often used to continue or expand upon critical or analytical discussions begun in class, and the prompts tend to require critical reading and writing skills that may be used to evaluate your rhetorical understanding of an assigned text or texts.

6.4.5   Reading Quizzes

Over the first half of the course, you'll probably be expected to take regular **Critical Reading Quizzes**, intended to encourage you to keep up with the assigned reading by fostering critical and rhetorical reading practices. You'll probably notice, however, that your quizzes expect more of you than to demonstrate you've read the text, watched the film, or listened to the music assigned. You may even notice that the types of questions your quizzes ask seldom have a single, simple "correct" answer. That's because the quizzes are designed to help you learn how to do more than simply regurgitate information about the texts.

They're intended to make you think about how and why texts are situated and constructed by modeling the type of open-ended questions about the rhetor, the audience, and the purpose of the texts that you will need to eventually ask on your own.

Ultimately you should think of your quizzes not so much as the end product of your learning, but the scaffolding for it. Rather than test your knowledge (or teach you how to take quizzes) they should support your learning process—to steady you a little bit—as you move forward into your Rhetorical Analysis and Rhetoric in Practice projects.

6.5   The Rhetorical Analysis Essay

You probably wrote essays in high school, and so you may think that you know how to write an academic essay. And in a general sense, you probably do. But if you've learned anything in 39B so far, it's that every text is rhetorically situated. Practically speaking, that means that while most academic essays have some things in common—an introduction, a thesis, body paragraphs that develop the thesis using credible, cited evidence, and a conclusion—it is unlikely that the essays you wrote in high school were rhetorically situated the same as will be the specific type of academic essays you'll be asked to write at UCI.

That doesn't mean you should throw out everything you've learned about essay writing in high school or that you won't be able to apply what you've learned about rhetoric from this class to construct effective essays in your own major. One of the primary objectives of this class is to help you develop the rhetorical know-how and flexibility to respond to a range of rhetorical situations.

For this particular assignment, you will be asked to write to an academic audience that is familiar with your theme and text; you'll have to pay close attention to the expectations of a scholarly audience and adhere to the conventions of the particular kind of essay you are being asked to write: **rhetorical analysis.** If you haven't already, you should read Chapter 3 on the process of composing (specifically, the process of composing an essay for an academic audience).

6.5.1   Objectives

As the name implies, the primary objective of this essay is to evaluate your ability to form an *analytical* thesis about a particular text(s), structure an analytical essay, and then develop it with an appropriate level of detail. The content focus of the assignment is the *rhetorical* aspects of a text(s); additionally, you will continue to learn how to evaluate and respond in writing to the rhetorical situation of a formal academic assignment.

Another important objective of this assignment is to build upon the positive benefits of writing as a process that you began at the outset of the course, as you continue to practice the social dimension of improving your critical reading and writing skills by reading and commenting on your classmates' essays and receiving comments from them on your own work.

In short, the Rhetorical Analysis Essay is designed to further the critical reading and writing skills you've been practicing in your CC & CR assignments.

6.5.2   The Prompt

Write an informative, thesis-driven essay that analyzes an aspect of rhetoric in a text covered by your class this quarter. The essay should be written for an academic audience that is interested in your text and your class theme. This essay may also be written as a comparative rhetorical analysis of two texts (covered by your class).

Multiple drafts, peer review and revision are required elements of the assignment; failure to complete parts of the process will result in a lower final grade. The final essay must be 6–7 pages long and be presented in MLA format.

A total of five (5) sources must be used to develop the essay (the text being analyzed counts as one). Include a Works Cited in MLA format.

The prompt tells you the purpose (informative), genre (essay), medium (print— although you will also be asked to turn it in electronically), audience (academic and interested in your text/theme), and something about conventions (MLA, page length, and sources) and process (you must write drafts and conduct peer review). In a nutshell, you now know the rhetorical situation for your text. Now for the harder part: content. How do you analyze an aspect of rhetoric in a text?

How a Text Works

At its simplest, a rhetorical analysis looks at how a text works. It's not concerned with explaining the meaning or interpreting the message of a text; rather, it's concerned with analyzing *how* specific elements within the text create an impact on a particular audience, within a particular genre or medium, or reflect something about the culture or time period when it was constructed.

Analysis means breaking something into parts and looking closely at each part. Once you've looked at the broken down parts, you also want to have a look at how they operate together to create the whole (for more description of how to write an analysis, see Chapter 4, section 4.11).

Rhetoric focuses on the construction and situation of a text: who wrote it and for whom, what form it takes, how it appeals, etc. So a rhetorical analysis is breaking into parts some aspect of how the text communicates to an audience within a context.

A **Rhetorical Analysis** might explain why a given element in a text is there by analyzing *how* that element works on a particular **audience**. The elements you choose will vary according to the type of text you are analyzing. For example, with a literary text, you might analyze how metaphors, symbols, or a particular writing style impact a specific audience; for a film text, you might analyze how a particular style of film editing or camera placement and movement impacts the audience's response.

A rhetorical analysis might also explain *how* a textual element is constituted or influenced by conventions of its **form** (**genre** and **medium**) or explain the cultural and/or historical **context** in which it was composed (and how that impacts the audience).

In essence, then, a rhetorical analysis examines some particular interplay of communication in a text by looking through the prism of the **rhetorical situation**. It might help to think about which aspect of the situation you'd like to use as your primary focus.

The Rhetorical Situation

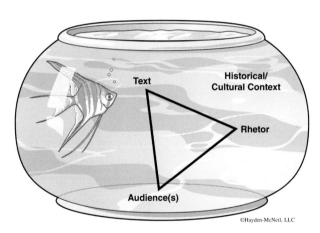

©Hayden-McNeil, LLC

Planning Your Rhetorical Strategy. Before you sit down to write your essay, here are some of the types of questions you should ask yourself about the text you've chosen to write about. Keep the rhetorical situation in mind as you read through these questions. Depending on what you decide to emphasize—rhetor, audience, message, or context—and what element(s) from the text you'll be breaking into parts for your analysis, not all of the questions will apply equally to the rhetorical focus of your essay.

What is the primary *purpose* of the text? Is it to entertain? Inform? Persuade? Explore an emotion or some stylistic element of the genre? Or a combination of some of these?

To what primary *audience* does the text address its message? Think about the audience in terms of **demographics** and **psychographics**. What categories do they fit into within the larger society (demographics) and what do they think or believe (psychographics)?

Demographics are things like nationality, locale, gender, race, economic class, age, educational background, and occupation; psychographics are things like specific interests, political affiliation, or religion, to name just a few. Keep in mind that some texts may appeal to multiple audiences by including several elements which each function separately to address subsets of a broader audience. Think of market segmentation in advertising or narrowcasting in political media.

To which *genre* does the text belong? By what medium (media) is it communicated? And how does it either meet or disrupt the audience expectations (conventions) of the genre/media? Whether an action film, a TV-show satire, a war poem, a music video, a print ad, an academic essay, a political speech, or a commercial web site selling products, all texts either conform to or contradict a conventional set of practices that an audience accustomed to those practices will expect to see. These practices are often conventional because they work well, but sometimes disrupting them can emphasize part of the text's message. For more on determining a text's genre/medium, see Chapter 2.

How does the text ask the reader to identify with its *rhetor* or its *message*? A text that appeals to ethos may ask the audience to identify directly with the rhetor (or, in fiction, a character). It argues that these two parties share similar values, morals, concerns, and worldviews and it asks the audience to trust the rhetor as a result. An audience identifies with a message (an appeal to logos) when they see themselves in the narrative or situation the rhetor describes, or when they respond to the logic of argument. A text appeals to pathos when an audience responds emotionally to a character created by the author or to the set of values to which the rhetor appeals.

What conventions or contextual and historical knowledge does the text assume its audience knows? A rhetor seldom gains anything from alluding to events, facts, details, names, etc., that his or her primary audience will not know (though sometimes obscure references can be part of a rhetor's strategy of representing a text as more informed than the audience). An audience will often therefore be defined by its ability to decode references in a text. Furthermore, a text will be more likely to seem relevant to a contemporary audience if it responds to concerns from a contemporary context in terms with which the audience is already familiar.

To which values and beliefs does the text appeal? Most texts will appeal to a given set of values (psychographics) that the audience is assumed to share. Values are not mutually exclusive, so frequently emphasis on one value implies an argument for its priority. If an audience agrees with the basic values that inform the reasoning of the text, and if the rhetor can make the connection apparent, the text will be rhetorically effective.

What narratives does the text tell or access? A novel or short story is usually quite obvious in its narrative structure, but essays, speeches, and even visual texts also have narrative elements. They can set up a hero, a conflict, and argue for a resolution or climax to that conflict. Some audiences identify strongly with narratives, even more so than arguments from reason (logos), because they encourage emotional investment (pathos) and comparison between the reader and the character in the narrative. A text can also be successful with an audience by accessing (through allusion, comparison, or contrast) pre-existing narratives, frequently cultural myths, with which the audience is already familiar and already identifies with in some way.

What specific rhetorical techniques or devices do you notice the text using, and for what purpose(s)? Does it use them to tell or access a narrative, to appeal to values or shared context, to play with generic expectations, or to ask the audience to identify with its author or message?

The rhetorical techniques or devices are often specific to a medium. For example, films use composition, camera movement, color grading, editing style, mise-en-scène, montage, frame rates, sound design, voice-over, focus, sequence, and special effects. Speeches and poems tend to use techniques like alliteration, anaphora, catachresis, hyperbole, figurative language, similes, imagery, and extended metaphors (conceits)—though longer texts like novels and short stories use these too. Both films and longer texts tend to use narrative elements like sympathetic characters and emotionally stirring climaxes, though shorter texts frequently use those as well.

How is the text structured? All texts organize a series of elements either spatially or temporally, and the structure is tied to audience, genre, and medium, or historical/cultural context. The choices reflected in the way a text is organized can communicate emphasis, elicit emotion, or suggest logical connections to an audience.

A narrative tends to follow a chronological organization. But, even within a narrative that follows a given sequence of events, a particular commentary offered on those events or the techniques used to highlight them can be placed at one of several different points in the narrative. As a result, the author must choose the most effective point in the narrative at which highlight the values, concepts, or other arguments he/she wants to illustrate. Sometimes this takes place at the climax, sometimes in the introduction, sometimes in the dénouement.

Finally, now that you have a pretty solid idea about what a **rhetorical analysis** does, it's probably a good idea to clear up a few common misconceptions about what a rhetorical analysis doesn't do by spelling out exactly what it isn't.

A Rhetorical Analysis Is Not

1. **An extended summary of the text.** Keep your summary of the text or its parts to brief statements to provide context for the analysis you are doing.

2. **An in-depth examination of the meaning of life (or the text).** While your analysis should arise in part from some meaning or message that you have gleaned from the text, this theme or "meaning" should help you frame your analysis, but it should not be the point of the essay.

3. **A laundry list of rhetorical observations.** Don't simply identify every rhetorical device you think you see in the text. Once you've identified them, decide which one or two you think are most important to conveying the point or premise you will use to frame your analysis.

4. **A literary analysis.** While some of the elements you identify in your analysis may be literary devices like symbols, metaphors, or textual allusions, remember that in a rhetorical analysis, the purpose of identifying these elements is not to prove to the reader **what** they mean. Rather, your job is to explore **how** they contribute to meaning: how is the rhetor using these literary devices and what effect might they have on an audience? How are they consistent with the conventions of the genre or the expectations of an audience, or the practices of the text's historical/cultural context—or how do they challenge what is expected?

5. **The kitchen sink.** Don't throw in every random bit of summary, metaphorical meaning and interesting trivia about the text that you can think of just to fill pages. Use the rhetorical situation to focus your approach to the text—choose one aspect of the situation and use it to frame your analysis. Be selective about the evidence you choose to include in your essay—don't just throw in everything that might look good. Consider your purpose and your audience to help you decide what is most relevant to the focus of your analysis.

A Note About Academic Objectivity

Part of understanding the context of a text is assuming a degree of academic objectivity in the way you think and write about it in a formal academic essay. Academic objectivity is an act of the imagination: you have to imagine how people different from yourself experienced the text. If you are analyzing rhetoric from the past, say Plato's *Republic* or Swift's "A Modest Proposal," you have to take into account historical factors such as gender assumptions, politics, economics, technology, and religion. These cultural and historical assumptions formed the context in which the audience of that period found meaning in those texts. Even contemporary rhetoric often requires you to exercise your ability to imagine other points of view. Every time you watch a movie from a gender or cultural perspective not your own, you find yourself challenged to perceive and understand the world differently.

For example, from the point of view of our current cultural-historical situation, the old black-and-white TV sitcoms of the 1950s can seem very boring. This is true for most viewers today when you consider how much more contemporary TV technology offers in terms of color, sound, and action. However, if you are writing about a text composed in the 1950s, an episode of *I Love Lucy*, for example, you have to make the imaginary leap to the rhetorical situation and perspective of that audience. Then you can explain how Lucy's original audience experienced that program as new and exciting; or, you can compare and discuss how a current audience might respond differently than the original audience. No doubt, you will have to simplify these audiences so that you can handle writing about them in an essay, but you should still strive to be as accurate, objective, and specific as possible.

You may need to do some background research so that you can imagine how an audience that had previously received its home entertainment in the form of dialogue on radio shows might find the ability to *hear* comic dialogue and *see* corresponding images on TV in a multicultural sitcom format as revolutionary. In fact, since you are required to use at least four outside sources in your essay, you can consider this background research as necessary (don't forget your classmates' Headnotes, either—you can use them as a source).

You would have to imagine how unusual it was for many of the 1950s American viewers of the time to see a Latino, Desi Arnaz, co-starring in the show and to hear the Afro-Cuban music that he played. Likewise, you have to make similar, though not so extensive, cultural adjustments in your point of view when you watch older episodes of *The Simpsons* that make references to Bill Clinton and events of the early nineties.

Finally, before you get started, remember that 39B is a course in which each assignment builds upon the previous assignments; you have already done some of the preparation and planning for your Rhetorical Analysis (RA). Everything you have done so far—headnotes, critical reading quizzes, blogs, class discussions and presentations—all these have helped you develop rhetorical reading and writing skills that are directly applicable to what you should be doing in this essay. In some cases, you may be able to use material that you have written for a blog or from an in-class essay, for example, as material for your working draft.

6.5.3   The Nuts and Bolts of the RA Essay

The Thesis

Like most academic essays, the RA is a thesis-driven essay, which means that it starts from a very focused and specific premise that guides the development and structural organization of the essay.

Attributes of an Effective RA Thesis

Specific: The focus of the analysis is narrow—the writer has a specific rhetorical focus and a specific textual focus. It covers only what can be convincingly argued within the page requirement.

Sophisticated: It goes beyond the obvious and superficial and shows a depth of thinking about the text and how it communicates. It is not something that has already been said many times. It recognizes the important relationships and interplays of communication within the text and its rhetorical situation. It offers a useful or compelling insight.

Structured: It foreshadows the organization by which you will proceed in your essay.

Polished: The sentence (two at most) has been revised to make it clear, detailed, precise (not wordy), and readable. If it is a long sentence, it uses punctuation or parallelism to make it easy to read.

Remember, it will help you come up with a thesis if you first decide which aspect of the rhetorical situation you'll focus on in order to approach the text.

Approach From the Rhetor(s)

A thesis focusing on the rhetor's construction of the text might analyze how a particular style, genre, or motif is part of his/her signature, and how that influences the impact of the text on the audience. For example, this thesis addresses a director's signature visual style and how that impacts the audiences attracted to his films:

- Guillermo del Toro's penchant for huge clockwork settings and heavily tinted scenes creates a unique visual style that delights both steampunk and dark fantasy genre audiences.

Approach From the Audience(s)

A thesis focusing on audience might analyze who is in a particular text's audience or how the rhetor/text appeals to particular viewers or readers. An audience-based analysis might also focus on differing reactions within the primary audience or within audiences in different cultures or times (a sort of "reception history" for the text). For example, this thesis analyzes how one genre with similar conventions and content comes out quite differently based on two different audience types (and the audience is constructed by the type of medium):

- *Dexter* and *CSI: Miami* both follow some basic conventions of the current TV crime drama such as the wisecracking detective character and the creation of elaborate crime scene sets, but because the CBS network audience is so different from the pay-cable Showtime audience, these conventions are constructed differently by each series.

Approach From the Text

A thesis that starts with the text might analyze the genres to which the text belongs, the medium by which is it communicated, or a device of its genre/ medium that it uses for a particular rhetorical impact on the audience. For example, this thesis focuses on how conventions of the comic book medium are used for a particular rhetorical impact on the audience:

- In the 3-part graphic novel *We3*, Grant Morrison and Frank Quitely use frames and gutters in highly unusual and unique ways so that readers can experience the pathos of the narrative from the point-of-view of the three animal protagonists.

Here's a text-based thesis where the structure of the narrative as well as a cinematic device are used to analyze a particular rhetorical impact:

- Christopher Nolan's use of crosscut editing throughout *The Dark Knight* structures the way the narrative is presented, thus forcing viewers to construct their opinions of Batman and the Joker as intertwined.

The approach from the text is the trickiest focus to pursue without getting caught up in explaining what the text means. Make sure if you decide to approach from the text that you are focusing on HOW it communicates to its particular audience or within/because of its cultural/historical context. Although this thesis includes the words "reader" and "culture," the focus is on what the text means, and therefore it's a literary analysis thesis instead of rhetorical:

- Morrison and Quitely's use of unusual frames and gutters helps the reader understand their message that animal cruelty should be questioned by our culture.

Approach From Historical/Cultural Context

A thesis that starts with the culture or historical time period in which the text was published might analyze the conventions or contextual/historical knowledge that the rhetor assumes his/her audience knows (because they are also part of that culture or time period). For example, this thesis analyzes how a director uses the recent common experience of Americans—the 9/11 attacks on the World Trade Center—in order to create pathos within the narrative of his film.

- In *Avatar*, James Cameron constructed the scenes depicting the fall of Home Tree to visually resemble the falling of the twin towers on 9/11 in order to be able to transfer the pathos of that historical time period to the pathos of his fictional narrative, thereby gaining sympathy from his viewers for the Na'vi.

One more thing about your working thesis: Expect it to change significantly as you write and revise your essay. Your initial thesis is intended mostly to help you stay focused as you develop your essay. If you're doing the required work, you *will* refine your understanding of the text as you write your essay and you *should* revise to better reflect what you've learned about the text and your own writing voice as your essay progresses from first to final draft.

The Introduction

Once you've got a working thesis, it's time to start building an introduction to your essay around it. The first thing to consider is the purpose of your introduction. While its general purpose may seem self-explanatory—the purpose of an introduction is to introduce—there are many rhetorical elements you will need to set up in order to provide context for your reader: the text you are analyzing, who constructed it, the context of its construction, in what medium, for what audience, and what purpose.

This means that you'll need to specifically identify the text by title, rhetor, and medium, and probably genre, as well. Don't forget to name the rhetor (author, screenwriter, director, songwriter, poet, or essayist) by first and last name on first reference, and by last name, thereafter. Always use specifics—don't just keep writing "the author this and the director that"—because the use of specific detail and word choice increases your credibility as an expert. If you're analyzing a film, let the reader know what genre (or genres) it fits: dark comedy, horror, sci-fi, romance, etc. Do the same for any other type of text and be as specific as possible, because specifics help increase our expertise and credibility.

You're also going to want to provide a short thumbnail sketch of what the text is about. This means a short—one or two sentences, max—plot summary if the text is a film, a novel, or short story, or a thesis summary if the text is a nonfiction article or essay. Even texts like still images, songs, or poems can be summarized with the rhetorical purpose of providing a sense of the emotional or evocative thrust of the piece. The point is to provide a big picture idea of the text to provide the reader with a concrete foundation from which to consider your analysis.

If the perspective and historical context of the text is different from your reader's, you may also want to provide some additional explanatory information about the rhetor, the medium or genre, or any historical or cultural events or assumptions you think your reader may need to know to understand any aspect of the text or its context that might not be clear to her. In order to provide specific, helpful contextual information, you'll most likely need to do a bit of research and reading about the text's rhetorical situation (just like in the Headnotes). Since you are required to use at least five outside sources as you write your RA, the introduction is a good place to use some of these.

Finally, you will need to establish your rhetorical approach to your analysis: what you plan to argue, and how you plan to do it. That's the thesis part of your introduction. But before you launch directly into your thesis, don't forget to create a bridge, or transition, between your background commentary and your argument.

That's a lot of "stuff" to cover in a single paragraph. So much, in fact, that you might want to consider extending your introduction into a second or even third paragraph; the first paragraph might introduce the text, the second summarize context, and the third transition into your thesis. Of course, you can structure your introduction any way that makes sense. The point is to not feel constrained by the Five Paragraph structure. Instead of letting that formulaic structure control your ideas, let your ideas control the structure.

In addition to providing basic information that will help your reader understand how you will frame your analysis, the introduction also sets your readers' expectations about you and your ethos (credibility with the reader). Just as a polished introduction can incline a reader to trust you enough to forgive the occasional leap in logic or awkward sentence construction, so can a careless or incomplete introduction lead the reader to doubt the logic or veracity of every little detail that follows. Use your introduction to establish a strong academic ethos and set your readers' expectations high.

A Body of Evidence

After you've established the rhetorical approach you'll be taking to the analysis of your text in your introduction, it's time to turn to the body of your essay. Once again, do not feel obligated to follow the Five-Paragraph-essay form, because that structure isn't usually robust enough to contain a nuanced and sophisticated academic essay. Just as you will likely need more than one paragraph to provide enough relevant background information about your text to set up your thesis, you may need more than one paragraph to adequately cover each of your thesis points. What's important is not how many paragraphs you have, but how many you need to fully and logically develop each point you make.

The Paraburger

Your argument (minithesis) is the top bun

Your development is all of this—it looks like most of the paraburger (because it is!)

©Hayden-McNeil, LLC

Quotes from the text or a source are the ketchup, mustard, and mayo (a little goes a long way!)

The bottom bun relates the paragraph back to the thesis/message and transitions to the next paragraph

In general, each body paragraph should be a mini-essay of its own, containing one major focus and the details and specifics to develop it. Additionally, your paragraphs should integrate all evidence using the three-step method discussed in Chapter 4, Using Sources: Appealing to Authority, section 4.10.

Saying Doesn't Make It So. As you develop your paragraphs, remember that just because you say that a symbol or a metaphor represents "maturity" or "love" or "evil" doesn't make it so. In fact, any assertion you make about any rhetorical element of the text you are analyzing must be supported by evidence (from the text, from something the rhetor or a critic has said about the text, or from some concrete correspondence with a historical or cultural event or assumption) and you must not only quote or paraphrase the specific passage or outside evidence that supports your claim, but explain the connections you are making, and their significance to your larger point.

Ingredients of a Good Paragraph

1. Strong topic sentence or controlling idea that the entire paragraph strives to develop.

2. Credible, relevant evidence that directly supports the point being made.

   Analyze and explain the significance of the evidence in your own words (that is, make the explicit connection between the evidence and the paragraph's controlling idea in your voice).

   Offer enough concrete evidence (from the text you're analyzing and/or outside sources) to fully support the point you are making.

3. No unsupported or overly general statements.

4. Logically ordered sentences that follow a clear, connected progression of thought.

5. Explicit transition phrases to guide the progression of ideas between sentences and paragraphs.

6. Clear, precise language and sound grammar.

The Connective Tissue

Once you've said everything you think you need to say in your body paragraphs, and you've provided enough evidence to support and develop your ideas, it's time to take a final look at how you've structured your argument. Take a look at your thesis statement. Compare what you've said you're going to focus on with what you actually wrote about in the body of your essay. Do you actually develop the points you've promised your reader that you will? And are the points in the same order as you promised in your thesis? If not, decide what you need to revise to improve the overall structure of the essay.

If your essay reads smoothly, moving from the simplest or most obvious points to progressively more complex ones that build to a logical conclusion, you may want to revise your thesis to more accurately reflect the structure of your argument. If, however, your thesis seems to make a logical "mini" argument, but your essay seems to bounce from paragraph to paragraph with no real connection to either your thesis or the points you made before or after each individual paragraph, perhaps you need to reorder your essay to follow the roadmap you laid out in your thesis.

Either way, once you've settled on a coordinated structure between your thesis and the body of your essay, take another read through to be sure that the transitions between your paragraphs provide the necessary guideposts to lead your reader clearly through your analysis. Try to avoid "list" transitions such as *first, second, third,* and *in conclusion.* Why? Because these are too facile and will work against your rhetorical purpose: to impress the reader with your sophistication of thought and eloquence of language.

Think about picking up a key phrase from your previous paragraph and echoing it in the topic sentence of your next paragraph with a transition word such as *likewise* or *similarly* to show a direct connection between the two points, or a transition such as *however,* or *on the other hand,* to show how the points diverge. In other words, use transitions to do more than order your points. Use them to show how the points are logically connected.

And in the End

As long as we're debunking the Myth of the Five-Paragraph-Essay-as-Model-for-College-Essays, let's finish the job with a word about conclusions. Try to avoid the summary conclusion that merely restates your thesis. And be sure to leave enough time in your composition process to come to a satisfying conclusion. Use the conclusion of your essay to tie up any loose ends and leave your reader with something else to chew on—nothing out of the blue, mind you. But something original or thought provoking that arises from your analysis or is a logical extension of the argument you've made.

Rhetorical Analysis Essay Rubric Breakdown

	6=Highly Effective (A Range)	5=Somewhat Effective (B Range)	4=Satisfactory (C Range)	3=Developing (C−)	2=Poor (D Range)	1=Unsatisfactory (F)
Thesis	Thesis offers an exceptionally insightful idea based on rhetorical concepts, and is specific, sophisticated, structured, and polished	Thesis offers an insightful idea based on rhetorical concepts, and is specific, sophisticated, structured, and polished	Thesis offers an insightful idea based on rhetorical concepts. It may lack one or two of the characteristics of an exceptional thesis, but is enough to carry the essay	Thesis offers an idea, but it may not be insightful or based on rhetorical concepts. It lacks some of the characteristics of an exceptional thesis, but is enough to carry the essay	Thesis offers an idea, but it may not be insightful or based on rhetorical concepts. It lacks several characteristics of an exceptional thesis, and may not be enough to hold the essay together	No thesis, or thesis offers an idea that is not rhetorical or not enough to hold the essay together
Expertise	Expert knowledge of topic throughout essay	Clear knowledge of topic throughout essay	Generally good grasp of topic throughout essay	Intermittent or inconsistent familiarity with topic	Little evidence of familiarity or expertise with topic	No evidence of familiarity or expertise with topic
Conventions and Audience	Exceptional understanding of essay conventions and academic audience	Clear understanding of genre and audience	General understanding of genre and audience	Inconsistent or inaccurate understanding of genre and audience	Little awareness of genre and audience expectations	No awareness of genre and audience expectations
Objectivity	Writer is consistently objective and scientific in presentation of text and ideas	Writer is usually objective and scientific in presentation	Writer is generally objective and scientific in presentation, although in a few areas may lapse into biased or fan-like admiration for text/ideas	Writer is sometimes objective and scientific in presentation, but frequently lapses into biased or fan-like admiration for text/ ideas	Little evidence of objective ethos throughout essay; bias and opinion rule	No evidence of objective ethos throughout essay; bias and opinion rule
MLA Conventions	Consistent use of correct MLA style throughout, including margins, page-numbering, in-text citations and Works Cited	Consistent use of correct MLA style in most of essay, including in-text citations and Works Cited	Overall correct use of MLA style, but some particulars of the style are not followed	Some use of MLA style, but many errors in how to apply the style throughout essay	Little use of MLA style, or incorrect use throughout	No MLA style is present

I. Rhetorical Knowledge

2. Analysis & Evidence

	6=Highly Effective (A Range)	5=Somewhat Effective (B Range)	4=Satisfactory (C Range)	3=Developing (C−)	2=Poor (D Range)	1=Unsatisfactory (F)
Analysis vs. Summary	Insightful development throughout; summary is expertly used to develop writer's ideas	Insightful moments of development; summary is used to develop writer's ideas	Development is logical (if obvious); summary may overpower student's own ideas	Development is used indiscriminately: summary may overpower student's own ideas	Little evidence of development; summary overpowers student's own ideas	No evidence of development; summary overpowers student's own ideas
Rhetorical Analysis of Text	Analysis is consistently developed using rhetorical aspects of the text itself, its medium/genres, its audience, or its cultural/historical context	Analysis of text is usually developed using rhetorical aspects of the text itself, its medium/genres, its audience, or its cultural/historical context	Analysis of text is sometimes developed using rhetorical aspects. Analysis may sometimes be literary instead of rhetorical	Analysis of text is rarely developed using rhetorical aspects. Analysis often focuses on the literary instead of rhetorical	Analysis of text is rarely developed using rhetorical aspects. Analysis often focuses on the literary; or no analysis overall	Essay shows no understanding of rhetorical analysis
Specific vs. Generalized Analysis	Analytical claims are based on specific and well-chosen excerpts from the text or its situation	Analytical claims are based on specific and usually well-chosen excerpts from the text or its situation	Analytical claims are based on specific, although sometimes obvious, excerpts from the text or its situation	Analytical claims are sometimes based on specific, although sometimes obvious, excerpts from the text or its situation	Analytical claims are usually not based on specific excerpts from the text or its situation, or there are too few analytical claims	No analysis—only summary and opinions without evidence
Sources: Credibility and Relevance	Sources are consistently credible for essay's purpose/audience, well-chosen for their relevance to the subject	Sources are usually credible and/or relevant	Sources are sometimes credible and/or relevant	Sources are intermittently credible and/or relevant	Sources are rarely credible and/or relevant	Sources are not credible and/or relevant
Sources: Integration	Consistently effective rhetorical choices concerning how writer introduces and situates sources	Effective rhetorical choices concerning how writer introduces and situates sources	Some rhetorical choice is evident in how writer introduces and situates most of the sources	Inconsistently introduces and situates source material; no rhetorical choices regarding source integration	Little introduction and situation of source material	No introduction and/or situation of source material

	6=Highly Effective (A Range)	5=Somewhat Effective (B Range)	4=Satisfactory (C Range)	3=Developing (C−)	2=Poor (D Range)	1=Unsatisfactory (F)
Thesis Follow-Through	Effectively focused throughout essay, follows through on the thesis	Clear focus throughout essay, follows through on the thesis	Generally good focus throughout essay, usually follows through on the thesis	Inconsistent or illogical focus throughout essay, sometimes follows through on the thesis	Weak or inconsistent focus throughout essay, little follow through from thesis	No clear focus in essay, thesis and essay do not match
Paragraphs: Coherence	All paragraphs display coherence by effectively covering a single topic	The majority of paragraphs display coherence by clearly covering a single topic	Paragraphs frequently display coherence by covering a single topic	Paragraphs sometimes display coherence by covering a single topic	Paragraphs lack coherence and usually cover more than one topic	No clear use of paragraphing, or little/no coherence within paragraphs
Paragraphs: Structure	All paragraphs display effective internal organization	The majority of paragraphs display effective internal organization	Paragraphs frequently display internal organization, but the organization may sometimes be ineffective or illogical	Paragraphs sometimes display internal organization, but the organization may be ineffective or illogical	Paragraphs lack internal organization or the organization is usually ineffective or illogical	No clear use of organization within paragraphs
Overall Essay Structure	Organization expertly enhances the development of ideas	Organization clearly enhances the development of ideas	Organization is logical and supports the development of ideas	Organization is somewhat logical, but may also be formulaic	Generally lacking clear organization; ordering of paragraphs does not help develop ideas	Lacking organization; ordering of paragraphs does not help develop ideas

3. Structure

		6=Highly Effective (A Range)	5=Somewhat Effective (B Range)	4=Satisfactory (C Range)	3=Developing (C−)	2=Poor (D Range)	1=Unsatisfactory (F)
4. Language	Correctness and Readability	Idiomatically effective prose that is a pleasure to read	Idiomatically correct prose that conveys meaning clearly; essay is easy to read	Idiomatically correct prose that usually conveys meaning clearly; essay is readable	Errors and non-idiomatic sentence constructions intermittently impede meaning; essay may be difficult to read—decoding is necessary	Errors or non-idiomatic sentence constructions impede meaning; essay is difficult to read and must often be decoded	Invasive and multiple errors or non-idiomatic sentence constructions impede meaning; essay is difficult to read and must often be decoded
	Eloquence: Tone, Style, and Word Choice	Tone, style, and word choice are credible and effectively enhance the reading experience	Tone, style, and word choice are credible and often enhance the reading experience	Tone, style, and word choice are generally credible and sometimes add to the reading experience	Tone, style, and word choice are sometimes detracting and inconsistently add to the reading experience	Tone, style, and word choice usually detract from readability	Tone, style, and word choice consistently detract from readability
	Sentence Structure	Consistently displays rhetorically sensitive and effective sentence structure and variety throughout essay	Usually displays rhetorically sensitive and effective sentence structure and variety throughout essay	Generally displays effective control of sentence structure and variety throughout essay	A few sentences might be effective in structure and variety, but there is little evidence student can control sentences	Repetitive sentence structure with little evidence student can control sentences	A majority of sentences are either grammatically broken or simplistic in structure

One Last Thing. After you're satisfied with your essay's continuity and content, be sure to read it through one last time to check for formatting, spelling errors, and sentence mechanics. Remember that while this is the last thing you'll check for, it's the first thing a reader will notice about your paper. First impressions are important. You wouldn't think of showing up for a job interview wearing a stained shirt and torn jeans. So why incline your reader to think less of your essay by presenting it in a carelessly put together package?

Make sure the RA essay is formatted according to **MLA standards** (Modern Language Association). This is the style used by scholars in the Humanities—since Composition is a part of the School of Humanities, that's why we ask you to practice using this formatting style. However, be aware that each scholarly discipline pretty much has its own formatting style. Believe it or not, even the style of your formatting (whether you include a year of publication in a parenthetical, whether you use footnotes or endnotes, etc.) takes rhetorical know-how: your ethos is determined by how well you follow the rules of conversation in your field, which includes how you format your writing.

Make sure, also, that your essay is free of spelling errors and typos. While we can't all be "great" writers, we can all be careful writers. Run your final draft through your computer's Spell Check program before you turn it in. But don't stop there. While Spell Check can catch a lot of careless typos and spelling errors, it's not perfect. It can't tell, for instance when you mistake one correctly spelled word like *there* for *their*. And sometimes, when you're too far off in your spelling, it corrects for the wrong word. Be sure to read through your paper one last time to look for what Spell Check can't catch.

Here's a trick that professional editors use: on your final proof, read your essay from the bottom up. Often, especially after we've read a text over and over, we see what we expect to see, not what's actually on the page. By reading your sentences last to first, you disrupt those expectations and are more likely to catch word omissions, transposed letters, and other careless errors.

6.6   Rhetoric in Practice

In the first *Spider-Man* film, Peter Parker says, "Whatever life holds in store for me, I will never forget these words: 'With great power comes great responsibility.' This is my gift, my curse. Who am I? I'm Spider-man." While you may not have been bitten by a radioactive spider and you may not be able to elude the Green Goblin-esque attacks of 39B by scaling the walls of the Social Sciences Lab, you *have* been given a certain measure of power: you have been given the Rhetoric in Practice project. (We'll wait for the celebratory cheers and hi-fives to die down before proceeding.)

If pop culture quotes don't do it for you, here's what Eleanor Roosevelt said about a very similar subject: "Freedom makes a huge requirement of every human being. With freedom comes responsibility. For the person who is unwilling to grow up, the person who does not want to carry his own weight, this is a frightening prospect." While the final sentence of this quote is probably a bit harsh when applied to the setting of 39B, there is some truth in it (as well as what Peter Parker had to say) for us.

The Rhetoric in Practice project affords you considerable freedom (and a little power, too), because it compels you to design your own rhetorical situation. Even if your instructor defines the project by limiting you to a certain *genre*, you are nevertheless responsible for the creation and execution of a purposeful text intended for a particular audience in a particular time and place. In real life, you will probably not be given the comfort or confinement of a prompt that specifies exactly what you must do, so this assignment will give you practice with being resourceful when presented with communication tasks.

6.6.1   The Project

Throughout the quarter in 39B, you've been learning the fundamentals of rhetoric and gaining valuable rhetorical conditioning through practice. You've learned about the **rhetorical situation**, you've learned the major categories of rhetorical **appeals** (logos, pathos, and ethos), and you've analyzed specific texts leading up to and including the RA Essay. In writing the RA, you were not only analyzing the rhetoric used by a particular **communicator**, but you were also writing as one.

In fact, all quarter long you have been adopting the conventions of a variety of writing modes and genres for different audiences, which means you have been **practicing rhetoric**. For assignments completed prior to the **Rhetoric in Practice** (RIP), your **audience** was your peers, your instructor, or a more generalized academic audience. For assignments such as blogs, forums, and class

Wikis, you have adopted the appropriate ethos for the situation and carried out your rhetorical purpose accordingly.

The RIP is a capstone assignment that allows you to use what you've been learning for the past several weeks. For this project you will:

Choose a topic and message related to the theme(s) of the course that will make it possible for you to include text(s) you've covered in class as source material. Based on your specific focus (topic), create a thesis or main message for your project.

Choose a specific audience (i.e., 18–25 year old American filmgoers, business professionals in healthcare, a local government official, teenagers from SoCal, the UCI community, students taking a particular class, etc.) and a specific genre (i.e., letter, review, presentation, essay, web page, etc.). Be as specific as possible when targeting your audience; for example, if you decide to write a book or film review, then it will help you to further define your audience if you choose a particular publication where it could be published. No matter what audience you choose, please remember that since you'll be workshopping your project with other members of the class, your audience also includes your classmates. Another important member of your audience is your instructor, who will be evaluating (grading) your success in addressing the particular audience you have defined.

Choose the delivery vehicle, or medium (i.e., written text, visual, audio, electronic, or a combination) which will convey your particular thesis most effectively; in many cases, the genre you choose will determine the delivery vehicle.

Use critical reading and rhetorical analysis to develop the ideas to have a particular desired impact on your target audience.

6.6.2 Objectives

The primary objective of this project is to give you practice in analyzing a rhetorical situation (of your own making), and then in developing a type of communication that is appropriate to that context. The focus of the assignment will depend upon the rhetorical situation you choose and the assignment you decide to prepare in response to it; however, remember that you must use analysis in the development of your text.

The RIP takes your experience as a communicator and asks you to expand on it by creating your own **rhetorical situation,** which includes defining all the textual elements you've identified and analyzed in other texts throughout the quarter: **message, audience, purpose, genre,** and **context.**

After defining these elements, you will create a text that executes a complex **rhetorical strategy** (comprised of a thorough variety of appeals) that will effectively achieve your stated purpose. The rhetorical situation you design will incorporate your class theme—as a result, this assignment is partly a demonstration of your awareness not only of rhetoric in general, but also of its applications in a particular set (realm? galaxy? is Pluto still a planet?) of texts.

6.6.3   Designing a Rhetorical Situation

Your first spark of an idea may be related to any of the above listed textual elements: you may decide that you want to make a public announcement video (genre, medium) to persuade suburban SoCal teenagers to eat Brussels sprouts for breakfast (purpose, context, audience). You might have a message in mind such as, "Brussels sprouts increase student performance on chemistry mid-terms in suburban high schools when eaten 3–6 hours prior to test time." Once you've got that first spark, you'll have to define the other textual elements.

The creation of a text is a critical process, and as Chapter 2 suggests, it is important to ask questions as you proceed. If you have a message in mind, then ask, "Who needs to hear this message?" If you have a context in mind, then ask, "What message and purpose are appropriate to this context?" You get the picture—when you have one element, ask yourself about the others. It is important, though, not to settle for the easiest answers to these questions. While you might be able to create an adequate text by offering yourself easy answers to your questions, you will have a much greater chance of creating an excellent text if you give yourself a hard time (though not such a hard time that your dueling voices develop into a dissociative disorder—please remain just one human!).

Executing the Design

A successful RIP project usually includes innovative elements, whether in the design of the rhetorical situation or in the rhetorical devices used in executing the design. Innovation requires creativity, and creativity requires you to surprise your audience. That is, your text should not be predictable—it should not merely imitate others of its kind; instead, it should add to what we already know about its genre, context, or about rhetoric itself. You write, at least in part, to generate new knowledge and as a writer, your texts have the opportunity to *teach* your peers and your instructor.

In order to add to what we already know, you'll need to become a certain kind of expert. In order to make an effective short film, you'll need to study the conventions of that genre. You'll need to know what other short films do, so that you can select the techniques most suitable to your own film. To execute a film, you must be able to acquire a camera, lighting, sound equipment, actors, a script, editing software, and more. A word to the wise: don't try to execute a project with which you have no prior experience or expertise. If you don't know how to shoot and edit a film, don't try to learn for the sake of the RIP—perhaps you can just produce a script instead.

If you plan to write a magazine article, you'll have to select a specific magazine, analyze its articles, advertisements, and layout until you achieve a workable understanding of its audience and of the techniques it uses to appeal to that audience. No matter what your situation, you'll need to demonstrate *expertise* as an element of your writerly ethos. (Because this is also a project for a grade in a class, this demonstration of expertise will let your instructor know that you have understood her/his lessons well enough to incorporate them into your own work.)

Is Anybody Out There?

Audience is often the most difficult, overlooked, and over-generalized element of a rhetorical situation. When analyzing a text, you may have found it challenging to identify its audience in a way that was productively related to the text's rhetorical strategy. In some cases, you might have thought about audience as a demographic group—a group of people who share one or more characteristics. In others, you may have had to consider audience in terms of values, desires, fears, or other human qualities (psychographics). In all cases, you have had to consider **context**, as well as the text's specific appeals, before you could be satisfied that you had come to a productive understanding of audience.

A RIP project without a well-defined audience is like a homeowner woken in the night by a mysterious noise in the backyard, who peeks his head out the bedroom window and whispers, "Hello? Hello? Anybody out there?" He is likely to receive no response, because it is likely that the noise was caused by a raccoon rummaging through his trash (and we all know raccoons aren't interested in our RIPs). If you have chosen a worthy message, purpose, genre, and context for your purpose, don't waste them whispering to a raccoon. He's just hungry, so maybe toss your leftover pizza out that window instead.

6.6.4   The RIP Proposal

Because the RIP allows such latitude in the design of your project, it is important for your instructor to approve your plan before you execute its design. You will be required to write a proposal outlining your intended rhetorical situation; you may also be asked to meet with your instructor to discuss your plan. Once you have been given your instructor's approval and guidance, you can begin to carry out your RIP. Your instructor will give you specific instructions regarding the proposal.

6.6.5   RIP It Up: The Writer's Memo

Once you have completed your project, you will be asked to write a memo describing it and your rhetorical strategy, which you will submit along with your final draft. Instructors have a variety of names for this component of the RIP, but the most common name is the "Writer's Memo." In the memo, you will introduce your project to your instructor by defining the elements of its rhetorical situation: Rhetor, Message, Audience, Purpose, Genre, and Context. You will need to do so in enough detail that your instructor will be able to identify and acknowledge your level of rhetorical awareness (not to mention all the hard work you put into your project!).

RIP Writer's Memo Rubric

1. Does the writer clearly (and with details) summarize the rhetorical situation for his/her RIP text? Rhetor, Message (Medium & Genre), Audiences, Historical/Cultural Context?

2. Does the writer clearly state what ethos he/she will adopt for the situation? Or if a fictional work, is the ethos of each character carefully described?

3. Does the writer provide ample detail and specifics about the demographics and psychographics of the target audience? Has the writer clearly spent time analyzing the audience?

4. Does the writer clearly describe the medium (or multi-media) to be used for this project and list specific conventions expected of texts in this medium?

5. Does the writer clearly describe the genre(s) to be used for this project and list specific conventions expected of texts in this genre?

6. Did the writer choose and describe a specific place of publication for this text? Did the writer describe some of the conventions of other texts in this same publication?

7. Does the writer clearly describe his/her purpose for creating the text (what he/she wants the audience to know, feel, think, how he/she wants the audience to react)?

8. Does the writer clearly describe what he/she intends as the primary message of the text? Has the writer distinguished between purpose and message?

9. Has the writer explained how he/she will use analysis as part of the creation process for this text?

10. Is the writing clear, specific, and understandable, lacking errors? If this is an individual project, is the Memo at least two pages, double-spaced typing, MLA format? If this is a group project, is the Memo at least four pages, double-spaced typing, MLA format?

In the same way, each RIP will be evaluated with slight differences, depending upon the genre, medium, and purpose. A film review of *Into the Wild* for *Rolling Stone* magazine will be "read" differently, for example, than a YouTube video parodying a Nike shoe commercial or a mock comic book that analyzes a scene from *X-Men* or a PowerPoint presentation on the underlying environmental themes of *The Simpsons Movie.*

Most important is that your RIP project, whatever form it takes, demonstrates a clear understanding of the rhetorical principles we've been reading about, observing, analyzing, writing about, and practicing all quarter long. To do this, your RIP should clearly identify and target a specific audience, convey a specific message and purpose, and show an awareness of the conventions of the medium and genre you choose to work in. The rubric for the RIP is below.

RIP Rubric

1. After one reading (viewing, listening), is the main point, message, or thesis easy to determine? Was analysis involved in order to create the message?

2. How well does the RIP target its intended audience? Are the conventions the audience expects for this type of text followed?

3. Does the ethos of the writer(s) fit the rhetorical situation?

4. Does the RIP show awareness of its historical and cultural context?

5. Is the medium used effective for this particular message for its particular audience? Are the conventions of this medium followed?

6. Was the genre a good choice for delivering this particular message to its audience? Are the conventions of the genre noticeable in the text?

7. Overall Message: How well does the creator(s) communicate the message for the audience (within the medium and genre chosen)? Is the message clear? Will the audience feel convinced that the creator is an expert? Will the text make its audience feel, think, react, respond in the way the creator intended?

8. Overall Execution: How well is the text executed? Rate the quality of execution. (If writing, then quality of writing; if something like a film, then production values; if a sound text, is the sound clear and strong?)

Chapter 7

WR 39C, ARGUMENT AND RESEARCH

WR 39C: Argument and Research is an introduction to academic argument and research designed to help you succeed in upper-level University courses. You will learn how to analyze the construction of arguments and how to conduct academic research in the library and online. You will also learn to engage responsibly and effectively in democratic discourse. Finally, you will write a connected series of academic essays based in credible research in order to make a persuasive argument.

You have probably heard UCI referred to as a "research university." That means that the faculty is responsible not only for teaching, but also for conducting research that generates new knowledge in various disciplines. Writing is most often the means of forming and conveying knowledge gained through research, and is therefore an essential activity for students attending research universities.

The process of making knowledge continues as other scholars read what has been written, test its arguments and findings, and then build upon it to create more knowledge. In your composition courses at UCI, you will participate in this great process of making meaning by reading, researching, and extending the knowledge of your writing community—your class.

Today, technology continues to improve the ease with which information, misinformation, and disinformation can be disseminated and acquired. So how do you know which information to trust or even where to find the necessary information? How do you decide what part of a source to use? Then, once you've sorted through all that information, what's the best way to integrate research information into an academic argument?

39C is a course dedicated to helping you learn how to research effectively, how to shrewdly evaluate the sources you find, and how to integrate research into an academic argument. Throughout the quarter, you'll learn and practice using methods for finding, contextualizing, evaluating, and organizing information, and, finally, for effectively using it to build persuasive arguments.

7.1   Class Community and Participation

Writing is a social activity. We communicate in different social contexts, sometimes in specialized communities. This class will also become a writing and research community, and several assignments ask you to write within this community, responding to other writers and communicating in more or less formal contexts.

Two graded components of this class—Community (Blogs/Forums) and Participation—provide you with a number of different writing opportunities that are meant to help you practice your responses to class materials, shape your thinking about complex issues, and practice writing in a variety of rhetorical situations.

Your instructor will explain the kinds of weekly writing and response assignments that will comprise your grade for both community and participation. Blogs or forums provide a less formal (or "low stakes") writing environment in which to try out responses and ideas. You'll be asked to respond to your classmates' writing here as well, which is yet another specialized writing task. Your teacher may also assign quizzes, reading response questions, peer review memos, individual or group presentations or freewriting assignments in class. Each different kind of writing assignment has its own purpose and objectives, though these objectives are meant, ultimately, to deepen your understanding of the class material, and provide you with an opportunity to sharpen your thinking and the articulation of your ideas.

7.2   The Arc of the 39C Quarter

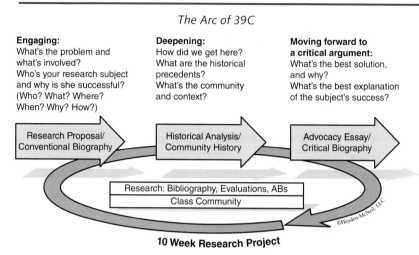

The Arc of 39C

Engaging:
What's the problem and what's involved?
Who's your research subject and why is she successful?
(Who? What? Where? When? Why? How?)

Deepening:
How did we get here?
What are the historical precedents?
What's the community and context?

Moving forward to a critical argument:
What's the best solution, and why?
What's the best explanation of the subject's success?

Research Proposal/ Conventional Biography

Historical Analysis/ Community History

Advocacy Essay/ Critical Biography

Research: Bibliography, Evaluations, ABs
Class Community

©Hayden-McNeil, LLC

10 Week Research Project

Think of it this way: first, you'll identify an interesting topic; you will choose your topic by starting with issues that have been reported by researchers, scientists, and journalists, or selecting an individual whose success is notable. You'll begin your research with some fundamental questions about this topic in order to discover what problem is most interesting to you or why other researchers, academics, biographers, or experts care about this topic or individual. Then, you'll dig deeper to discover how this problem came to be, what causes and factors led to the current state of affairs, or what community shaped the individual you've been studying. If you've been studying a problem, your final paper will advocate a solution (one proposed by a credible expert or group). If you've been writing about the nature of an individual's success, your final paper will make a critical argument about that success.

Why do you need to know all of the assignments now? Knowing the goal of the final essay will help you make a better choice in your research topic and will make your first phases of research more purposeful.

NOTE: You will be working on your class community and research assignments consistently (weekly) throughout the quarter.

7.3   Reading Your Core Text

The core texts for 39C sections deal with current or controversial topics that provide relevant backdrops for the kind of collaboration and focused investigation integral to the course. Each text provides a springboard to research that addresses a variety of scientific, technological, cultural, political, historical, economic, social, and ecological trends in our society.

Research topics need not come directly from the core text; think of the core text as a model for research and argument, rather than a textbook about your topic.

All core texts concern arguments made in the public sphere, and this is where we'll begin our study of how to read and write an argument. As you read—no matter the core text of your class—make notes about your author's rhetorical situation: What is the main thesis or argument? What other major claims are made? What evidence is presented? What is the purpose of investigating the material and then writing a book about it? What does the writer want her audience to believe when they finish the book? Who is that audience? How persuasive is the text? In other words, you will be asking the same kinds of questions of the class core text that you learned to ask in 39B when writing the rhetorical analysis essay.

In addition to noting the rhetorical situation of the core text in your section, you will be expected to conduct some research into the background of the text's author(s) and learn something about their field of expertise, professional interests, and rhetorical style. In other words, you will attempt to determine the credibility your author has with regard to the particular field he is writing about, what types of influences may have shaped his perspective, and whether the author has an ulterior motive that might be affecting the argument presented in the text. In addition, you will take notice of how he has selected, introduced, and used sources in the core text and whether he has objectively presented opposing views without skewing them for the purpose of strengthening his own argument. After all, research begins with an investigation of the sources themselves, and, as noted above, the authors of your core texts are a good place to begin this kind of examination.

Because the core texts focus on current and controversial issues you may find yourself at odds with the author. It is not, however, the purpose of the course to convince you of the author's views. Instead, each text provides an opportunity to study and analyze the rhetorical strategies of a talented writer, facilitates class discussion of the course topic, and offers a possible model for structuring your own research and argument.

7.4   Choosing Your Research Project

At the beginning of the quarter, you will be asked to select a research topic that's interesting to you (and then begin to identify a problem that has resulted from some key failure of human activity or inactivity or to identify why a particular individual attained a notable level of success). By the end of the quarter, you will become an expert on this topic, understand its background and causes, and develop a reasonable argument based on your research and in-depth reading.

Your most helpful resource at this point in the quarter are the articles and web sites found in the Links folders in the Writing Studio class environment; browse each topic/folder to see sample sources about the problems connected to your course theme. These Links files are not meant to define the problem once and for all. Instead, these are meant to be springboards to better, clearer research.

Be forewarned: it's a bad idea to choose a topic because you think it will be easy to investigate. Every research topic requires hard, though rewarding, work. A much better criterion for selection is whether you are actually interested; successful students often choose topics that they already care about, or that are related to their majors.

Once you have identified a *topic* that is of interest to you, begin considering what problems exist within that topic. Look for sites of conflict, disagreement, or debate. Read the materials in the Links folders not as impartial statements of fact, but as representations of a variety of positions on current controversies.

If you are in a "Defining Success" class, consider the kinds of examples Malcolm Gladwell gives in *Outliers* as inspiration for the kinds of research subjects you could choose. Most students find it works well to choose a major player in their own or a related field. For example, an Environmental Studies major might choose noted environmental activitist Rachel Carson. It's not important that your research subject be well known outside your field—many innovators don't end up famous or rich (which will help you push farther than "money and fame" when you're defining the nature of your subject's success).

Some students prefer to take a break from working in their own major, and choose someone they respect in another field. An exhausted Math major who loves jazz might choose Miles Davis, the seminal jazz musician, and that Environmental Studies major might go with Frank Lloyd Wright, an architect whose designs incorporated natural elements and materials.

7.4.1   Rule #1: Read Widely, with an Open Mind

Most of us have no shortage of opinions, and when you begin your research, you will probably have some ideas of what you believe is true, or what the best solution to the problem will be, and you will want your essay to support those reasons.

This is exactly the wrong way to approach a topic. Coming in with preconceived ideas means you go on a scavenger hunt, picking sources that support your viewpoint and discarding those that challenge or contradict it. You want to approach your topic as if you're a detective coming upon a crime scene. You don't know what's happened, you don't know who is responsible, and you need to find out. Collect the evidence and from there go for a broad overview of the problem first.

Real research—and real learning—means that there are stakes involved. You could be wrong. You might have to change your opinions based on acquired knowledge.

Preliminary Research

One of your first assignments in 39C is to do some preliminary research (primarily in popular media sources such as newspapers, web sites, magazines, television documentaries) to follow up on one of the Links articles to confirm if other writers or researchers are concerned about these issues.

The Bedford Researcher contains helpful information about how to begin your research process, how to conduct internet research and how to use these sources to branch out to even better research. Make sure you read those chapters carefully, even if your instructor doesn't cover that material in class.

Reading the News Early and Often

One habit you'll find helpful is to become a news junkie. Reading newspapers, listening to National Public Radio (NPR) and checking in with online news blogs will be enormously beneficial to developing your research. However, it's not always efficient (or even possible) to read all of the news every day. Instead, you can let the news come to you. Google lets you create a news alert so that every time your topic shows up in the news, you will get an email alert. These news alerts will help you stay up-to-date with important developments regarding the problem you are researching. If you're reading *Outliers*, you'll be surprised how often your research subject shows up in the news, no matter how long ago they may have lived. Successful people's lives have a way of continuing to be relevant.

Using Wikipedia Wisely

Wikipedia is a natural first stop for research. An encyclopedia should contain verifiable, objective information, and at first, Wikipedia seems reliable. The language of the articles is what most of us recognize as academic: free of emotional words and phrases, clear of obvious bias.

Unfortunately, Wikipedia's strength—that anyone may submit information—is also its weakness. The Wikipedia editors trust that time and multiple contributors will weed out the incorrect data. What this means for you, as a researcher, is that Wikipedia isn't always a trustworthy source: you might get an article that is correct in its information or you might get one that's misleading. When consulting a Wikipedia page, scroll to the bottom to see if the article cites credible sources. Go to those sources next. If you have trouble locating any of them, your library orientation will help you do so.

Developing Better Keywords

Keywords are terms which, when put into an internet or library search (Google or ANTPAC, for instance) produce results that will help you with your research. The more words you use, the more specific your search results will be.

Different ordering and combinations of keywords will also produce different— and sometimes better or worse—results. If you aren't having much luck with a particular combination, don't give up and assume there's simply no information on your topic. The research process is full of trial-and-error experiences—you'll have to stumble before you can walk, then run. Try another combination of words, or read another article to see if you can find a few more phrases that might produce some results. You can also consult one of many online, discipline-specific encyclopedias available through the UCI Libraries' web site.

Finding keywords isn't an exact science, and there isn't a precise formula you can follow each time to produce good results. However, there are a few tricks you can use to narrow your searches.

Tips for Finding Keywords

Look for:

- words which appear with high frequency in the article
- words consistently grouped together, such as "genetically modified"
- discipline-specific or technical terminology or jargon
- unusual words you haven't seen before
- names of organizations, corporations, and individuals

7.4.2   Rule #2: Keep Good Notes and Records

One of the important habits you should develop as an academic researcher is to keep track of all your good information and sources. Every time you find a source that you find instructive or valuable, copy the URL or save the URL in your favorites. Then, you should select, copy, and save the bibliography and the keywords into a separate file at the Studio, or in a word document or notebook.

Topic Prewriting

1. Briefly summarize what you already know about this topic and the issues surrounding it. Begin the process of taking notes on what you find—either in the Writing Studio, a word document, or a notebook.

2. Read the section "Preliminary Research," above, before beginning your research. Then use Google to find general sources that will provide the background to your topic: a recent newspaper article, encyclopedia entry, FAQ from a related organization, Wikipedia, etc.

3. As you read through the first few general sources you locate, make a list of keywords associated with the issue. Keep a running list of keywords and add these to your notes.

4. Identify two passages from your sources for closer reading. These should be passages that you think you'll be able to use in an essay, perhaps where the author is defining or contextualizing a problem, either explicitly or implicitly.

5. Begin the process of evaluating your sources (explained in more detail later in the chapter). This process can provide clarity about the author, the source, and the topic.

7.4.3   Rule #3: Look for Academic Sources

Google will help you find good initial sources, but for an academic essay, the genre you'll be writing in 39C, you'll need to find specialized and discipline-specific sources as well. These specialized sources are usually not free—a subscription fee must be paid. Fortunately, you attend one of the best research universities in the country, which means we have an extensive library collection that includes subscription-only databases. Your class library orientation will help you become more familiar with the databases and resources available to you.

Your instructor will require you to develop a working bibliography that contains a variety of sources. As the quarter progresses, you will find that you will develop a kind of hierarchy of research.

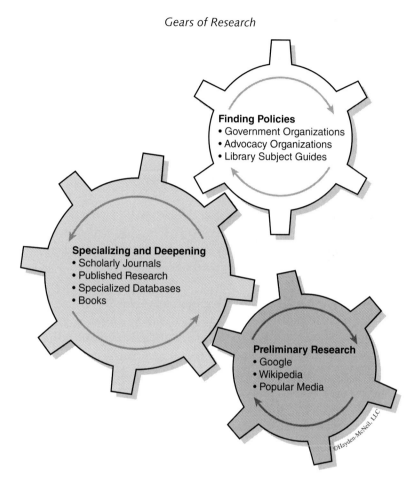

Gears of Research

Finding Policies
• Government Organizations
• Advocacy Organizations
• Library Subject Guides

Specializing and Deepening
• Scholarly Journals
• Published Research
• Specialized Databases
• Books

Preliminary Research
• Google
• Wikipedia
• Popular Media

©Hayden-McNeil, LLC

Though the quarter begins mostly with popular media sources, you should quickly move to include scholarly and academic sources, government sources, and sources from advocacy groups. As you keep track of your work, you should make sure that you have books, government publications, scholarly essays, reports from investigative journalists, and articles from peer-reviewed journals. You can even develop your own independent research by conducting interviews, visiting key sites important to your research project, or emailing scholars about your topic.

Why Do You Need Academic Sources?

Academic sources are written by scholars in a particular field, for other scholars in that field. This means that these sources are held to a high standard by people who know what they're talking about, and you can trust authors of academic sources to have done their homework.

Further, using academic sources lends your own writing credibility. Knowing where to look for authoritative, trustworthy expert support for your own points, and integrating that source material smoothly, is the hallmark of strong academic writing in college and beyond.

Finally, academic sources almost always feature arguments—scholars develop opinions about their research, and they write academic articles and books to contribute to or change the research in their fields. That means you're not just getting information; you're getting great models of how to construct an academic argument persuasively. You may find that reading academic sources gives you new ideas about how to approach your own research and writing.

Of course, you should practice your critical reading skills on academic sources just as you do on any other kind. You don't have to agree with an author, and you can certainly challenge his or her credibility—especially if you find opposing evidence and arguments in other academic sources.

7.4.4   Rule #4: Accept the Fact that Research Takes Time

All researchers gather some information they end up discarding. Remember that even if you don't end up using some of the sources you've found and read for your final 39C essays, the process of finding and reading them has contributed to your journey to becoming an expert on the topic, which then forms a key part of your academic ethos.

 RESEARCH ADVICE FROM PAST 39C STUDENTS

Take Your Time. Do preliminary research to make sure you have a good understanding of your topic so you know exactly what aspect to research.

—Erika Odegard

Don't pick the first source you see. Read it, analyze it, do some background research, then make an educated evaluation of the credibility of the source and how it relates to your topic.   —John Costumbrado

Try to do some research every day.   —Selena Gunggavakin

Do not limit yourself to only one search engine. Give your research some variety.

—Brendan Gilbert

Don't expect to find an excellent source in a matter of minutes. Research takes time! Also, I don't just throw out "bad" sources because even the weakest ones can give you keywords or hints that will lead you to better ones.

—Amanda Patrick

Use sources that would prove both sides in order to strengthen your argument.

—Tiffany Cheng

7.5   Developing Your Working Bibliography

Since your writing for this course depends on using credible sources, it is extremely important that you spend time researching, reading, and evaluating sources continuously throughout the quarter. Each time you find a source worthy of your attention (even though you may not end up using it in an essay) you should enter this source into the Bibliography tool at the Studio.

This assignment is the principal component of your research grade for the course and is based on:

- consistent addition of sources to the Bibliography in the Studio throughout the quarter.

- the quality, quantity, and variety of those sources (typically, approximately 40 sources).

- the quality and quantity of the source evaluations.

For more information on the Bibliography assignment, objectives, and a formal rubric, please visit the Studio.

From your Working Bibliography, you select material that you cite in your essay—the Works Cited page. Read the following two Works Cited examples (and remember that these pages represent only a fraction of the students' full range of research).

SAMPLE WORKS CITED #1

Ball, Ian. *Turning the Tide: Power from the sea and protection for nature.* Joint Marine Programme, December 2002. Web. 20 November 2008.

Bond, Sam. "Barrage bad for birds." *Edie.* 10 July 2006: Web. 14 October 2008.

Crumpton, Neil. *A Severn barrage or tidal lagoons? A comparison.* Friends of the Earth Cymru, January 2004. Web. 12 November 2008.

Green Energy Study for British Columbia Phase 2: Mainland. Triton Consultants Ltd, 24 October 2002. Web. 30 November 2008.

"Severn Tidal Fence Group set up." *Renewable Energy Focus.* 23 July 2008. Web. 30 November 2008.

"Severn tidal 'fence' idea floated." *BBC News.* BBC, 16 July 2008. Web. 20 November 2008.

Technology: Tidal Lagoons. London, United Kingdom: Tidal Electric, 2008. Web. November 15, 2008.

"Tidal Fence across Bristol Channel is rival to Severn Barrage." *Evening Post*. 18 July 2008. Web. November 3, 2008.

Turning the tide: Tidal power in the UK. Sustainable Development Commission, October 2007. Web. October 14, 2008.

Walters, Rod. *TIDAL ENERGY: BARRAGE VS LAGOONS—THE WRONG DECISION?*. Abergavenny & Crickhowell FOE, October 2007. Web. November 12, 2008.

Why do we need to take care of our birds?. European Commission, November 2004. Web. November 12, 2008.

SAMPLE WORKS CITED #2

Bettleheim, Adriel. "Presidential Power Has Bush overstepped his authority in fighting terrorism?." *CQ Researcher* 12.40 (2002): 945–968. *CQ Researcher Online*. CQ Press. Univ of California Irvine. Web. 19 October 2008.

Gordon Adams. "The United States Should Not Pursue Military Expansion." *Opposing Viewpoints: Military Draft*. Ed. Viqi Wagner. Detroit: Greenhaven Press, 2008. *Opposing Viewpoints Resource Center*. Gale. Univ of California Irvine. Web. 25 November 2008.

Glennon, Michael J. "A Conveniently Unlawful War." *Policy Review* 150 (2008): 75–91. Print. 2 December 2008.

Jost, Kenneth. "Rethinking Foreign Policy: Should President Bush's approach be abandoned?." *CQ Researcher* 5.17 (2007): n. pag. *CQ Researcher Online*. CQ Press. Univ. of California Irvine. Web. 14 October 2008.

Katel, Peter. "New Strategy in Iraq." *CQ Researcher* 17 (2007): 169–192. *CQ Researcher Online*. CQ Press. Univ. of California Irvine. Web. 14 October 2008.

Katel, Peter. "U.S. Policy on Iran." *CQ Researcher* 17.41 (2007): 961–984. *CQ Researcher Online*. CQ Press. Univ. of California Irvine. Web. 2 November 2008.

"McCain Blasts 'Vote of No-Confidence'." *USA Today* 5 February 2007. Web. 25 November 2008.

United States. Cong. Senate. A bill to express the sense of Congress on Iraq. 2007. 110th Cong. Senate Bill 470. Govtrack. Web. 1 December 2008.

The sample work and sample paragraphs throughout this chapter do not necessarily demonstrate superior work. Look carefully at each example and the subsequent questions and try to determine if the work is superior, good, etc.

RHETORICAL ASIDE

Works Cited Peer Review Questions

1. What can each Works Cited page tell you about the project? What is the issue that the writer is researching?

2. Where do you think that the writer stands on the issue in question?

3. Which writer do you think has the stronger ethos? Why?

4. What would you say to the author of the weaker Works Cited list? What specific things could she improve?

5. What errors or problems, in format, style, or sources used, do you notice in either of the lists?

6. Reflections: Look at your own Works Cited page. Does your collection of sources indicate anything to you about where your project is heading? Is there anything new to consider about where your interests seem to lie?

7.6   Evaluating Your Sources

It's one thing to find sources; it's quite another to use this source material well. To help you determine how to use this material (or, even, if you should use it at all), you're asked to both summarize and evaluate your sources. The annotated bibliography (AB) is a way to quickly summarize the main aspects of the text's rhetorical situation: who created it, what medium and genre it is, what evidence is used, and the audience and purpose. You're required to write six ABs for the quarter (of your six best sources). See Chapter 4, section 4.2, to review how to write a proper AB.

Next, you'll complete source evaluations for approximately half of your sources. A source evaluation is different from an AB in that it provides an opportunity to show that you have read it carefully enough to reflect on its quality. The Studio, where you will post your evaluations, asks that you use relevance, evidence, author, publisher, comprehensiveness, and timeliness as evaluative criteria. Those criteria are fully explained on the Studio itself. Here are two examples of source evaluations:

● SOURCE EVALUATION SAMPLE #1

ICAO. *ICAO Environmental Report 2007*: Environmental Unit of the International Civil Aviation Organization, 2007. Web. January 13, 2009.

This report argues for various policies that will help curb greenhouse gases in the future. The report was written because greenhouse gas emissions are growing and must be curbed somehow. It provides statistical evidence and interviews with various experts in this field. It is a report for both the scientific community and those who are interested in this topic. This is one of the best sources in my bibliography. It is very comprehensive and easily readable. It details important trends and problems facing aviation. The part most useful for my topic is Global Emissions. That section provides information regarding aircraft emissions and potential biofuels to replace jet fuel. It discusses the potential rewards and losses to using biofuels, and tries to be as unbiased as possible. Like many other reports, it also gives information regarding the process on making biofuels and the properties of biofuels. This report is definitely credible and citable.

● SOURCE EVALUATION SAMPLE #2

Watkins, Kevin, Jung-ui Sul. "Cultivating Poverty." *Oxfam International* (2002): 1–35. Web. March 4, 2009.

Relevance:

The information is helpful in understanding the causes of the problem and the necessary steps to take in fixing the problem. It includes facts and figures that are specific to only Mali, but the solutions it suggests are general, which is fine because the solutions can be applied to all African cotton growing countries. The information includes a background on the problem, history of the problem, and statistics to help understand the scope of the cotton problem. There are plenty of quotes from authoritative figures such as Ann M Veneman, U.S. Secretary of Agriculture, or firsthand witnesses of the problem such as Assita Konate, a Malian agricultural laborer. It also includes numerical figures such as the amount being paid to cotton subsidies at $3.9 billion in 2001/2002. The main point of this article was not to describe the problem, but to highlight the political causes and the political solutions to the cotton problem. I am using this source for my advocacy proposal, so it is very valuable. It even provides information about Brazil's dispute with the United States at the WTO.

Evidence:

There are plenty of sources, ranging from quotes from lobbyists, Malian farmers, American farmers, and other government officials. There are also cited statistics, such as estimates by the International Cotton Advisory Committee. At the end of the article, there are several graphs and tables that are cited and used to back up Watkins' claims. All in all, the evidence used appropriate because the quotes from Malian farmers come near the beginning where the scope/background is being explained, quotes from American farmers come next when the American subsidies are being described as part of the problem, and such. It sometimes seems that some of the evidence can be interpreted other ways, such as poverty comes directly from farming profits, but the journal comes from Oxfam and is well cited so I trust the information coming from this source.

Timeliness:

The decade when the source is published is accurate and still relative to my research. However, because it was written in 2002, it misses a lot of information. Such as the example of Brazil; since the article was written Brazil won its dispute against the United States. In response, the United States appealed the WTO decision and lost again, but has not undergone any changes. This source is timely enough that the information is still correct, but more research needs to be done.

Source Evaluation Peer Review Questions

1. **Format:** Does the writer include all sections? If it's not split into sections, does the writer include the most necessary content, as covered by the Writing Studio?

2. **Relevance:** Does the writer address not only that it is (or is not) relevant, but how it's relevant, for what case-specific reasons, and to what degree?

3. **Evidence:** Does the writer address specific types of evidence used, evaluate the accuracy and trustworthiness of the evidence, and explain its purpose and/or the context in which it's used?

4. **Author/Publisher:** Has the writer shown an effort to find out more about who the author is (other works, affiliations, areas of expertise), and indicated anything about the type of publication and the work they tend to publish?

(continued)

5. **Comprehensiveness:** Does the writer indicate the scope of the article, and relate it clearly to the scope of her own argument?

6. **Timeliness:** Is the writer clear about the relevance/usefulness to her project of the publication based on its publication date? If it's a scholarly work, is there any indication of whether the date range or evidence discussed within the paper itself is timely?

7. Are the sentences well written? Are there moments of overly informal tone, or very obvious grammatical errors? Is the bibliographic entry correctly formatted?

7.6.1   Annotation and Evaluation: A Comparison

An annotation of a source and an evaluation of a source serve different purposes for a researcher. Here's a back-to-back comparison of an AB and a source evaluation to review:

Annotation:

Thornton, Stephen P. *Freud, Sigmund [Internet Encyclopedia of Philosophy].* Internet Encyclopedia of Philosophy. 29 December 2010. Web. 3 April 2011.

Stephen P. Thornton, a professor at the University of Limerick in Ireland, provides an extensive factual outline of Sigmund Freud's life, work, and legacy, as well as a critical evaluation of his ideas. Thornton presents this vast collection of general information in the Internet Encyclopedia of Philosophy, a peer-reviewed academic collection of information on philosophers and related topics. Thornton makes extensive use of factual and anecdotal evidence to provide information, as well as quotes from authorities in the field of psychoanalysis to illustrate opposing viewpoints of Freud's ideas. Thornton's work generally appeals to those deeply interested in Freud's life and work, and accordingly, his purpose is to educate his readers in many aspects of Freud's life and legacy.

Evaluation:

Relevance: Like all of the other encyclopedic works, this source is directly relevant to the research subject. It is entirely factual, and is an excellent general resource for Freud's life, accomplishments, and ideas. The source does go in depth for an encyclopedia article, especially in topics related to Freud's ideas—thus it will definitely be useful both for general information as well as more in-depth information about his ideas.

Evidence: The author offers mainly factual support for his information. The source seems to be very objective, and where it is not (under "Critical Evaluation of Freud"), the author does not make claims himself, but rather gives the viewpoints of a number of experts. This factual evidence, along with some anecdotal support, lends the article credibility where it is used; however, since much of the source only provides factual information about Freud, not a lot of support is given (or necessary) for many claims.

Author/publisher: There is little background information about the author. He does, however, provide his name, research institution, and contact information. The organization he is an author for, however, lends much credibility to the information that he provides; the web site itself is an established academic resource, and is reviewed by many editors. The article cites all of its sources, is written in largely objective, academic language, and is formatted neatly, lending the source much credibility. Like other encyclopedia articles, this source stays away from providing biased information.

Comprehensiveness: The article is extremely comprehensive, providing a complete and thorough collection of information. The "critical evaluation of Freud" section is the only section that offers opinionated information, and the article manages to stay neutral and unbiased by providing a balance of opposing opinions.

Timeliness: The source was updated in 2010, which is considered recent in terms of the research subject. Not many developments have occurred which would change the information offered about Freud; the Critical Evaluation portion might benefit from another year's worth of research, but it is unlikely, as no large developments have occurred in the field of Psychoanalysis for years.

Peer Review Questions

1. Read both AB and evaluation. What information is in the AB that is not included in the evaluation? How is the evaluation significantly different from the AB? What purpose does each form serve?

2. Where could the writer have been more detailed or nuanced (in either the AB or the evaluation)?

3. In writing the evaluation, imagine that you're trying to decide if this is a good source to use. What information here seems the most useful? What might have been left out?

7. 7   The Research Proposal/Conventional Biography

The first formal assignment in 39C is the Research Proposal, or the Conventional Biography for "Defining Success" classes. They're similar. The Research Proposal is a short, thesis-driven prospectus of a research project that identifies a specific problem related to your course theme and lays the groundwork for your research throughout the quarter. The Conventional Biography is a short, thesis-driven presentation of your research subject's life story, emphasizing the particular nature of your research subject's success, and identifying elements in that life story that led to that success. Here are some specific objectives for this first assignment:

- learn to write in a new genre that is common in research and academic communities.

- find, evaluate, and analyze a number of different sources. In effect, this is the first step in entering into a conversation among experts and researchers related to a specific topic, and you'll build on that knowledge to develop your own argument.

In the larger context of a research institution, research proposals are used to apply for funding or other kinds of support. Likewise, your research proposal in this class is meant to show your instructor that A) you've learned enough about a current problem to be able to continue with the next two essays and B) that you have a plan for future research. The more specific your topic is from the beginning, the more convincing and profitable your work on the research proposal will be.

In order to be convincing in this first assignment, you must demonstrate that you have already completed some reliable research. To that end *you must quote from at least three current, relevant sources in the proposal and cite them properly using the MLA guidelines.* You are also required to turn in a Working Bibliography of at least ten sources, and create Annotated Bibliographies for the best two sources from that list.

7.7.1   Defining Success

For "Defining Success" sections, the first essay defines the specific nature of your research subject's success, and reviews the life story of your subject, emphasizing the elements that contributed to his or her success. The essay demonstrates a confident, comprehensive grasp of your subject's biography and accomplishments, so that in the later essays you can dig beneath the surface.

What is success, beyond money and fame? The respect of one's peers? Being remembered decades or centuries after one's death for contributions to one's field? Changing the way people understand the world or each other? Exploring these questions will help you begin thinking about the qualities that make a truly successful person.

Once you've chosen a research subject, your initial research goal should be to become familiar with how your subject is remembered and written about from various points of view. The essay itself should offer a narrow, specific definition of this particular person's success, and should organize the presentation of that person's life story in a way that supports that definition.

⬤ SAMPLE INTRODUCTION #1

Amelia Earhart acknowledges three sources that attracted her to aviation: "the many trips she made with her father..., her love of sports and games usually restricted to boys, and her lifelong propensity for experimentation" (Ware, 32). In a short period of 10 years, Amelia Earhart established herself as a successful female pilot and earned celebrity status through her record breaking feats and many "firsts." Her courageous and fearless spirit, unconventional upbringing which installed her belief between the equality between men and women, and the revolutionizing ideologies of the women's movement in the early twentieth century, drove her to accomplish the many deeds she did. As she made herself a name in the public, Amelia Earhart became an iconic female role model inspiring young women to embrace their strength in a period of time when women were breaking free from traditional perceptions.

⬤ SAMPLE INTRODUCTION #2

Four men in four different places were all after one goal in 1967: the first successful human-to-human heart transplant. Teams of surgeons gathered in New York, Virginia, California, and South Africa waiting for the moment when a suitable donor heart would rush through the emergency room doors and provide the key to the surgery. Each team had different motives, patients, and apprehensions towards the surgery they were all about to embark on. The surgeons in the United States were the first to attempt the surgery and the first to fail. It was South African Christiaan Barnard who would be the one to convince a father that his brain dead daughter would be better off dead so that he could take her heart and save another man's life (McRae 189). Barnard flourished after finally taking the step to create one of the most historical medical moments in history on a Saturday evening in December of 1967. His overnight stardom allowed him to pursue his own interests. His handsome looks and charm along with his popular image allowed him to finally bring attention to important aspects of medicine and the corrupt politics of South Africa. His influence proved not only powerful in medicine, but also in reforming his native country that he adored so much.

Peer Review Questions

1. How do these intro paragraphs define the nature of their subject's success? Which one is more effective? Why? How could either of them be improved?

2. Are these introductory paragraphs making an argument about why this person is remembered, or are they just remembering them?

3. Do these introductory paragraphs suggest what kind of body paragraphs will follow? How might those paragraphs be organized?

7.7.2 Research Proposal: Defining a Problem

The first step in your work on this project is to clearly define a problem. To aid you with this process, your instructor may assign exercises that help you research current events and define current problems. This is important, because in the advocacy essay you must propose a solution to your problem. Keep in mind that there may be many problems associated with the topic you've started researching, and the problem may be defined differently based on your point of view, expertise, interests, or agenda.

Rather than trying to take on too broad a topic in a ten-week quarter, it is crucial to narrow your focus to just *one* problem. A research proposal that focuses on more than one problem or that defines that problem inadequately will be rhetorically ineffective. As you develop your research proposal, make sure that you can identify the following:

Names of Key Players

Take notes every time you read about people involved with the issue—those who are experts on the topic, those who influence public perception, organizations, universities who have done studies, political groups, or government agencies.

Key Events

Take notes on key events that have occurred leading up to or surrounding your problem. (Hint: this will help enormously when you need to consider historical factors in your research proposal and later in the Historical Analysis essay.)

Key Places

Keep track of **where** the problem has occurred and had a significant impact (this may be locally, nationally, or internationally). You will need to name a specific place where your research is targeted in the research proposal.

Legislation (Laws) or Public Policies

Look for mention of laws, acts, or proposed policies, whether by the government or by organizations in the public sphere. Keep track of both those related to your problem historically and those that might lead to possible solutions.

7.7.3   RP Introduction and Thesis

The introduction is where you attract the attention of your academic audience, providing important information about a specific problem and its seriousness in order to make them care about reading the rest of your proposal. A successful introduction must do the following:

Define the current problem (this should include defining any key terms related to your topic).

Establish the fact that it is a problem that has not already been solved (this may involve quoting from your sources briefly or using convincing statistics).

Write a focused thesis (no more than two sentences) that establishes WHAT the problem is, WHERE it exists, WHO is causing it, and WHY it is an important and pressing problem that we should be worried about solving.

Remember that your thesis must focus on one very *specific* problem, so rather than talking about nuclear energy problems in general, for example, you might talk about problems with storage containers that leak.

● SAMPLE THESIS STATEMENTS

1. While special education can be beneficial to students with certain needs, it has a perverse effect for the numerical majority of minority children across the country who are wrongly placed in these programs due to cultural differences.

2. Old pipes leak in contaminants that add to the impurities of the water. The quality of tap water in Los Angeles is negatively affected by the aging pipe system, thus endangering the health of its residents.

3. Henceforth, as climate change becomes a more pertinent problem, viticulturists must develop these new techniques or strategies for the cultivation of wine grapes in California in order to save the industry and effectively California's economy.

4. Recently, workers in this less developed area have not been able to keep their children in school or buy food for their families. Something has to be done about these American subsidies so as to provide these less fortunate people a fair chance at survival.

RP Thesis Statement Peer Review

1. Compare the previous thesis statements. Without the full introduction to fall back on, can you still answer the following questions: A) What is the problem, B) where does it exist, C) who is causing it, and D) why is it important? (And, perhaps, when did it arise?) If any one of these elements is missing, what suggestions would you give for revision?

2. Organization: Do the answers to *what*, *where*, *who*, and *why* follow each other in a logical order and create a distinct picture, or do the facts seem arbitrarily "thrown together"?

3. Make sure for each thesis that this problem hasn't already been solved and that it is potentially solvable. If the problem doesn't meet one or both of these two criteria, suggest a revision.

4. Is the problem addressed in each thesis sufficiently specific? If not, how might you narrow it further? Be specific.

5. Is each thesis well-written and appropriately formal?

7.7.4   RP Background/Context

In this section, you are responsible for demonstrating the depth and range of your research and your knowledge of how your specific problem developed. This section will likely be several paragraphs in length, and must show your reader that you are thoroughly informed on the scope and context of the problem. This section will:

Explain more about the context of the problem. If the problem is regional, you may need to explain why the problem is confined to this region. Is the problem connected to other issues—for example, a recent war or economic downturn?

Include some information on the scientific, cultural, economic, societal, and/or political influences on the problem. In other words, what types of events led up to your specific problem? This is information that you will later integrate into your thinking on the historical analysis essay.

Use specific, cited evidence to give a full picture of the severity and importance of the problem. This is probably where you will include the three cited sources (be sure to integrate your quotations and use correct MLA citation style).

Here's an example of one paragraph of background information. As you read this, consider how clearly the student describes the context, which influences are key, and what kind of evidence the student draws on to make his case:

SAMPLE BACKGROUND INFORMATION PARAGRAPH

A problem that eventually led to the movement away from the electric car was rooted in its design. Due to its low speeds and the long amount of time it took to recharge the battery, the electric proved to be suited only for limited use, and the design was mostly pushed aside by 1920 ("Automobile"). Gasoline vehicles became more popular, propelled by Henry Ford's mass production of his famous Model Ts. As the price to purchase a car went down and gasoline remained reasonably priced, most American families became car owners by 1925 (McShane, par. 4). The gasoline-powered vehicle became a viable and appealing option to the public, and it took over the reigns from the electric vehicle. America held the top spot as the most automobile-dependent country by the close of the twentieth century, and was accordingly also the nation with the heaviest reliance on petroleum. By the year 1990, the average family owned two cars and the mileage per year increased (McShane, para. 16).

> ## Background Information Paragraph Peer Review Questions
>
> 1. Paraphrase the problem. Does it seem viable (narrow, solvable, urgent)?
>
> 2. Understanding that you are missing information from the Introduction of this sample, can you tell who or what is hurt by this problem? What is the extent of the hurt? Who or what has caused the hurt?
>
> 3. What purpose is this particular paragraph serving? Does it provide information about the influences on the problem? Which influences does the paragraph highlight (notice organization)? What evidence does the writer use to make the case?
>
> 4. Does it give a sense of context, scope, or urgency? How clearly does it describe these aspects?

7.7.5 RP Research Questions

In this section, you will lay the groundwork for the historical analysis and advocacy essays by establishing what questions you need to ask in order to understand the historical development of and solution to the problem. The best proposals do not simply present a list of brainstormed questions. Instead, the authors use a mixture of statement, analysis, and questioning to give a clear sense of their direction for the next ten weeks. They also demonstrate that they have already answered most basic questions about their topic, and will be moving on to more complex issues.

> ## How to Generate Research Questions
>
> 1. Start by offering what you currently know about the historical causes of the problem (be prepared to offer at least one). This could be any causal event that directly influenced the development of the problem, whether political, scientific, technological, natural, etc.
>
> 2. Then begin a list of questions that will help you understand more about the problem and its context. In short, these questions should be even more complicated versions of the basic "who, what, where, when, why, how" questions.

(continued)

3. Next, develop a set of questions that help you explore why the problem still exists, and who is working toward a solution. Remember: you will eventually need to advocate a solution, so it's important to ask questions now about who would benefit from solving this problem, and who would benefit from the status quo. Start to identify the major players, the experts, and the activists who are involved in the problem and its resolution.

NOTE: *The Bedford Researcher* contains helpful tips on developing research questions.

7.7.6   RP Review of the Research

This final paragraph will summarize the research you have done so far, including a statement of the problem and its effects today, some of its causal history, and some likely solutions (here you are briefly re-stating what you have laid out in the research proposal so far). Also include a review of the research you have done: search engines used, types of sources, biases—if any—of sources, timeliness of materials, and anything else that is appropriate here. List the five best "keywords" you have found useful. Finally, conclude your proposal by briefly indicating your plan for continuing your research.

The Writing Process: From Draft to Final Copy

Your instructor will supply you with full samples of several research proposals, but for now, take a look at one student's progress on his introduction as he worked from draft to final copy.

 SAMPLE INTRO PARAGRAPH: INITIAL DRAFT

Imagine a calf being ripped from its mother, father, sisters, and brothers, and pushed into a crowd filled with others just like it. Screams of pain and confusion jump from its lips as it cries for its mommy. She cannot hear it. The poor calf cannot even hear itself. Shoved along it eventually trips and twists its ankle rendering it immobile. The herders prod the calf along to get keep going but it cannot move. The calf's inability to move frustrates them and they pierce its skin with their sharp poking. Once dragged along the way it has no capacity to move, breathe, or even think. Presently, this is the horrific treatment that cattle used for slaughter face on a daily basis so that humans may buy their meat at the supermarket. The fact that humans kill other living creatures to feed themselves may be considered a problem itself, but the fact that they maliciously harm these living creatures right before their untimely end, is a problem that needs to be addressed at once. According to John Solomon Otto, Assistant Professor, American Studies Department at the University of Maryland, cattle were not always treated as walking food—they used to be creatures that were used mostly for grazing on the open range (Otto). As they became more domesticated, humans realized their potential for sustenance. In becoming domesticated, cattle began to be viewed as inferior due to their ultimate fate. Because they are seen as already dead, American slaughterhouses abuse cattle in a multitude of ways and it is not humane. Cattle should be treated with as much respect as cats or dogs get because they provide humans with labor, nutrition in milk and beef, and most importantly because they feel just as humans do; their treatment is directly related to the contributions they make to humans, therefore it is imperative that penalties on slaughterhouses that violate legislation need to be stronger and strictly enforced.

Introduction Peer Review

1. How does the introduction work organizationally? The final stage should comprise a definition of a problem, but how does the introduction begin? By telling a story, asking a question, delivering a powerful statistic?

2. Does the introduction give you an idea of the current state of the problem and does it convince you to care about the problem?

3. Does the introduction use evidence to back up its claims? Are the sources credible?

4. Comment on writing style and ethos.

5. Locate the thesis. Does the initial part of the introduction move seamlessly into the thesis?

SAMPLE INTRO PARAGRAPH: FINAL COPY

The Need for Stronger Enforcement and Surveillance in Cattle Slaughterhouses

Imagine a calf at the abattoir. Shoved along, this particular calf twists its ankle rendering it immobile. It stops, but herders prod the calf along. The calf's inability to move frustrates them and they pierce its skin with their sharp poking. This goes on for several minutes before the calf is dragged to the killing floor by its neck. Presently, this is the horrific treatment that cattle face so that we can have meat. The fact that humans kill other living creatures to feed themselves may be considered a problem itself, but that they harm these living creatures right before their untimely end, is a problem that needs to be addressed at once. According to John Solomon Otto, Assistant Professor, American Studies Department at the University of Maryland, cattle were not always treated as walking food—they used to be creatures that were used mostly for grazing on the open range (18). As they became more domesticated, cattle began to be viewed as inferior. This then eases our conscience and facilitates inhumane treatment. Cattle should be treated with respect: they provide humans with labor, nutrition in milk and beef, and there is evidence that they are creatures with emotional lives. Their treatment should be directly related to the contributions they make to humans; therefore, it is imperative that penalties on slaughterhouses that violate legislation be stronger and strictly enforced.

Working Draft to Final Draft: Review Questions

1. What do you notice immediately about the two versions? How are they different from one another?

2. How does each version work structurally? Identify the leading idea of each paragraph in the final copy, and note how they transition from one to another. Can you identify the same ideas in the draft? Are they ordered differently?

3. What stylistically and/or in terms of the writing itself has changed or improved?

You might find that there are still things that could be improved in the student's final copy. If so, that's good, since you want to develop your ability to revise and edit your own work.

7.8   Historical Analysis/Community History Essay

The Historical Analysis or Community History essay assignment builds on the research and writing you did for your first assignment. Between the time when you write the first formal assignment and the time when this essay is due, you will have had a chance to continue researching and reading about your topic; therefore, significant revision and rethinking is expected and required for a superior grade on this assignment. Keep in mind that the next essay (either the Advocacy Essay or Critical Biography) will build on the work you do in this essay, and the strength of the argument you make in that final essay will depend, in part, on the clarity of the researched knowledge you gain regarding the historical context of a problem or community. Here are some specific objectives for this essay:

- To research and read more deeply about the topic you've been researching.
- To develop an analytical argument about history (not just a report on history).
- To think, read, and write critically about the sources you've found.
- To integrate your own ideas with these sources.
- To write a formal, academic essay, and to understand the conventions of an academic audience.

Your essay must have a focused thesis that outlines your perspective on the primary scientific, cultural, financial, societal, and/or political events, trends, and/or perceptions that have shaped the history of your problem or the history of a community; the body of the paper must demonstrate that you understand how events or trends shaped various outcomes, and therefore it can't simply be a listing of events. The moments that you include should have a clear rhetorical purpose. Your essay should be thesis-driven, focused, descriptive, specific, argumentatively sound, and targeted to academic readers.

7.8.1   Examining the Prompt

What does it mean to analyze history? First, you'll have to have a pretty good understanding of what you're writing a history about: "the problem" or "the community." Then you'll have to research and read until you can develop a historical timeline of your problem—events, people, places, and things that constitute the development of the current problem or of a community. After you have a good general understanding, you'll have to break history into parts: choose a few moments (interactions, artifacts, people) that represent the most important moments in this history.

The prompt for the Historical Analysis assignment says, "Write a thesis-driven historical analysis of a problem that has developed because of human activity or inactivity," and the prompt for the Community History assignment requires the same thesis-driven historical analysis. Let's take a closer look at what these prompts are asking.

Thesis-Driven

This means that you have thought out a compelling structure for your argument which will orient your reader. A thesis as foundational structural component is a convention of academic essays, although the type of thesis will change according to the demands of the assignment (your rhetorical situation).

Analysis

In WR 39B, you wrote a rhetorical analysis, breaking a text into parts to analyze their rhetorical impact. Now you are being asked to analyze "the history of a problem" instead of an assigned text. Although what you're analyzing is different, the basic method remains the same: break the thing being analyzed into logical, relevant parts and then look closely at each part and how each part fits into the whole. If you need a refresher on the meaning of analysis for an academic audience, see "Analysis" in Chapter 4.

Historical

For any historical problem, there will be more points in history than you can write about in a short essay; therefore, you have to pick the most important moments to focus on.

In an historical analysis, you are arguing that these events are the most important moments for understanding how this problem has developed. Research and revision will be necessary before you will be able to develop a focused thesis that outlines what you believe to be the primary scientific, cultural, financial, societal, and/or political events, trends, and/or perceptions that have shaped the history of your problem.

Problem

Your task is not to write the history of a problem in general. Instead, you must analyze how particular events, trends, or other factors shaped or contributed to the development of the problem as it currently exists.

Community

The term "community" can refer to a place, a city, state, or region from which the subject originates or resides. However, it can also refer to something temporal, like the "late '80s" or "the Depression." It can refer to a social or political milieu, like "the Civil Rights Movement," "the Dixie-crats," or "Grunge." Or it can describe a certain loosely-defined subset of people who have a shared interest, like "the scientific community" or "the business community." Be careful to define your "community" narrowly enough so that you can investigate it usefully in six pages. This may require some temporal and/or spatial limits on a broader community; for example, "the Chicago business community in the early 1940s."

7.8.2 Historical Analysis or Community History Thesis

A thesis provides the framework of an essay, making the essay's structure clear and giving it a sense of direction. Before drafting your thesis, you should research wide and deep: look for political, cultural, economic, ecological, sociological, and other facets of the history of this problem or community, and look for multiple perspectives.

It is hard to write a thesis if you haven't done enough research. At the same time, it is difficult to do research if you don't at least have a draft thesis to direct your research. Do enough preliminary research to at least draft a preliminary thesis that anticipates where your research might lead. Then, you can do the research necessary to "test" your thesis, and revise it to reflect what the actual evidence reveals.

As you research and read, it will become clear to you which moments you should highlight in your brief history; these will be the seed of your thesis statement.

Be Concise and Specific

A thesis statement should be concise. If, when you first draft your thesis, it is several sentences long, try to revise it down into one compact statement. Revising into one sentence will help you focus on what is most important.

Focus on Specific Historical Moments

Your thesis should mention the specific moments that you will argue contribute to the history of the problem that you will analyze. The following thesis does not focus on specific moments:

- Piracy, thought to be a problem of the past, is alive off the coast of Somalia because of Imperialist intervention in Somalia and its waters.

Go Beyond Historical Narrative

Your thesis should go beyond just telling a story and also foreshadow your analysis about this community's influence on your subject. The following thesis does not predict analysis (or mention a problem):

- Chocolate has changed from a liquid that was only available to the elites to a solid that is available to everyone; chocolate is now common and is produced everywhere.

Connect the History to the Problem

Your thesis needs all three: *analysis* of the *history* of a *problem*, and there should be connections between them. The following thesis infers analysis and a problem, but doesn't mention specific history, and doesn't make connections between the three elements:

- Although scientific as well as societal sources have encouraged against the use of tobacco, teenagers today continue to use tobacco as a result of social trends, cultural perception, and their different economic backgrounds.

Do More than Argue "This Is a Problem"

You cannot just state that your problem exists and contend that it is significant—you must analyze the history of the problem. The following thesis designates a significant problem without analyzing its history:

- Successful floral cultivation and productivity require the use of pesticides "to reduce crop loss and improve the flowers' appearance" (Gale). The use of pesticides is important to keep the cut-flower industry profitable and in business. However, pesticides have been described as potentially threatening to the health and safety of farm workers, the environment, and consumers.

◯ SAMPLE HA THESIS STATEMENTS

1. Despite consumers' tendency to focus on the positive aspects of the drug advertised and overlook its negative aspect, the FDA allowed the distribution of Direct to Consumer (DTC) ads. Since the FDA lifted the 1982 moratorium, the use of DTC ads have increased so rapidly that the FDA has failed to competently regulate them, which allows the broadcast of misleading materials and ultimately jeopardizes public health.

2. The issue of child labor and slavery in the growing of cocoa beans has been the result of many factors, the three most significant being the start of continuous economic dependence of African countries on cocoa export since the 1970s, cocoa's fluctuation and drop in prices since 1977, and also the failure and shortcoming of efforts such as the Agricultural Appropriations bill and the Harkin-Engle Protocol made in 2001 in response to the issue.

3. The inadequate use of tPA can be attributed to neurologists' resistance to adopt the drug, controversy regarding tPA's manufacturer, Jeanne Lenzer's article in the *British Medical Journal* attacking tPA with false accusations, and the failure of the American government to complete action on the Stroke Treatment and Ongoing Prevention Act of 2001, collectively shaking medical professionals' confidence in the drug and preventing adequate public awareness (Zivin); (H.R. 3431).

HA Thesis Peer Review Questions

1. What is the problem that will be discussed and elaborated upon in this essay? How is the problem defined?

2. Does the writer clearly identify specific moments in the history of the problem?

3. Is the statement concise and accurate? What words, phrases, or even sentences might be deleted?

The thesis for the Community History paper, specifically, should be a cause-effect argument about a particular, influential community in history. As such, it answers the question "Why," and should offer an answer: "Because." Why did this community arise at this particular point in history? Why did it become significant and influential, and in what ways?

⬤ SAMPLE COMMUNITY HISTORY THESIS STATEMENTS

1. The Great Depression decade shaped cinema's role as the outlet for rage against government and law and escapist fantasies for the poor, thus attracting citizens of all ages to indulge in film.

2. The Black Panther Party was created with the goal of framing a new impression of civil rights in the local and national media, upholding the full title of the Civil Rights Act of 1964, and policing the rising rate of police brutality in predominately black neighborhoods.

Community History Thesis Peer Review Questions

1. Can you identify the "why" and "because" these essays probably offer about their respective communities?

2. Is it clear from the thesis what topics or events the paper will discuss?

3. Do either of these thesis statements provide more than just a narrative about the history?

7.8.3 Historical Analysis or Community History Introduction

Your introduction is the first thing your reader will see—you're making first impressions that will have a lasting effect on your reader. Make sure that it sets an academic tone and establishes your ethos. Take your time, introduce everything that needs an introduction, use the best sources you can possibly find, and revise often for precise and concise word choice. Don't worry if your introduction is more than one paragraph long.

Your Introduction Should Include

1. An introduction to the current state of the problem or scope and significance of the community that makes the reader care about it.

2. A frame for the aspects of problem you'll focus on and its historical timeline (your perspective on the problem). For the Community History, a clear statement of the focused history related to this particular community.

3. Highly credible sources.

4. A thesis statement that forecasts the rest of the essay's content (specific historical moments for analysis) and structure.

The Writing Process: From Draft to Final Copy

Below, there are two sample introductions, the first from an early draft, and the second from the final copy.

 SAMPLE INTRODUCTION: INITIAL DRAFT

As crime rates began to soar in the 1970s, drastic measures were introduced by the United States government in hopes to alleviate the supposed chaos that was looming. One of the biggest social reforms that they adopted was the anti-drug campaign launched in 1971 by President Richard Nixon who blamed illegal pharmaceuticals for the existing problems within society. The notorious "War on Drugs" was intended to discourage the production, distribution, and consumption of narcotics. The advocates of the movement, however, never thought of the devastating consequences that would follow, like overcrowding in prisons, which is a prevalent issue that Californians are facing today. The social sentiment of that era was targeted towards the general welfare of the public by reducing crime, thus the government creating harsh criminal justice policies that would emphasize longer prison stays as punishment for offenders. The epitome of these policies would be the 1994 California Three Strikes Law which required a life sentence after a third felony conviction. The "War on Drugs" and Three Strikes Law attempted to rid the streets of drugs and crime to benefit society as a whole, but in turn led to the over capacity of prisoners in the California Penitentiary System.

 SAMPLE INTRODUCTION: FINAL DRAFT

Over the past three decades, California has made numerous attempts to stop the soaring crime rate; however, it seems as though plans have failed with prison overcrowding creating an even bigger issue. Since the 1970s, drastic measures have been taken to inflict harsher sentencing guidelines to emphasize strict criminal-justice policies. Consequently, the prolonged stay of prisoners as a form of punishment has resulted in correctional facilities unable to provide adequate resources for their inmates, in addition to billions of dollars spent by taxpayers annually. The ongoing cycle of high recidivism and crime rate has plagued California for years, with mass incarcerations burdening legislators and citizens alike.

With social and political reforms centered on public safety, laws were created to alleviate the chaos stemming from crime. The biggest of these reforms was the War on Drugs campaign first introduced by President Richard Nixon in 1971. Nixon, along with his administration, blamed illegal pharmaceuticals for the problems existing within society. The "tough on crime" sentiment continued as these newly established laws were ratified, incarcerating thousands of prisoners each year for longer periods of time. The cornerstone of these hard-on-crime policies was the California Three Strikes Law (AB971) enacted in 1994, which required a life sentence after a third felony conviction.

Currently, California houses more than 173,000 inmates in thirty three prisons meant to hold half the existing population, where 16,000 of the inhabitants are forced to resort to cots, gyms, hallways, and classrooms for livable space, reports Jennifer Steinhauer, a New York Times writer (3). Due to the burgeoning prison population, members incarcerated have been subjected to unsanitary living conditions, neglectful mental/medical healthcare, and substandard security. The policies resulting from the War on Drugs and the Three Strikes Law are the prime causes of overcrowding in the California Penitentiary System due to their emphasis on the political slogan "tough on crime."

Peer Review Questions

1. Based on the changes from draft to final copy, what kinds of comments do you think the writer received?

2. What's clearer in the revision?

7.8.4   Presenting Evidence

In 39B, you practiced writing unified, fully developed paragraphs. Even though your particular writing challenge in 39C may be different, the principles of writing good paragraphs remain the same. You will need to write paragraphs that have clear, focused topic sentences that are clearly connected to your overall argument. Each subsequent sentence, in turn, must connect to and make logical steps derived from that topic sentence. Below you will find one writer's analysis of some of the causes of the overuse of pesticides in the pineapple fields of Costa Rica. Read the discussion questions that follow the passage carefully. Your instructor may have you write out the answers to the questions or she may use them for an in-class discussion.

⬤ SAMPLE HA EVIDENCE PARAGRAPH

Price wars are not the only cause of pressure for producers to operate cheaply, as Wal-Mart factors in as well. Producers do not set their own prices for the product they cultivate; instead, the ultimate buying power falls in the hands of the big retailers like Wal-Mart. If the big sellers like Wal-Mart do not buy pineapples from the producers like Del Monte and Dole, then their profit falls significantly. In March of 2006, Wal-Mart acquired a majority of shares in CARHCO, the Central American Retail Holding Company, and changed the name to Wal-Mart Central America (Rasine). In April of 2006, Wal-Mart Central America made an announcement that it would begin directly exporting pineapples from Costa Rica into the U.S. Chairman of the Board of Directors Fernando Paiz highlighted in a 2007 interview a recent contract for shipments of pineapples to be sent directly to the U.S. from Costa Rica (Rasine). In other words, Wal-Mart gained the ability to directly use their buying power in Costa Rica to put the squeeze on the producers operating there. Wal-Mart uses this extreme buying power to set the prices for the fruit, and pressure for lower prices caused companies like PINDECO to resort to methods such as replacing workers with chemicals, and in Costa Rica there is nothing stopping them from doing so (Tocco, Sneidelman).

HA Evidence Peer Review Questions

1. What is the topic sentence of the paragraph? Does each other sentence develop it?

2. Does each sentence connect to the next, and make logical steps derived from the topic sentence? Are there any sentences that seem to be unconnected to those around them? Do you have suggestions for the writer to help us understand undrawn connections? (Logic words—but, however, because of—can help)

3. What types of evidence are used to develop the point? Is there enough evidence? How credible is the evidence? Does it inform, illustrate, or support the writer's argument?

4. How effectively does the writer introduce her sources as authorities? How credible are the sources?

5. How well integrated are the sources and their evidence into the writer's argument? Are there places where the writer lets the source *make* her argument instead of using it to *help it*?

(continued)

6. Are the sentences well written? Are there instances of overly conversational tone, or glaring mechanical errors? Are transition words used correctly and effectively? Notice tense shifts, and the use of passive versus active voice, and note whether they are necessary.

7.8.5   Integrating a Graphic Illustration

Your graphic may be a map, cartoon, table, chart, graph, drawing, or photograph—but it should not be merely decorative. Indeed, proper use of graphic evidence requires as much thought as using any other evidence.

Using graphic evidence poses three main challenges: finding an effective graphic, explaining its relevance to your argument, and displaying and citing it using MLA conventions.

Finding a Good Graphic

Review your sources. Often, professional or scholarly texts will include good graphic illustrations that you can cite, just as you cite their words. You can use Google's "Images" search or the UCI Libraries' LexisNexis "Statistical Universe." Or, you can prepare your own graphic illustration: a chart or table of statistical information that you locate in your research. However you find the graphics, choose from among them one that efficiently communicates the point that you want to make.

Explaining Your Graphic's Relevance

Chapter 4, section 4.10 introduces the "Three-Step Method" for integrating quotations. Implicit there is the idea that facts don't speak for themselves. Like quotations, the facts of a graphic require explanation. Your graphic should not puzzle or confuse your reader, or lead her to come to the opposite conclusion from you. So you must explain how exactly the graphic makes your argument. This is true whether you use the graphic to show the problem's severity, or to show a key moment or moments in the problem's historical evolution.

Displaying and Citing Your Graphic According to MLA Conventions

In the essay itself, display the graphic with a label, such as "Fig. 1." and provide the publishing information that identifies where you got the graphic. Subsequent graphics, if any, should be labeled Fig. 2., Fig. 3., etc.

Double-space this publishing information below the graphic and divide it with two double-spaced lines from the text of the essay that follows the graphic. (Use MLA "note form.") When properly cited in your text, graphics do not need to be included in your Works Cited. Like all MLA matters, this formatting is neither optional nor insignificant.

Practice: Integrating Graphics

Writers of Historical Analysis essays are frequently attempting to answer one or more of the following questions when using graphic evidence: "Who or what is being harmed?" "What is the extent of that harm?" "How has this problem come to be?" What are the writers below attempting to accomplish with regard to these questions?

● SAMPLE GRAPHIC #1

In 2006, EPA and USDA recognized agricultural production as the largest phosphorus contributor to the Chesapeake Bay according to their *Evaluation Report: Saving the Chesapeake Bay Watershed Requires Better Coordination of Environmental and Agricultural Resources*:

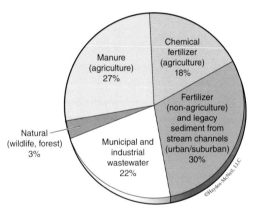

Note: Wastewater loads based on measured discharges; rest based on an average-hydrology year.

Figure 1. Sources of Phosphorus to Bay from Bill A. Roderick and Phyllis Fong; "Evaluation Report: Saving the Chesapeake Bay Watershed Requires Better Coordination of Environmental and Agricultural Resources"; EPA and USDA, 2006; Web; 15 Oct. 2010.

As shown in figure 1, contributing 45% of the Bay's phosphorus, agricultural production needed to be changed to better sustain and improve water quality in the Bay. Large loadings of inorganic nutrients such as phosphorus from agricultural fertilizer entered the Bay and resulted in the future oxygen-removing algal blooms that would plague the Bay during the summer to this day.

SAMPLE GRAPHIC #2

The next crucial turning point in the history of the automobile industry was from the early 1950s to the late 1960s when the demand for automobiles saw an enormous increase, which established America as a nation of personal rather than public transportation and further increased America's carbon dioxide emissions. From 1900 to 1929 the United States automobile industry saw automobile sales increase from just about 0 cars per United States citizen to around .2 cars per United States citizen (Smith 37). However, in 1929 automobiles sales were thwarted by the great depression, and sales remained relatively stagnant for the ensuing 20 years. According to Michael Boskin, a Stanford university economics professor, when the economic times were challenging, as they were from 1930s to 1950s, citizens would rely more on public transportation such as trains in order to fulfill their daily transportation needs, and consumers simply could not afford to purchase new automobiles (para 7). However, after World War II the United States economy had rebounded drastically, and America maintained the largest GDP per capita in the world.

The influx of wealth into United States directly caused an increase in automobile sales. From 1950–1968, vehicles per U.S. citizen rose from .2 per U.S. citizen to .6 per U.S. citizen, roughly a 300% increase (Smith 41). America's Population from 1950s to the 1970s doubled, which consequently increased the need for transportation. The increase in transportation needs had devastating effects on the environment, because it is clear that America's carbon dioxide emissions increased with the greatest velocity from the 1950–1970. Below Figure 1 is a graph from the Carbon Dioxide Information Analysis Center of the United States Department of Energy which illustrates the immense increase in North America's carbon dioxide emissions from 1950–1970, which can be directly attributed to the increase in automobile sales.

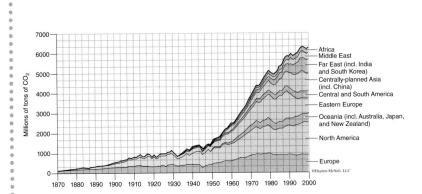

Figure 1. Global, Regional, and National Fossil Fuel CO_2 Emissions from G. Marland et al., In *Trends: A Compendium of Data on Global Change*; (Oak Ridge: Carbon Dioxide Information Analysis Center, Oak Ridge National Laboratory, U.S. Department of Energy, Oak Ridge, Tenn., United States., 2003) 253. Print.

Although figure 1 is not limited to carbon dioxide emissions from just automobiles, and again according to the World Resources Institute, the transportation sector of America's economy makes up 25% of all carbon dioxide emissions. The 1950s–1970s established the notion that personal transportation was necessary for all Americans, and this troubling notion was paralleled by an historic increase in carbon dioxide emissions.

Graphic Evidence Peer Review Questions

1. The graphic is evidence to support an argument being made by the writer. What is that argument (or claim)? Does the evidence seem to support a major aspect of the argument, or an inconsequential one?

2. Briefly summarize what the writer says about the graphic's meaning. Has the writer interpreted the graphic accurately and sufficiently?

3. Does the writer do enough to introduce the graphic and then explain it? Does he remember to use the graphic evidence as he would a written quotation—introduce source, integrate evidence, analyze evidence?

4. Are there any potential pitfalls with the graphic or its integration? Is anything unclear? What might we warn the writer about?

5. What would you like to know about this topic that could be represented graphically? Give two examples, and indicate what the labels on the x- and y-axes would be.

7.8.6   Historical Analysis Conclusion

Concluding paragraphs must be just as carefully developed as introductory paragraphs. While introductions often craft appeals to draw a reader into a discussion or argument, conclusions signal where your argument ends and where the reader's work (in the real world, for example) may begin. Introductions and conclusions provide the frame—or bookends—of your argument. Therefore, they need to be just as appealing as the argument they are framing.

Conclusions leave a lasting impression on your reader about your research quality, argument, and academic ethos. Don't undermine a superior and well-crafted argument by dashing off a generic paragraph or dumping in leftover research. Here are some tips for better conclusions:

- Avoid restating your thesis or repeating claims and evidence from the essay; instead, you could reiterate the seriousness of the problem and the urgency of its resolution.

- Develop pathos here by engaging the reader's emotions—you may want to appeal to values of morality, guilt, activism, or compassion for the affected people, ecosystems, and/or environment.

- Reconnect to the broader context of this issue—globalization, industrialization, urbanization, healthcare/school/food policy reform, etc.

- Give yourself time to revise your conclusion several times.

Consider the following models for concluding paragraphs:

- **Barrier to solutions:** Think of the one thing that may not have necessarily caused the problem but is the biggest barrier to solving the issue: Government ineffectuality? Too much partisanship? Corporate monopoly? Consumer apathy?

- **Good intentions gone wrong:** Sometimes solutions become part of the problem. Is there a particular law that was enacted to suit the needs of that time but now has actually made the crisis worse?

- **Cumulative effects:** One cause by itself may not have been bad enough but multiple mini-causes may seriously damage an already-compromised situation.

- **Update:** What is new about your problem today? What may have changed over the past week or month that could change the problem for better or worse? Weak economy? Newly elected Congress members? Proposed budget cuts? Rising unemployment or poverty rates? A natural disaster?

- Is there enough political will to solve your problem or is the solution more likely to be postponed yet again because other crises may have supplanted it?

- Looking forward: Now that we know about the problem, causes, and effects, we can think about effective solutions. Is there a particular organization, group, or agency that may be proposing reform and change? Is there a viable solution that a city or state may have already adopted to solve this problem that could act as a model? Is there a solution/bill that was passed recently which you think may not be a good solution and will worsen the crisis?

- Awareness: Are American citizens and consumers more aware about this issue today than they were months or years ago? How may you use this new awareness to create a sense of urgency and call to action for your reader?

- Is there a last image/idea you want to leave with your reader so that they are forced to think more deeply about this issue after finishing your essay? An anecdote, statistic, quote, or factoid?

● SAMPLE CONCLUSION #1

In conclusion, the global overfishing of Blue fin tuna has reached a critical state and is a threat to the species survival. The chain reaction of events rendered the Blue fin tuna in a critically endangered state. The inability of groups like the ICCAT to regulate Blue fin tuna coupled with wide consumer appeal for the taste of tuna are the biggest barrier to solving this issue. For decades this remains a problem and time is running out to save the Blue fin tuna. Today, stronger quotas are set that try to put a halt to overfishing, however the ICCAT still fails to establish any sort of management on global fishing. The WWF is one of the leading advocates of saving the Blue fin tuna and they are constantly trying to persuade and influence ICCAT's role in preventing overfishing. Currently, aquaculture (fish farms), offer a temporary solution to the demands of consumers but does not solve overfishing as a whole. A likely long-term solution to overfishing is stronger action and a bigger involvement by ICCAT to really crack down on overfishing. They need to take a stronger stance to convince the nations responsible for the most consumption of Blue fin tuna to limit their activities and impose punishments for violations of protection laws. However, judging by ICCAT's past actions on this topic, immediate action will most likely be delayed as many do not seem to care about the Blue fin tuna. There needs to be a sense of urgency dedicated to solve this problem as soon as possible or else things will continue they way they have been since the beginning of this crisis. The world needs to realize how critical this situation is and if nothing is done to change it, then the Blue fin tuna will disappear from the face of the Earth completely.

SAMPLE CONCLUSION #2

Financial aid for the middle class, from the beginning with private aid from top colleges to the overlapping grants awarded to the lower class, has had little to compensate for times of tuition increases and heightened competition with a large student population. Without foreseeing the need to fix a system that unjustly grants upcoming college students from middle class families, there will be a dilemma keeping students enrolled should there be a crisis in the work force and overall the economy and families having to pull their students out of college. Placing the burden on middle class families to bear the brunt of the price of education, would lead to the population as a whole to value less of the worth of higher education. Because education is an investment, middle class families may rationalize that it is better off to save money for times of uncertainty instead of taking a risk which once again repeat the cycle in reinforcing the belief that only higher class students can afford a higher education.

Concluding Paragraph Peer Review Questions

1. Do the opening sentences create a sense of urgency?

2. What kinds of appeals does the writer use? Are they persuasive?

3. Do you get a sense of the writer's analysis/argument and its significance and relevance to the big picture or the broader theme of the class?

4. Does the paragraph make the reader look ahead to what the next step may be in the cultural or political discussion of the issue?

5. How fluidly is the writer able to switch tenses in this paragraph?

6. Does the conclusion leave you with a positive final impression about the writer's ethos and problem's possible resolution?

7. What are the strengths and weaknesses of this paragraph?

7.9   The Advocacy Essay or Critical Biography

All quarter, you have spent time researching, reading, and writing about a current problem or about the success of a particular individual. You've been developing expertise on this topic, and you probably find that, now, you have a strong point of view as well.

As you've developed expertise on the problem's causes and effects, you've likely begun to consider what could be done to address it. The Advocacy Essay assignment asks you to do just that: to argue in favor of a specific policy that will fix the problem, or lessen its severity. Advocating a solution to your problem is an important next step in your development as a researcher. Not only does this project provide you with a chance to refine your research and revision strategies as you apply what you've learned from the Research Proposal and Historical Analysis assignments, it also gives you the opportunity to take on yet another rhetorical stance as you develop a persuasive argument.

For the "Defining Success" classes, you'll use what you've learned about the life of your research subject, plus the in-depth research skills you have acquired while investigating one specific community that influenced your subject, to build an argument about the specific factors that made it possible for this individual to become successful, framing your own argument about the nature of this individual's success.

As you'll recall from the first chapter of this book, rhetoric is both an interpretive and a productive art. This means rhetoric offers you a set of tools not only to analyze texts and ideas of others, but also to communicate your own ideas persuasively. The writing you've done so far this quarter has emphasized your analytical skills: you considered the influence of a writer's purpose, audience, and context on the argument in a source, and developed a sense of the historical context from which your research topic emerged. Your persuasiveness as a writer has been something you've thought about all quarter as well. For instance, you established your own credibility through the effective use of sources and considered the effect of one organizational method over another on your audience. The purpose of this final essay is for you to hone those abilities even further as you take on an argumentative stance and persuade an audience of other academics and committed stakeholders. The assignment is an exciting platform to draw on everything you've learned throughout your writing classes as you enter into the discourse community of this research topic.

7.9.1   Advocacy Research: Finding a Solution

One of the biggest challenges of this assignment is finding a solution to advocate. You have undoubtedly come across a number of policies in your research thus far. Still, to fully prepare to write the Advocacy Essay, you should research as many different proposed solutions as you can. These policies, solutions, initiatives, or plans may come from many different sources: corporations, advocacy groups, or local, state, federal, or foreign governments. Once you have found a wide range of possible solutions, you will advocate the one you think is best. This section will help guide you through the process.

What Is a Policy?

There are several definitions of the word "policy," but the one probably most useful for this project is from *Webster's Third International Dictionary*:

> Policy: a definite course or method of action selected (as by a government, institution, group, or individual) from among alternatives and in the light of given conditions to guide and use to determine present and future decisions.

From the definition, you can see that a policy is a method of action selected from among alternatives. In short, you do not have to find only legislative solutions to problems. Solutions come from a number of different places, and the government is only one place to look.

What Solutions Have Worked in the Past?

Before you start looking for a solution to be followed in the future, you should first understand what kinds of solutions are currently in place to help with the problem you've defined. These solutions might have come from a governmental body (laws, codes, statutes, regulations, ordinances, treaties, or similar international agreements). Other policies might be developed by non-governmental organizations (NGOs), business groups, unions, think tanks, and more.

In your previous research, you should already have identified some discussions about existing policies. You should already have identified the key players involved in or interested in the problem you've been researching, so before you dive into new research, read what you've already found. Chances are that the answer to "What's the best solution?" is in the research you've already discovered.

Where Can You Find Policy Information?

If a policy has been proposed by a government legislative body (international, federal, state, or local), try looking at government web sites where the policy was first proposed or the sites of politicians who support the policy. For U.S. federal policy, for example, look at **thomas.loc.gov** and **opencongress.org**. If the policy you are researching has been proposed by a private organization, look at that organization's web site.

If a known government agency, U.S. or international, has the official responsibility of implementing or enforcing a policy, their web site will provide good leads as to existing policies and their proposed changes.

If you find you need more detail or background, the UCI Libraries' subject guide for 39C also provides specific web sites and databases to help you with finding a policy. The **Policy Information** tab gives a crash course on policies and who might propose them. The **Find a Policy** tab lists the most relevant databases to help you and sorts them by international, federal, state, and non-governmental policies.

7.9.2   Advocacy Essay Proposal

Before drafting your Advocacy Essay, you will send a policy proposal to your instructor via email or the Writing Studio. Think of this short assignment as similar in form to your Research Proposal. Your performance on this assignment will be part of your Advocacy Essay grade. Your instructor will "green-light" viable policies and may require revisions of policies that do not fit the problem as you've presented it in your Historical Analysis essay, are too old, or are no longer viable (e.g., bills "dead" in committee).

This brief (1- to 2-page) proposal includes:

- The policy or solution you wish to advocate. Explain who crafted it, when it was introduced, and where it is in its development. This is where you need to be sure that the policy is already being proposed by some public entity, since this paper is about advocating an *existing* solution.

- Why this policy is the best solution to the problem you've identified. This is a first draft of your thesis statement and, as such, should explain the reasons this policy is the *best*, not merely state what the policy will do.

- One source that supports your policy.

- One source that challenges your policy directly, or that offers an alternate policy.

- A Works Cited list.

7.9.3   Advocacy Essay or Critical Biography Thesis

Although how you frame the problem is foundational to your advocacy argument, it should not be the focus of the thesis. Instead, your *thesis should focus on the reasons why your policy is the best solution to this problem*. That bears repetition: your thesis should focus on the **reasons why** your policy is the best solution to this problem. For the Critical Biography, your thesis needs to advance an argumentative claim about how Malcolm Gladwell's argument in *Outliers* applies to your research subject's success. To what extent can Gladwell's claims help your reader understand how and why your subject became successful, beyond individual merit and hard work? Does your subject defy a Gladwellian explanation in some way?

Remember that you are seeking your audience's cooperation. Your audience may be composed of groups or individuals with a range of values and concerns related to the problem and its solution or the nature of the success you're discussing. Persuading such an audience is most effective when you take on multiple approaches to defending your solution and draw on a number of argumentative strategies. Accordingly, your thesis points should not merely state the things the policy does, but rather suggest, in an analytical way, *why* those things are the best ways to solve or lessen the severity of the problem. Writing your thesis this way will also give your subsequent research a clearer direction.

In the case of the Critical Biography, your thesis should be more than a list of ingredients of success; rather, the thesis should highlight the relationships between the elements you've isolated.

When developing your thesis, it may help you to keep in mind these analytical frameworks for argument:

Causation

What are the root causes of the problem? Does your policy significantly address those causes more effectively than other solutions?

Research Direction. If, while researching for the historical analysis, you found persuasive evidence of a particular cause of your problem, research to find policies that directly address that cause.

> The renewal of the International Coffee Agreement is the most viable solution to the issue of small coffee farmer exploitation as the collapse of the original agreement allowed for the beginning of the problem in the first place. This new agreement provides for the participation of small farmers in the debate, providing environmental sustainability and helping small farmers stay afloat and compete in the world market.

Coverage (Comprehensiveness)

Does the policy satisfactorily address the problem for a significant number of those most affected by the problem? If so, consider using the policy's comprehensive approach as a reason for its superiority.

Research Direction: To support a coverage analysis, you will need to show how many people, or what groups of people, will be affected; for example, you might present demographic data or studies that quantify the effects of the problem and solution on different groups of people.

: The World Health Organization's "Rolling Back Malaria" program (RBM) cov-
: ers a large number of individuals worldwide including those currently infected
: with malaria while also protecting others from contracting this fatal disease.

Cost/Benefit

Do the policy's benefits exceed its costs?

Research Direction: To support a cost/benefit analysis, you will need to detail how much the policy will cost to implement, what benefits will come from it, and how long it will take for benefits to be seen. Although this will often take the form of an analysis of financial costs and benefits, other factors—like human well-being—can also be used. For federal policy proposals, the Congressional Budget Office may have budget estimates available; some think tanks may also have this information.

: The United States government bailout of insurance industry giant AIG was
: undoubtedly expensive, costing many tens of billions of dollars thus far. In ex-
: change, the government received nothing. The proposal to nationalize AIG, on
: the other hand, while costing several billion more, would offer complete gov-
: ernmental control of the company, and is therefore the best proposal available.

Feasibility

Is the policy feasible? Is it more realistic than other solutions? Is it easy enough to implement, without significant negative consequences for other social interests? Does it have enough support from significant parties to make it likely to be passed and implemented?

Research Direction: To support a feasibility analysis, you will need to present evidence to show that implementation of the policy is feasible in terms of money, time, and support. You will want to show that there is enough political or popular will to support the policy and/or that implementing it would not be overly difficult or expensive. You might present budget data, public opinion polls, as well as politicians' statements and voting records on similar proposals.

- Because it has the support of both the American and Botswanan governments, the UN Aids education program is the most likely to mitigate the problem of Aids orphans in Botswana.

Comparison

Comparison is usually a *type* of feasibility argument. To make a comparative argument, you ask: has a similar policy worked significantly well in another comparable context?

Research Direction: To support a comparative analysis, you will need to present evidence to show that a similar policy has worked before in a similar context (i.e., in another city, state, or country, or at some time in the past). In addition to showing that the policy worked well in the other context, you want to make it clear that the other context is relevant and likely to work in the current circumstances. You may want to look at historical data or policy reviews, for example.

- In the European Union, where legislation like the GM Labeling Bill is already in place, consumers have been given more information about their food, and have been able to make successful dietary changes. Therefore, it only makes sense to adopt such a bill in the United States.

From Draft to Final Copy: The Advocacy Thesis

SAMPLE THESIS: INITIAL DRAFT

- This bill provides a superior solution over others because it is cost effective, feasible, addresses the core of the problem, and is comprehensive.

SAMPLE THESIS: FINAL COPY

- The "Voting Opportunity and Technology Enactment Rights Act of 2009" is the superior solution because it is more cost effective than Charlie Crist's solution, addresses the software problem, is feasible in an economically tough time, and fixes all the touch screen machines in the United States of America.

Thesis Draft to Final Copy Peer Review Questions

1. What do you notice immediately about the two versions? How are they different from one another?

2. What does the writer gain by using concrete facts and tailoring the analytical frameworks to his specific solution?

Not all thesis statements must be contained in one or even two short sentences. For this paper, it is possible to weave the elements of your thesis statement through a full paragraph, narrowing down as you go. Look at this sample to see some possible benefits.

● ALTERNATE SAMPLE THESIS 1

The ecosystem of the Sacramento-San Joaquin Delta has been deteriorating over past decades and will only continue to worsen unless a change is brought about. As the circle of ongoing predicaments indicates, what is ultimately needed to solve the problem of the Delta's declining ecosystem is to create a peripheral canal, which would simultaneously meet the demands of water exportation. First proposed in 1963 by an Interagency Delta Committee and re-emerging with the recent election of Governor Jerry Brown, a peripheral canal would transport water around the Delta instead of directly through it, addressing the root cause of the Delta's current canal design that is threatening its ecosystem. Although another viable solution would be to end water exports altogether, since it would be best for Delta fish, it is unrealistic to cut off Southern California's major water supply because doing so would be exceedingly costly. A peripheral canal would be the best solution because it would address the necessities of a reliable water supply and improve conditions for Delta fish, working toward restoration of the Delta's ecosystem while maintaining cost-efficiency. By providing reliability, a peripheral canal would also relieve public insecurities created by the worsening condition of the Delta's current infrastructure. If the existing infrastructure were to fail, California would lose complete use of Delta water; the state's primary water supply. Furthermore, although support for a peripheral canal depends on where people live, this solution would ultimately benefit California as a whole.

Thesis Peer Review Questions

1. Does the writer succinctly reintroduce the problem she will have laid out in the (unseen) introductory section?

2. From this paragraph alone, does the writer convince you that she understands the causes as well as the current state of the problem?

3. What are the writer's strategies for persuading the reader of the importance of this topic?

4. Locate the thesis. Note that it's not confined to just one or two sentences. How does the extended length of the thesis work for the argument?

(continued)

5. Does the thesis answer the question: Why is this solution the best solution to the problem? How many reasons does the writer give you as to why this solution is the best one? Do the reasons seem logical and persuasive? How well do the reasons given in support of the policy match the problem?

ALTERNATE SAMPLE THESIS 2

Bruce Lee once said, "To hell with circumstances; I create opportunities!" This is a true statement, since Bruce had done away with circumstances that held him back, such as the lack of money, racism, and a back injury, and instead used them as a stepping stone to success. According to Malcolm Gladwell's *Outliers: The Story of Success*, "achievement is talent plus preparation," but it does not stop there; in addition to having some sort of "innate talent," the person must be prepared to achieve (38). Furthermore, Gladwell states, people are the "beneficiaries of hidden advantages and extraordinary opportunities," and do not reach success just because of their hard work (19). Bruce Lee, many could argue, was a man who achieved success merely because he was dedicated to what he did—martial arts and acting—and kept doing it. To the public eye, Gladwell's "ten-thousand hour rule" is an obvious facet of Bruce Lee's success, since he did not stop practicing his martial arts and honing his skills and physique from day one. But on the deeper level, there are several aspects of success that apply to Bruce Lee, outside forces that manifested themselves, that in turn allowed him to get this practice time. Growing up in harsh conditions caused him to take up Kung Fu as a form of defense, the Chinese culture and philosophy regarding martial arts had him hooked to learning and forming his own ideas, and being in an America that was not familiar with any Chinese martial arts allowed him to be the first to introduce and popularize Kung Fu in the form of popular media.

Thesis Peer Review Questions

1. Does the writer succinctly introduce the research subject, as well as Gladwell's argument?

2. From this paragraph alone, does the writer convince you he understands the obvious and underlying causes of the research subject's success, and the relationship between them?

3. What are the writer's strategies for persuading the reader of the importance of this research subject?

7.9.4 Anticipating the Opposition

> If you know the enemy and know yourself you need not fear the result of a
> hundred battles. If you know yourself but not the enemy for every victory
> gained you will also suffer a defeat. If you know neither the enemy nor yourself
> you will succumb in every battle.
>
> —Sun Tzu, "The Art of War"

Argument is not war, but the idea behind Sun Tzu's philosophy applies: to win
an argument, you have to understand the opposition. And you need a persuasive
response to any criticism they might have about the plan you're advocating.

There are two basic ways that you can introduce an opposition argument into
your advocacy essay:

Find Opposition to the Policy You Advocate

To find opposition to a particular bill or policy, take a broad view of opposition
itself. For example, although you are unlikely to find anyone who is publicly
"pro-obesity," you will undoubtedly find individuals or organizations who oppose spending money to support anti-obesity programs, or who oppose your
policy's approach to addressing the problem.

Find an Alternative Solution to Compare

Because you are dealing with an important problem that has an effect on many
people, you can be sure that more than one solution has been proposed. An
alternative policy is, implicitly, an opposition to your policy.

Consider searching for trade or industry perspectives on the solution. The **ABI/
Inform** and **Business Source Complete** databases are very good sources of trade
information. As a general rule, you can assume that opposition to a proposed
course of action will come from politicians who object to spending money to
implement programs and/or from industry representatives who object to governmental regulation of their activities. Look at politicians' and organizational web
sites for various perspectives about the problem or the solution.

If you have a good sense of who is for your policy, you will have an easier time
figuring out who is against it. You may have to read the text of web sites that
support the bill to determine what opposition they anticipate. Other resources
that can give you ideas about who might be opposed to a particular course of
government action, and more importantly, why they are opposed to it, are the
Opposing Viewpoints database (available through the UCI Libraries) and the
"Issues" page of Politics1.com <http://www.politics1.com/issues.htm>.

Practice: Addressing the Opposition

 SAMPLE: OPPOSITION PARAGRAPH

Compared to other proposed solutions, Roll Back Malaria has been severely criticized for making its goals too ambitious to be achieved, mostly for fiscal reasons. Gavin Yamey of the British Medical Journal has already called RBM "a failing health initiative" (Yamey 1086). Yamey comes to this conclusion because he believes that donors have not been providing the donations and aid they initially promised (Yamey 1086). Additional RBM criticism is mentioned an article titled "Roll Back Malaria? The Scarcity of International Aid for Malaria Control" written by Vasant Narasimhan and Amir Attaran, both part of the Center for Human Rights Policy at Harvard University. They come together to argue that the total amount needed to reach such a goal far exceeds available financial aid (Naraisham and Attaran 1). However, with the amount of support RBM has already gained, reaching complete malaria eradication is not too ambitious. Roll Back Malaria has a great potential to reaching its goal because big name supporters strongly believe in this policy and have already promised to donate and fund the cause. The World Health Organization initially introduced this policy and has taken on the role to become the main backbone; foreseeing that this policy makes progress and stays on the right track. Along with WHO, major names such as UNICEF, UNDP, and the World Bank have made a commitment to make RBM one of their priorities. Even the United States has shown their support through the President's Malaria Initiative. In 2005, President George Bush announced a "$1.7 billion aid package for Africa, $1.2 billion of which was to go to combating malaria infection" ("Poverty in Underdeveloped Nations"). This money is to be used in towards insecticide spraying and improved drug technologies. Both the Global Fund and the World Bank have also pledged a combined total of 2.7 billion dollars (Roberts 26). Not only are countries and major organizations contributing large amounts of financial aid, but Bill Gates of the Gates Foundation had funded $150 million towards development of an improved antimalarial drug in support of Roll Back Malaria (Sachs 124). With these noted contributions, along with others not mentioned, the "funding for malaria control [has] jumped from $51 million in 2003 to an estimated $1.1 billion in 2008" (Roberts 26). This significant increase in funding shows that this policy is gaining substantial support which makes it a feasible task. Because of RBM's practicality, it is without a doubt that monetary funds will still continue to come in throughout the next couple of years.

> ### Opposition Paragraph Peer Review Questions
>
> 1. Does the writer present the opposition in a balanced way? Does the writer maintain the academic ethos of fair and accurate representation of opposing views?
>
> 2. Does the writer effectively rebut the opposition? How so or how not? Are you persuaded that the writer's proposed policy solution will be better than the alternative?
>
> 3. Identify places where the writer gives credit to the opposing views, and identify places where the writer rebuts those views. How are these moments organized? Does the writer start with the views of the opposition and then knock their arguments down, or does the writer bolster her own views first, and bring up the opposition's as clearly weaker? These are both viable options, but it's important to be intentional about the order of information.
>
> 4. Note style and mechanics. Are there any sentences that could be more graceful? Are transitions between sentences smooth and logical?

7.9.5   Structuring the Advocacy Essay

The structure of your Advocacy Essay can vary based on the different strengths of your solution and on your rhetorical approach. Your thesis lays out the analytical frameworks you will work within, so there are a few ways to think about structuring your paper. The opposition paragraph is a good touchstone.

You might start out with your opposition paragraph, or you might wait to unfurl it until the end of your paper, depending on how you believe your readers will initially feel about your solution. If your solution is a radical one that will meet with deep-seated cultural resistance (maybe you're arguing for the legalization of steroids), you might find that immediately acknowledging opposition is useful so that you can clear your reader's minds of their preconceptions before moving on. If rebutting the opposition is less urgent and you are confident of your readers' support (you are advocating for better protection for US troops abroad) you might address opposition later, to clear up loose ends based on more practical complaints (such as economic cost, in our example). In select cases, you might choose to address opposition within your own analytical frameworks. If the opposition has a point based on cost/benefit, address it in your own cost/benefit paragraph and then address their point about feasibility when you address feasibility. While still giving credence to the opposition's concerns, this argumentative strategy allows your own voice to naturally carry more weight.

SAMPLE ADVOCACY BODY PARAGRAPH

Other bills have attempted to reach the same goal as the Torture Outsourcing Prevention Act. A closely similar bill, Convention Against Torture Implementation Act of 2005 (S. 654), was introduced by Senator Patrick Leahy (D-VT) on March 17, 2005 and had the same basic provisions as H.R. 952, only it allowed more excusable purposes for the rendition of detainees (Legislative). This bill, however, was never reintroduced to the 110th Congress once it expired, likely because it managed to gain only 8 cosponsors (S. 654 [109th]) (Legislative). Senator Dick Durbin (D-IL) tried to prevent extraordinary rendition by attaching an amendment (S.A. 4341) to the Defense Authorization Bill (S. 2766) that would penalize countries which torture detainees that have been sent there by the U.S (Current). These countries would be taken off a list of acceptable places in which the U.S. could rendition detainees if they failed to enforce their diplomatic assurances that they would not torture (Current). After being passed by the Senate, this bill was never referred to a committee before the next session of Congress and therefore died. Since then, it has never been reintroduced. Thus far, Representative Markey's bill appears the most likely to put an end to extraordinary rendition as Markey has proven that he is willing to continue reintroducing the bill and regaining the support of fellow Congressmen until it passes.

Advocacy Body Paragraph Peer Review Questions

1. What is the paragraph's topic sentence, or controlling idea? Does it clearly introduce the point to be discussed? Does it mention a specific reason for supporting the problem?

2. What kind of analysis does this paragraph set out to do? a) Causal (the solution will address the root cause of the problem), b) Comparative (e.g., the solution has worked before in another, similar context), c) Analysis of coverage (the solution will cover the most or most-affected people), d) Cost/benefit (in terms of money, energy, time, people's well-being), e) Analysis of feasibility (the solution can be implemented quickly, cheaply; it has a lot of support). Keep in mind that the topic sentence is not required to make the type of paragraph overt, since this is not a formulaic essay. You'll need to take the whole paragraph into account. The paragraph can even, sometimes, do more than one type of analysis (though it's usually more fruitful to stick to one).

(continued)

3. If it does none of the above, perhaps describing something about the policy without arguing **why** this means the policy is **the best** solution, what would you tell the writer about how its information could be used in service of one of the five types of analysis?

4. What kind of evidence is used? Is it relevant to the paragraph's argument (go back to the topic sentence)? Is it recent? Credible? Is there enough? If not, what points need more support? What kind of evidence would you look for if you were the writer? Any suggestions for research?

5. How does the paragraph conclude? Does it seem like a wise choice? Can you imagine what the next paragraph might say? (Or, for that matter, the previous paragraph?)

7.9.6 Concluding the Advocacy Essay

One possibility in concluding an advocacy essay is to spur your reader to concrete action. After all, you have spent the quarter researching a problem and concluding that something very specific should be done to remedy this problem. If you've done your job effectively, your reader may be moved to agree with you, and even wonder what she can do to help. So, instead of simply summarizing your opening argument, point to actions that the reader may take. Examples of possible actions include, but are not limited to, petitions, letters to Congress, boycotts, and joining an advocacy group.

Before you offer specific actions, you might decide to exhort the reader. In convincing them that concrete action is truly needed, it might be useful to refer again to the *harm*, this time framing it less with the issues caused by the current state of the problem and more with what new or exacerbated harms will result if your particular solution is not adopted—or if alternate solutions win out. On the other hand, you may decide that using vivid language and concrete examples to show the *benefits* of the solution will profit your argument. When you choose which harms and benefits to focus on in your concluding paragraph, consider using those that might resonate personally with your readers.

Note that some of these tactics, while they might cover similar ground content-wise as points you made earlier in your essay, are not mere summary; instead they take known information and tailor it towards real action and your readers' real lives, ushering your reader out of your paper and into advocacy. Whatever you write, be sure you use compelling, concrete language and that you continue to use sources and evidence, just as you have throughout your essay.

Read the two sample concluding paragraphs below.

SAMPLE AE CONCLUDING PARAGRAPH #1

Since the UC IPM program successfully advances sustainable methods of agri-culture that reduce pesticide use, increased public awareness and more robust funding for its research and teaching grants must be encouraged. Currently $620,000 is dedicated annually to the first and $75,000 to the latter (Grants). However, one research project can be as much as $45,000 thus limiting the total number of research projects. If the California Legislature can increase funding for both grants, then more innovative and sustainable methods can be discovered and increased number of demonstrations will allow more farmers to implement such practices thus increasing the reduction of pesticide use and slowing down the pesticide treadmill. However, currently, the treadmill situa-tion appears bleak; California will consider legalizing condmethyl iodide, a pes-ticide that is "used in the laboratory to induce cancer cells" and has the ability to "kill everything" to replace methyl bromide, which depletes the ozone layer (Fimrite). Fortunately, the spread of IPM can, at least in the case of methyl bro-mide, prevent the dilemma of choosing between protecting human health or the environment and may also lead to a change in public perception- a demand for pesticide-free and sustainably grown food. Public opinion will pressure the government to steer favor away from corporatized monocultures and their in-herent problems thereby increasing the quality of health and the sustainability of the environment. As Professor Altieri contends, "ecological change in agri-culture cannot be promoted without comparable changes in the social, political, cultural and economic arenas that also conform [and determine] agriculture".

SAMPLE AE CONCLUDING PARAGRAPH #2

In an era where financial instability has resulted in concern over the future of the price of education, the Student Aid and Fiscal Responsibility Act of 2009 will usher in a new sign of recovery for students from not only the lower class but also for students who are in the middle class who are struggling with sec-ond jobs. Without the passing of this act, the future of student enrollment would become bleak when tuition rates continue to increase and the future of the economy still not on stable ground. Along those terms, without limitations on the interest rates for loans issued by private companies, middle class fami-lies who are forced to take out advancements for tuition may become indebt for a longer period of time or it may also discourage students from attend-ing colleges due to the fear of not having the results expected from a college degree. Should students decide to drop out of school it would only worsen the economic condition of the schools as well because competition would drop meaning that the quality would decrease since students would lack peers that would otherwise attend college. Lastly without the support from the national government for aid with student tuition prices despite the rising costs of attendance, a national spark could occur with outrage similar to that of the modern day protests of the public colleges within California causing anger and outrage harming the trust in the government as a whole.

AE Conclusion Peer Review Questions

1. What strategies does each writer use to end his or her paper?

2. What differences do you notice in the tone of the two samples? Thinking about what rhetorical appeals the writer makes may help: does she appeal to emotion? To logic? Authority?

3. Which paragraph do you feel is more effective? Which paragraph convinces you more? What aspects of it make it convincing? In answering this question, address language and style, examples and evidence, and concrete actions offered.

7.10   Pitches and Public Speaking in 39C

> Whatever be the subject of a speech, therefore, in whatever art or branch of science, the orator, if he has made himself master of it, as of his client's cause, will speak on it better and more elegantly than even the very originator and author of it can.
>
> —Cicero

Imagine that you have invented a new medical device that will save lives, and the woman who can help bring your invention to the world just stepped onto the elevator with you. As the elevator doors close, you realize you have only a minute or two (before the elevator doors open and she is no longer a captive audience) to convince her to invest in your project. Could you do it?

While you may not have experienced anything as dramatic as this, we've all had to defend a position, argue a point of view, persuade an opponent—and if you haven't yet, you will. Not all of us, however, have had much practice at speaking in public, and fewer of us would say we like it.

But being able to speak comfortably in front of a group—large or small—is something that you'll have to do at some point in your life, whatever career you pursue. In your 39C class, you may have at least one opportunity to develop your public speaking skills in a focused presentation we call a "pitch." This term comes from the "elevator pitch" described above. In the real world, a pitch is im-promptu, extemporaneous, and is usually successful only when you really know your stuff and are able to speak with clarity and passion.

In our class, this "knowing your stuff" is precisely the point. You'll have to do research, and as the great Roman orator Cicero says, become the master of it in order to speak effectively and persuasively.

7.10.1   Pitch Objectives

Being able to speak comfortably in public is only one of the goals of the pitch. There are other important purposes and objectives to this assignment:

• Practicing your rhetorical know-how by carefully considering the relationship between modality (i.e., speech instead of writing) and audience.

• Editing carefully—after all, you have only one or two minutes to hook your audience, state your purpose, give some pertinent evidence, and make your case. Every word counts.

- Focusing your research and your message. In most cases, you'll deliver your pitch as a prewriting assignment for your longer essays—and the confidence you gain from your pitch will help you write your argument with much more clarity.

7.10.2   Pitch Assignments

When your instructor assigns your pitch and how long your pitch will be depends, in part, on the purpose of the pitch.

For example, at the beginning of the quarter, you may be given this kind of assignment as prewriting for a longer essay:

> In a one-minute pitch, you will address the class as if they are an audience unconvinced about the existence of a problem or the severity of the problem. If your class is reading *Outliers*, then your task is to convince your audience that this famous individual requires further study, or poses interesting research challenges in terms of identifying the nature of the individual's success. This will require that you do some research—so that you can convince the class that this is a research topic worth pursuing, and so that you can identify fruitful avenues of future research.

At the end of the quarter, you may be given this assignment as a capstone oral presentation:

> In a two-minute pitch, you will address a specific audience of your choosing. Your pitch to this audience must have a particular purpose: to gain support, to get funding, to drum up votes in congress, to get a particular community on board with a project, etc. Both your audience and purpose must be clear, specific, and appropriate to the solution you're advocating.
>
> Your pitch must include the following elements:
>
> - A persuasive, clear and specific introduction to the problem—either with anecdotes, statistics, a narrative or details from recent studies.
>
> - A brief explanation of the root or direct causes (or recent history) that have made solving this problem particularly difficult or have made this problem particularly bad.
>
> - A pitch for the solution you wish to advocate. You must have clear, specific, and persuasive arguments for the need for this solution, and reasons why this solution is not just a good choice, but the best choice.
>
> - End your pitch with a clear, unequivocal appeal that directly addresses your purpose.

- Your pitch may include visual elements—but you should use these with caution. All visuals should enhance your oral argument—and you should avoid reading from a PowerPoint presentation. The graphics should enhance what you say, and should not get in the way of your appeal.

These are just sample assignments, but demonstrate that each pitch assignment has a specific purpose; your pitch must be carefully tailored to both audience and purpose for it to be a success.

Note: *Experience has shown that students who practice their pitches with a timer—many times—are the most successful and engaging.*

Think about the career path you have chosen, or one that you might choose. What situations might require you to do a pitch like the ones described here? Who would be your audience? What would be your purpose?

Thinking about how this pitch assignment may have a real-world analogue will certainly highlight the usefulness of the assignment beyond the scope of 39C.

RHETORICAL ASIDE

Chapter 8

FIP, FIRST-YEAR INTEGRATED PROGRAM

The First-Year Integrated Program (FIP) is a year-long experience for freshmen introducing students to the ways that different disciplines approach similar topics. Program participants become members of a unique learning community, including faculty from several different disciplines, graduate teaching associates, and a small number of other freshmen—the maximum enrollment is 80. Writing provides the thread that enables students to connect the various perspectives across three quarters of study.

Successful completion of a FIP sequence satisfies several lower-division course requirements, including composing a capstone research project in fulfillment of the second quarter of the lower-division writing GE requirement. Concurrent enrollment in WR 39B during fall or winter quarters is also a requirement of the course.

8.1   Writing in FIP

Writing assignments in FIP vary from course to course, but every sequence will require students to critically read and evaluate discipline-specific texts and to compose several academic and other types of writing assignments. All students will propose a project topic, conduct research and produce an evaluation of the sources located, and compose a capstone research paper based on that research, usually in the form of an academic essay. Other assignments will vary according to discipline-specific guidelines in a field. Some will learn to write a scientific water measurement report; others may compose a blog in the style of Baudelaire or write a letter to a newspaper editor as a part of learning to compose texts with different audiences and purposes. Students will produce multiple drafts and use the process approach in composing written assignments for a FIP course.

8.2   University Studies FIP Sequence Topics 2011–2012

8.2.1   Uni Stu 13: Environmental Studies

"Environmental Studies" introduces students to the Earth as a system, the physical and biological resources on the planet, and the impact of humanity on those resources. Students will become aware of the unique features of Earth that allowed the origin and evolution of life, the intrinsic values as well as the resource values of species and ecosystems, the extent of damage from historical and current overexploitation, efforts to restore endangered species and ecosystems, and the difficulties of reaching a sustainable relationship with the resources available in the face of increasing human population numbers compounded by increasing economic activity.

Writing assignments will include a source evaluation essay, a topic proposal presentation, and the capstone research paper. Other assignments are likely to include a well-kept field notebook, a consumer guide examining environmental impacts, an analysis of legislation designed to impact the environment, and a letter to someone who can do something about what you come to believe are issues concerning the planet. This sequence is intended to help students become more informed citizens and decision-makers and is ideal preparation for present or future majors in the natural sciences, social sciences, or the humanities.

8.2.2   Uni Stu 15: Consciousness

"Consciousness" explores the enigma of human consciousness from the perspectives of scientific research, philosophy, art, and literature. Students will examine scientific ideas about how and why we are conscious, including behavioral and neurological experiments in sensory perception and motor response.

They will also read Freud's theories of the unconscious and think about the ways in which writers and artists depict consciousness and struggle with its mysteries. By the end of the year, students will have learned how different disciplines investigate consciousness, the vocabularies they use to describe it, and the theories they propose for understanding it.

Writing assignments will include an evaluation of your own attitudes about consciousness, literary and film analyses, an annotated bibliography, a capstone topic proposal paper, and the capstone research paper. Other writing assignments will focus on critical reading and analysis of different kinds of texts, disciplinary modes of argumentation, and creative approaches to textual analysis. This sequence explores the interaction of the humanities and the sciences and emphasizes the modes of inquiry and writing used in the Humanities.

8.2.3   Uni Stu 16: "How Race Is Made"

"How Race Is Made" examines the origins and consequences of race in America. The fall quarter course focuses on contemporary issues of race, ethnicity, and difference from the perspectives of biology, society, law, and culture. Students will explore both historical and current analyses of health, politics, identity, and inequality. During the winter, the construction of race in America will be examined through historical and contemporary artifacts of popular culture (political cartoons, popular music, television, film/video, comedy, and performance). Students will investigate particular discourses of "excess" as represented by the racialized body in America—voice/accent, hair, skin, sexuality, and movement—and the concomitant political and cultural affects these discourses activate—fear, desire, pride, shame, to name a few. The spring class opens with the world before Columbus set foot in the Americas and ends with today in California. The course will investigate how the idea of race formed and its effect on politics in the early United States. Students will also identify and understand modern social, legal, and political efforts to construct and deconstruct race and be able to apply this understanding to currently evolving issues particularly in California.

Each quarter of "How Race is Made" has four component parts: lectures, discussion sections, assigned readings, and assignments. No one of these parts can, by itself, convey the full meaning of the course. Students in the sequence are the ones who will be doing all of these things at the same time: listening to and participating in lectures, reading books, articles, and documents, discussing the readings and lectures in sections, taking quizzes in section, and writing papers and taking exams. It is the students' task to integrate the four parts of the course so that they can develop their own viewpoints on how race was made in America.

8.2.4   Uni Stu 17: "Water"

In the Fall quarter, "Water" addresses water from scientific and engineering perspectives (global issues, land–sea interactions, and urban water), then moves in the Winter to a historical case study of water in the US, particularly the American west. The sequence culminates in the Spring with a course that explores water policy with the overall theme of water as a contested resource across space, time, and peoples. Wherever possible, examples are drawn from the local environment.

Writing assignments will include a source evaluation essay, a topic proposal, and the capstone research proposal. Other assignments are likely to include a technical report, an essay on the social and historical impact of environmental factors, and a policy analysis of some aspect of problems resulting from the scarcity of water. This sequence is intended to help students become more informed citizens and decision-makers and is ideal preparation for future majors in the sciences, social sciences, or the humanities.

8.3   A Portfolio of Assignments

8.3.1   Uni Stu 13: Capstone Research Project

A primary task of this final quarter will be to compose a "capstone" research project. To begin, you will compose a one-page overview or précis of your proposed capstone research topic. Your thesis here should describe your capstone research paper topic and the reasons why you have chosen it.

The Précis

In your overview, discuss how you will proceed to explore your topic when you write your capstone essay. Refer to any research and sources you might use.

Your topic here and for the capstone must focus on the question of the *sustainability* of one of the resources or systems you select from the list below:

- **Natural Resources**
- Local habitat (e.g., restoration of Back Bay via dredging project)
- Wetlands
- Freshwater resources
- Air
- Biodiversity
- Land cover (forest, desert, grassland)

- **Systems**
- Agriculture
- Energy production/use
- Local, state and national parks (e.g., Great Park plan)
- Transportation
- Waste management (Superfund, nuclear waste, human waste, plastic, etc.)
- Urbanization

Select the topic that interests you the most from the above list and consider the question of "sustainability" on this issue.

Speak to your TA about your topic selection, and compose a "scratch outline" of your proposal to present to your peer group for peer editing.

Propose your topic, rather than launching into a discussion about it. Save the analysis for your capstone project.

The Sources

In a separate document, list and annotate at least six academic sources on the topic (list them alphabetically) in an Annotated Bibliography with two parts:

Part One: A bibliographic entry using CSE style.

Part Two: A four-sentence annotation in which you state in your own words:

- The author's thesis
- The significant kinds of evidence used to support and illustrate the thesis
- The author's purpose
- Instead of the intended audience or reader for this text, include how you might use this information in your capstone research project

➡ *See Chapter Four for more specific instructions on how to compile an Annotated Bibliography.*

Write an argumentation essay approximately 1500–2000 words in length that examines a "sustainable" way to manage a natural resource or system and makes a recommendation for action. This essay should be on the topic you proposed in your previous paper.

Breakdown:
In your introduction, be sure to define the concept and practice of sustainability.

Your thesis, which also goes in the introduction, should make a claim about the sustainability of the resource or system you're focusing on, given the current management practices. Briefly describe these practices. Either in the thesis or as a result of your examination of the current practices, you should also offer a recommendation for making management of the resource or system more or even completely sustainable.

In developing your argument, remember to consider the economic, ecological, and legal implications of current and proposed management practices and the question of whether or not these make the resource or system sustainable.

In your conclusion, re-state your thesis and explain how the evidence you have offered supports it. Also make or repeat your recommendation for action.

SAMPLE UNI STU 13 CAPSTONE RESEARCH PAPER

Sustainability of Plastics Recycling

By Toan Nguyen

A plastic is any synthetic solid material that is typically composed of polymers of high molecular weight that can be made into objects, films, or filaments, for the manufacture of industrial products. Plastics are a huge industry with overwhelming consumer reliance on plastic-derived products for their relative cheapness, durability, and ease of ductility. The dominance of plastics in American consumer markets however has led to an increasing volume of plastics in solid waste and given their long-lasting qualities, are resistant to environmental change and can remain in the environment for a long period of time before they are broken down naturally. The majority of plastics utilize petroleum as feedstock and energy during their manufacture, which is a cause for concern as plastics processing contributes to carbon dioxide emissions in the atmosphere. Due to heavy societal dependence on plastics and their adverse effect on the environment, it is important that alternative and more "sustainable" plastics be found. According to the Brundtland Commission, a United Nations commission convening in 1983 to address sustainable development, sustainability is "development that meets the needs of the present without compromising the ability of future generations to meet their own needs," meaning that for something to be labeled "sustainable" it must maintain productivity in the future. For a plastic to be considered sustainable, it must be manufactured using organic, carbon-based material derived from a renewable resource and capable of biodegradation or being broken down rapidly by the natural environment. Sustainable plastics, or "bioplastics," unfortunately have not gained widespread use as a result of them being a more expensive alternative to the already cheap synthetic plastics and relative lack of suitable infrastructure for the compost of biodegradables in conjunction with recycling traditional plastics. Thus traditional plastics continue to dominate the market and are typically disposed through recycling and incineration, but usually tossed away with assorted solid waste. However, current practices in the disposal of petroleum-based plastic are hardly sustainable and inefficient to resolve the issue of excess solid waste, calling for a change in consumer practices and making sustainable plastics such as biodegradables a much more attractive alternative in regards to the future.

Since the 1950s, plastics have been a major industry and have been utilized in thousands of applications such as packaging material, medical equipment, appliances, toys, and a diverse variety of industrial and consumer goods. Innovation in the all-pervasive industry is common due to plastic's flexible molecular polymers and has led to the development of groundbreaking plastic types such as polyethylene (PET), Nylon, polyvinyl chloride (PVC), and polystyrene (PS).

The more prominent and fastest growing type of plastic is PET for its tough barrier qualities against gas and moisture. PET is typically used in single-use consumer products such as plastic bags and water bottles. The tremendous popularity of plastic products such as PET has also led it to become the fastest growing segment of the municipal waste stream in the U.S. and second to paper in waste by volume going into landfills. Plastics in waste streams accounted for 0.5 percent in 1960 to 13.8 percent in 1999 (Gibson and Pratt 2003). Though light weight in comparison to other heavier solid waste, plastics make up a larger volume of the waste in landfills and take up a disproportionate amount of space. As a result of landfills exceeding their capacity in conjunction with consumer inconsideration, some plastics get displaced into streams by urban runoff where they will eventually enter the oceans. While most plastics may break into smaller pieces given sufficient time in the water, the pieces do not effectively biodegrade in the environment and are still present in the water albeit not as visible to the naked eye. A study from the University of Plymouth found that the plastic particles concentrated toxic substances from the surrounding seawater to the point where it was a thousand times more potent than in the surrounding water on the surface of the plastic (Shukman 2008). Aquatic organisms could confuse the toxic plastic matter for food and ingest them, raising the possibility that the toxins may then be transferred directly to the animals themselves, which the infected animal would then be caught for consumption and pose a potential health hazard to humans or predators.

In an attempt to curb excess plastic waste and conserve natural resources, common current waste management plans for plastics are municipal recycling and pyrolysis or waste-to-energy production. Recycling is the most popular method to reduce waste in landfills and can significantly contribute to conservation of raw petrochemical products as well as save energy. PET bottles made out of recycled material require 23.6 million BTUs of energy, while PET bottles made out of purely virgin content require nearly four times as much energy (Weeks 2007). Recycled materials can be utilized for a wide variety of applications ranging from making the same product out of recycled material to using them to reinforce concrete. Although using recycled materials is much more efficient than using raw materials, recycling is marred by technical limitations that restrict full utilization of the reusable materials in plastic waste (Siddique 2007). Plastics must be cleaned of stains or leftover food before they are recycled to prevent contamination of plastic waste with foreign materials and damage to reprocessing equipment; vary in molecular structure or properties and cannot be recycled together; have relatively low densities and must be compacted en masse in order to reduce shipping costs. Application of recycled plastic in concrete requires a huge volume of material that makes them impractical to be used in all concrete-based buildings. The concrete that does receive recycled materials obtains plastic's reliable durability, but also receives its negative qualities and is much susceptible to abrasion and limited workability (Siddique 2007). Plastics recycling are also hampered by economical limitations as reprocessing equipment are relatively expensive and that consumption of plastics far exceeds regeneration of recycled products, leading to a net accumulation of plastics in the environment. Between the 80s to the late 90s, per capita consumption of bottled water increased from 21.6 to 104.5 liters (Mooney 2009). The popularity of single-use or "on the go" plastic products such as water bottles and plastic bags have exacerbated the rate of plastics production and their likeliness to end up in ordinary trash due to their casual usage. In order to prevent contamination and retain the integrity of recycled material, waste must be removed from plastic before it is recycled and it is currently impossible to automatically separate recyclable plastics already in landfills. Sorting plastics from trash by hand would prove to be far more expensive and time consuming. To make complexity worse, all plastics must be separated into different polymer types before they are recycled due to varying boiling or melting points. In an attempt to simplify the recycling process for consumers, the Society of the Plastics Industry (SPI) created a "resin identification coding system" in 1988 to identify common consumer plastics based on a scale of one through seven (American Chemistry Council 2007). But the resin codes do not guarantee that all plastics are will be recycled as recyclers mainly focus on heavily commercialized plastics such as PET rather than on the less developed markets of the other plastics on the identification chart.

Although plastics recycling are a sound first step for waste management, the rapid growth of plastics in the market or environment and the complicated, expensive nature of the recycling process prevent the method from taking into account the plastics haphazardly thrown into the garbage. The plastics recycling rate of 6.9 percent is the lowest of all other recyclable materials compared to 50 percent for paper, 35 percent for metals, and 20 percent for glass (U.S. Environmental Protection Agency 2006). Plastics that are not recycled are generally left in landfills or incinerated through pyrolysis as a source of energy. Pyrolysis of plastics greatly reduces the volume of garbage by 90–95 percent and providing an alternative energy source, but it produces carbon dioxide emissions that contribute to greenhouse gas content in the atmosphere as a result (Keane 2007). Incineration of some types of plastics such as PVC is also known to produce toxic emissions due to chlorinated dioxins that could lead to damage to the immune system or cause birth effects. Some pyrolysis machines are outfitted with filters that can house the emissions, but the ash gathered from the incineration has a risk of entering groundwater or pollute nearby soil. Pyrolysis is also an energy intensive process and suffers the same limitations of recycling in that plastics must be categorized by type before they are incinerated.

Through the complicated sorting of plastics and the limitations of recycling and pyrolysis, current methods of plastics waste management are essentially unsustainable both economically and environmentally given the rapidly growing pace of the plastics market. To control consumer waste tendencies, some countries around the world have taken legislative measures to force desirable consumer habits. In 2001, Ireland enacted a stiff tax on plastic bags that later caused a 90 percent decline of plastic bag consumption (Applebome 2007). Inspired by the effectiveness of the tax, some U.S. states such as New York and Texas have implemented their own taxes against plastics. Some have even gone as far as to ban non-biodegradable plastic bags in supermarkets or pharmacies such as San Francisco in 2007, the first major American city to do so. The banning or taxation of plastic bags would encourage consumers to consider more benign and reusable alternatives such as paper or biodegradable bags instead of relying on wasteful single-use plastic products. It would also reduce energy production costs and carbon emissions for the production of plastic bags as well as the volume of plastic bags in landfills. Besides affecting the attitudes of consumer waste, legislation against plastic products would also prompt manufacturers to seek more sustainable products or launch their own corporate-sponsored recycling program for consumers. In a sense, producers will be strongly encouraged to be responsible for the disposal of used products.

Besides legislative action to encourage a change in wasteful consumer and producer habits, developing a biodegradable and sustainable form of plastic would reduce plastics' durability against the environment. Biodegradation of plastics operates naturally by microorganisms and enzymes that are capable of breaking down the molecular structure of the material. The rate of degradation is largely determined by environmental conditions, the microorganism, and the type of plastic being biodegraded. Biodegradable plastics include synthetic polyester blends, polylactic acid, or starch-based blends of plastics. They are typically made from a variety of natural feedstock such as corn, rice, cellulose, or wheat fiber, and can be utilized in a wide range of applications like traditional plastics. It is possible to biodegrade petroleum-based synthetic plastics using certain microorganisms given the right isolated conditions, but this method is generally more of a hassle than simply just recycling and thus it is more favorable to simply manufacture plastics out of materials favored by common microorganisms in the environment (Shah 2007). Economic problems associated with the implementation of biodegradable plastics in markets are consumer confidence of the technical integrity of the plastic in comparison to petroleum-based plastics and concerns of reprocessing both plastics together. However these problems could be resolved by the gradual introduction of biodegradables to consumer markets by the national or state governments and public education of the qualities of the plastics to reinforce confidence. Another problem with biodegradables is the time and costs associated with their development, which could reach years and tens of millions of U.S. dollars in total. Although much more expensive than traditional plastics, the current price of biodegradables will eventually become a more economically viable option given sufficient research in reducing production costs and as the price of petroleum inevitably rises in the future as a result of its limited quantity in the world.

Given traditional petroleum-based plastic's finite re-usability and the inability of recycling or incineration to resolve excess plastic waste, it is important that more sustainable forms of plastic such as biodegradables be sought and established into consumer markets. For the meantime, it is also important that legislation be imposed against plastic products that would encourage consumers and producers to be more resourceful and limit single-use consumption of plastic products such as water bottles or plastic bags. Petroleum-based products are largely temporary materials in the long run that society currently relies too much upon. It is essential that action be taken to reduce consumer reliance on such products and rely on more future-proof materials or methods.

Works Cited

American Chemistry Council [ACC]. 2007. Plastic packaging resins. Available from: <http://www.americanchemistry.com/s_plastics/bin.asp?CID=1102& DID=4645&DOC=FILE.PDF>. Accessed April 29, 2009.

Applebome, Peter. 2007. Human behavior, global warming, and the ubiquitous plastic bag. The New York Times. <http://www.nytimes.com/2007/09/30/ nyregion/30towns.html>. Accessed April 29, 2009.

Brundtland Commission. 20 March 1987. Our common future: Report of the world commission on environment and development. United Nations. Available from: <http://worldinbalance.net/agreements/1987-brundtland. php>. Accessed April 30, 2009.

Environmental Protection Agency [EPA]. 2006. Municipal Solid Waste Generation, Recycling, and Disposal in the United States. Available from: http://www.epa.gov/epawaste/nonhaz/municipal/pubs/msw06.pdf

Gibson J, Pratt W. 2003. Plastics white paper: Optimizing plastics use, recycling, and disposal in California. California Integrated Waste Management Board.<http://www.ciwmb.ca.gov/Publications/default.asp?pubid= 1010>. Accessed April 8, 2009.

Keane, Mark. 2007. Catalytic conversion of waste plastics: focus on waste PVC. *Journal of Chemical Technology and Biotechnology* 82: 787–795.

Mooney, Brian. 2009. The second green evolution? Production of plant-based biodegradable plastics. *Biochemical Journal* 148: 219–232.

Shah A, Hasan F, Hameed A, Ahmed S. 2008. Biological degradation of plastics: A comprehensive review. Science Direct.

Shukman, David. 2008. Warning on plastic's toxic threat. BBC News Online. <http://news.bbc.co.uk/2/hi/science/nature/7316441.stm>. Accessed May 1, 2009.

Siddique R, Khatib J, Kaur I. 2007. Use of recycled plastic in concrete: A review. Science Direct.

Weeks, Jennifer. 2007. Future of recycling. *CQ Researcher, 17*, 1033–1060. CQ Researcher Online. <http://library.cqpress.com/cqresearcher/ cqresrre2007121400>. Accessed April 7, 2009.

Review Questions

1. Re-read the assignment for the capstone essay. Where in the essay do you find the writer establishing a context for sustainability that is specific to the topic? How does the writer justify the necessity for sustainable solutions to be implemented?

2. Locate what you think is the thesis claim or main argument of the essay. State it in your own words. Does the thesis provide enough information for you to anticipate the kinds of arguments the author will make?

3. Identify the topic sentence lead-ins in the body of the essay. Do they connect to the thesis claim? How does the order of body paragraphs affect the flow of ideas in the essay?

4. Review the concluding paragraph of the essay. Does it offer a re-statement of the main arguments of the essay?

8.3.2   Uni Stu 15: Capstone Research Project

You are asked to compose an essay, 8–10 pages (2000–2500 words in its final form) that argues for your own individual interpretation of Hitchcock's 1958 film, *Vertigo*. An argument is not just a description or a report: it presents an original theory, with which others may or may not agree. It has to be controversial enough that someone could disagree with it, so that your logical and evidentiary support is truly necessary. Support your argument with evidence from the film and from your research on it.

Although the paper proposal and the bibliography are due the same day, you have to have done some of the reading in order to come up with the proposal, so the bibliography is Stage 1 and the proposal is Stage 2.

Stage One: Annotated Bibliography

First you will research your topic and evaluate your findings in an annotated bibliography of book chapters, books, or articles in peer-reviewed scholarly journals. An annotated bibliography is a list of the texts you have read, with your notes on each. See Chapter Four for more specific instructions on how to compile an Annotated Bibliography.

Since the goal of the essay writing process is to develop an original idea of your own, the purpose of reading what others have written on the film is to help you understand how your own ideas are different from others' and therefore valuable to others. So, in searching for articles, try to find those that seem, from the titles and from the abstracts when abstracts are available, most likely to be related to your specific topic. There is some trial and error, though: it's not always easy to tell. It's also OK to look at some articles that sound particularly interesting to you even if they are not obviously related to your topic.

In reading articles on *Vertigo*, you need to (a) decide what the article is arguing (b) decide to what extent you agree and to what extent you don't agree, and why (where is the *evidence* weak and strong? where is the author's *logic* weak or strong? What fundamental *assumptions* do you share with the author, and which ones do you not share?), and (c) think about how your ideas reply to the author's ideas. The point of citing an article is not just to gather support for what you think: difference of opinion is probably even more valuable.

In the annotated bibliography, please list FIVE (5) journal articles or book chapters that you think are relevant to your project. To find five useful ones, you will need to have looked at more than five. For each article that makes your final list:

- Give the full citation of the text you read.

- Briefly summarize the argument of the text (2–5 sentences).

- Briefly indicate the strengths and weaknesses of the text (see [b] above).

The most helpful online databases for this subject are MLA (Modern Language Association) International Bibliography, JSTOR, and Project Muse. You may also want to check Google Scholar. And, of course, check ANTPAC for books on Hitchcock that may have chapters or passages on *Vertigo*.

You'll find that, because you are reading professional articles by scholars, many of the articles will treat *Vertigo* in combination with another film, another director, another theorist, in other words a lot of other stuff you don't necessarily understand. That's OK—research is always like that. Read the texts for what you do understand, and feel free to ask any of us if you would like additional help with anything or if you have any questions.

Stage Two: Paper Proposal

In a 250-word (1-page) essay, you will propose a topic for your capstone research essay. In your topic proposal essay, indicate:

a. Which topic you will be doing (see description of topics below).

b. What you currently believe you will argue.

c. A few examples of the evidence for your planned argument, including both details from the film and research you will argue with and against.

d. What we can learn about *Vertigo* from your paper. How does your argument help us to understand something about the film that we may not have noticed before?

Your discussion section leader will comment on your proposal before you go on to the next stage. We understand that the first draft of the paper may be quite different from the proposal. Please stay in touch with your TA so that you're sure that the latest version of your project has the green light from her.

Stage Three: First Draft

Compose a first, working draft (typed, about 1000–1250 words or 4–5 pages) of your capstone essay in which you propose and defend your own original theory, evidenced through your analysis and interpretation of Hitchcock's *Vertigo*, related to one of the following four topics. In developing your working draft, be sure to consider ideas from lecture about unconsciousness and consciousness, ambivalence, and the mind's tendency to associate ideas. You will also use evidence from peer-reviewed journal articles, scholarly books, and other sources that help to support and distinguish your argument from others' arguments. For this first draft, please use **only two sources**; using more than two sources in a paper of this length will distract attention from your original argument.

Your topic options are as follows:

Knowledge. The film emphasizes the question of what Madeline does or does not know about her actions and about Carlotta. Scottie is also shown to have some trouble knowing himself and knowing other people. He is also a detective, a profession in which information is supposed to be collected and synthesized. All together, what kind of picture does *Vertigo* give of knowledge, especially the way people know themselves and other people? What are the obstacles to knowing? What are or should be its goals? Why do some things in the film seem to be a lot harder for people to know than others? How much knowledge, and what kind, is really possible according to the film? What does the film want us to think about knowledge, and the way it is portrayed?

Femininity. In Hitchcock's *Vertigo*, women are compared to and substituted for one another by Scottie and also by the film itself (much as we saw in Freud's "Dream of Irma's Injection"). Women are also sometimes substituted for by portraits, costumes, false identities, etc. What does all this substitution and attempted substitution say about how Scottie and/or Hitchcock imagine women in the film? (To consider this question, you might ask yourself: what are all the substitutions? what happens because of them? how are the instances like and different from one another? which go together, which contrast? where does the film show imagination of the female figure going on or being discussed?)

Past and Present. The characters in *Vertigo* seem to labor under the burden of the past in various ways. Scottie both seems to want to repeat or recover the past and says at one point that he wants to be free of it. It is often said that something is "too late." So, according to the film, what relations can people have to the past? Is it possible to be free of the past? To what extent? Under what conditions? Should we want to be? If it is not possible, why not, and what relation to the past are we left with? What does the film want us to think about this problem?

Artifice. Midge is a designer, and (without giving away too much of the plot), there is also a lot of other designing and construction going on: schemes, for example, are planned and constructed, and characters invent or reproduce stories and images, act parts, and direct other people. The film itself is, of course, constructed and directed by Hitchcock and acted by the actors under his direction. What is the role that artifice and design play amid the other concerns of the film—sexual and romantic relation, power struggle, the struggle with a traumatic past? Why do characters want or need to design things and create artifices? What are the functions of this activity? Is it successful? If so or if not, in what way, for whom, and why? What is the film saying about the human impulse to design? How do Hitchcock's reflections on art and design reflect on himself as an artist?

Stage Four: Final Draft

Compose a final draft (typed, about 2000–2500 words or 8–10 pages) of your capstone essay in which you propose and defend your own original theory, evidenced through your analysis and interpretation of Hitchcock's *Vertigo*. This final essay will expand and further develop the argument you advanced in your first draft.

Writing Guidelines

Here are **general parameters** for composing your capstone essay, good for the first draft, revisions, peer editing and final drafts of your paper.

Focus. Use the topics above to develop **one idea** of your own. The questions given with the topics exist only to get your thoughts going. Structure your paper exclusively around your own idea; please do not follow their order or directly answer the questions.

Title. Be sure to give your paper a specific title that indicates not only the general subject but your specific angle on it. Please also note with your name and the title which topic you're responding to.

Thesis Argument. Your paper needs to have an original thesis—a developed theory about your materials in response to one of the topics. A college-level argument needs not only to be correct but to be interesting: if its claims are true but only repeat what everyone already agrees on, there is no real purpose to writing it; and if the reader doesn't understand why she or he needs to know the points you're making (what she gets out of being told about them), there is not yet an argument either. So, make sure that your claims are specific enough that someone could disagree with them, and make clear how other people's understanding of the film would benefit from your expression of your idea. In order for your idea to be "original," (1) it has to be at least possible for someone to disagree with you; (2) it has to be specific enough that readers can tell the difference between it and similar sorts of ideas; and (3) you have to let the reader know very explicitly what your idea contributes to debates about the film that one might have.

Order Your Argument. Get to your thesis right away in the first paragraph of the paper. You don't need to bother taking up a whole paragraph of such a short paper with "background" or atmosphere that just leads up to a point—put your energy directly into your point. The paragraph should give your main point, an idea of the evidence for it that will come in the body of the paper, and how your paper contributes to the understanding of the film. To do this, the first paragraph usually takes about 2/3 of the first page.

Coherence. Use clear topic sentences at the beginning of each paragraph to indicate what the subject of the new paragraph is. How does this paragraph build on the last one? What phase of your argument does it introduce?

Evidence. Support your points with evidence in the form of quotations from the film and texts you're writing about. It's hard to have too much evidence; and further, working with specific ideas and images helps to develop complexity within your thinking. Please use your notes on film scenes and images so that you can refer to them well. Make sure every claim that could be disagreed with is evidenced. **When writing about film, use direct quotations** from dialogue, as you would from a text. Also refer to specific visual moments. When citing the articles you read during your research, use exact quotations rather than paraphrase for much of your evidence.

Where relevant, remember to dwell on your quotations a bit after mentioning them in order to make sure the reader knows why you brought them up and to comment on their subtleties. Show us what you wanted us to get out of your citation.

Conclusion. In your conclusion, summarize what you have argued. In the very last sentences, see if you can take the reader to a place that clinches your argument or indicates its farthest reach. What reflection do you most want to leave us with?

Format. Your paper should be typed and double-spaced. Staple the paper in the upper left corner. Please provide another copy of your 1-page proposal with the final version of your essay. No need to put the paper in a binder or cover.

References. Use a consistent citation style. Humanities papers usually use the MLA citation style, and we recommend that because it is simple for our purposes. But you may use any style as long as it is standard and professional. See http://www.liu.edu/CWIS/CWP/library/workshop/citation.htm for more information on citation formatting. This link gives examples of how to cite different kinds of materials in each style: make your citations look like the examples. **Attach a Bibliography** (but not the annotated version) to your essay, listing all the sources you used. Bibliography styles, too, differ and you may use any style that is standard, as above. Here is a sample synopsis of *Vertigo*:

Vertigo (1958), one of Alfred Hitchcock's darkest and most complex films, tells the story of police detective Scottie Ferguson (James Stewart), who develops a debilitating fear of heights when he witnesses a fellow policeman fall to his death. When an old college friend, Gavin Elster, asks Scottie to tail his wife Madeline (Kim Novak), Scottie is drawn into a vortex of deceit and murder. With the motherly care and companionship of his former sweetheart Midge, Scottie attempts to rebuild his life and "cure" himself of his vertigo. But he quickly develops an obsession with the mysterious and delicately feminine Madeline Elster who shockingly falls to her death midway through the film. In the second half of the film, Scottie meets Judy, a look-alike of Madeline, and he attempts to re-make Judy in Madeline's image. Behind the scenes, Gavin, a master manipulator, works his devious plot. As the mystery unfolds, *Vertigo* explores how Scottie's inability to maintain the distinction between fantasy, reality, and deception is heightened, not cured. He pursues first the picture-perfect Madeleine, and then the mysteriously familiar Judy, who both turn out to be quite other than what they seem.

⬤ UNI STU 15 SAMPLE CAPSTONE ESSAY

Vertigo: The Ultimate Role Reversal

By Abigail Radaza

Within the Hollywood film industry, stereotypes litter the movies in the form of commonplace plots, themes, and roles. The mainstream narrative consists of characters such as the helpless and dependant woman, blinded by love and in desperate need of constant saving, as well as the dashing male coming to rescue her from imminent peril. In the 1950s, the time Hitchcock directed *Vertigo*, audiences deemed plots like these as acceptable and not at all startling or innovative. In fact, a set of guidelines for film directors called the Hays code, which censored content considered immoral or a negative influence on society, became instated and forced more films to incorporate the stereotypes of these times. In the movie *Vertigo*, the surface of the plot seems to fulfill the set standards as the male protagonist Scottie attempts to rescue the frail Madeleine from her fate. However, the film actually takes the conventional ideal of the male lead as the knight in shining armor and, through the use of various film techniques, turns him into the damsel in distress, thus creating a satire on Hollywood's commonplace stance on fixed gender roles in movies.

The film *Vertigo* has been analyzed from a countless number of differing perspectives, many of which, like the following, counter my own claims. In spite of the evidence supporting my argument that Scottie nowhere near resembles the typical strong male lead, but instead seems like a vulnerable woman, other plausible arguments oppose this. One could reason that Scottie does not possess any of the characteristics connected to the women in *Vertigo*. Unlike the females, who flounder about helplessly, Scottie takes matters into his own hands, such as when he tries to help Madeleine conquer her, albeit false, spiritual possession. He purposefully comes into the scene, intent on saving the damsel in distress from impending doom, not the other way around. In Glen Gabbard's article on female objectification in *Vertigo*, he comments that the film depicts a woman as "weak and dependent," implying that she needs a rescuer. Thus, Scottie relates more to Gavin, in that he uses these women as tools to gain what he desires. For instance, David Blakesley writes about Hitchcock's use of film rhetoric in the opening scene of *Vertigo*, in which "the criminal is the Id (which is set free), the police officer is the Superego (which is eliminated), and Scottie is the Ego left hanging (in search of a stable self)." The metaphor used here represents Scottie's mind and loss of his conscience (his Superego), and how he is driven to act solely on his desires. Therefore, this could explain why he never stops to think about the repercussions of his actions as he practically destroys Judy and forcefully transforms her into Madeleine. In this way, he resembles Gavin, the only other main male character of the movie, as he puts his personal gains first and foremost, controlling these women to reach his objective. Deborah Linderman, in her article concerning "the collapse of sexual difference" in *Vertigo*, also agrees with this claim, saying that Scottie and Gavin both created fictional women for their own purposes. She also mentions Scottie's unconscious power-play against Gavin in taking the position as the all-knowing male lead. This line of thought points to the conclusion that Scottie strives to regain his manly pride. Linderman provides further evidence by writing about the film's use of symbolism with the eye in the opening credits, saying that it symbolizes Scottie's vertigo, a fear of seeing heights used as a substitution for his inadequacies as a man, or, in her terms, his "metaphorical castration." Ultimately, Scottie wins against Gavin in terms of who has the most knowledge, as well as subsequently overcoming his vertigo. Additionally, Scottie tries to regain his masculinity by constantly attempting to save the women, failing to do so along the way. He takes on the role as the knight in shining armor, hoping that, by prevailing, his regains his dignity. This goes well with Berman's argument that Scottie traps himself in a "rescue fantasy," presuming that he has the power to save all these women. However, despite all these points, my argument still stands that Scottie falls short of Hollywood's standards of the clichéd knight, and the following will prove why.

First, *Vertigo* provides several parallels between Scottie and the women of the film, thereby illustrating the irrelevance of assigning certain characteristics to only one gender. Scottie, diagnosed with acrophobia, proves unable to reign in his irrational fear and becomes immobilized due to his vertigo. Likewise, Madeleine becomes powerless to a greater being, her actions not her own as Carlotta's spirit supposedly takes possession of her. Although one could argue this is all just a ruse, and so they do not actually share this similarity, the real "Madeleine," or Judy, truly falls prey to a higher being, in this case Gavin Elster. Figuratively speaking, "Madeleine" is possessed by her past relations with Gavin, and is forcefully compelled to do his bidding. Therefore, both Scottie and Madeleine face the same situation of being incapacitated by something out of their control. They seem even more vulnerable and helpless by the way the camera shoots them from a higher angle, looking down on them like an omniscient third-person. One example is in the scene in Scottie's home, where he speaks to Madeleine about taking her to the Spanish mission she dreams about, thinking that by going it will cure her. Scottie says, "It will finish your dream. It will destroy it, I promise you." Then, as he walks her to the door, the camera points downward from a high angle, as if some other presence knows differently, watching them to ensure that everything goes as planned. The shot appears to illustrate Gavin's figurative position as the omniscient god, playing with his pawns. Another comparison exists between Scottie and Judy, in that both stubbornly refuse to let go of their delusions of love and consequently become stuck in a fantasy. Scottie reassures Judy that he's falling in love with the real her, exclaiming "It's you too. There's something in you." However, he still continues to change her into Madeleine, contradicting himself and moving further away from reality.

Some may argue that only Scottie forces his ideals onto Judy, but the same could be said in reverse. Judging from her past failed relationships, Judy now desires a different man, one that will love and protect her, almost like a knight in shining armor ready to save her. As "Madeleine," she connects with the persona so much that she falls in love with her savior, despite not being in any real danger. She thrives off a love that does not truly exist, simply because she wants it just as Scottie longs for his desires. When Scottie meets her as Judy, she originally intends to make him love her as herself, not Madeleine. However, as it becomes more apparent that this will not happen, she does not leave him. In the scene where Scottie buys her Madeleine's gray suit, Judy says, "No, I won't do it...I want to get out of here." Yet, she does not leave the room, but stops and weakly protests. Then, the scene cuts to where she obediently tries on shoes similar to Madeleine's. She could have told him the truth and gotten herself out of the fantasy they created. However, she continues to allow Scottie to recreate her into Madeleine, knowing his true intentions. In a way, both are so blinded by their delusions of their ideal love that they do not wish to face reality and accept the truth.

Furthermore, this connects to how Scottie shares similarities with Midge and Carlotta, in that all of them pine after a lost love. Scottie and Midge both grieve over the ones they lost and, instead of accepting this, continue to devote themselves to something that can never be brought back. Although Scottie is the only one diagnosed with melancholia, the same illness applies to Midge, indicated by the disappearance of her character in the second half of the film. Perhaps that by finally realizing that Scottie loves another woman, Midge accepts that she truly lost him, and so now she can move on, thus vanishing from the storyline. Meanwhile, the characters that remain have yet to accept the truth, such as Scottie and his refusal to let go of Madeleine or Judy and her inability to see that Scottie does not love the real her. These two characters continue to search for some hope of restoring something lost. Similarly, Scottie shares this trait with Carlotta, who wanders the streets of San Francisco, desperately searching for her loved ones and never truly finding peace. *Vertigo* symbolizes this through visual rhetoric by setting the story in San Francisco, with its large hills and winding streets that denotes chaos and dizziness. Lost and confused in a large city, all of them become vulnerable to Gavin Elster's scheming. Scottie plays the naïve fool, Judy acts as the puppet, Madeleine becomes the disguise, and Carlotta turns into the unwitting villain. Ultimately, Scottie and the women of the film become interconnected in some way, showing that male leads do not always emulate superiority within a film.

To further prove that the male protagonist does not necessarily have to be superior to all others, *Vertigo* contrasts Scottie to Gavin, the only other male lead that the protagonist has nothing in common with. Gavin is a cunning character that remains in control and possesses the most knowledge pertaining to the situation at hand. In contrast, Scottie is a naïve pawn in Gavin's game. Scottie does not possess the characteristics of the omniscient male lead and cannot see the truth set out before him. In this case, Scottie resembles the women in that they too do not know everything. The real Madeleine did not realize that her husband was plotting her murder; Midge did not know the entire situation that Scottie placed himself in; and Judy, despite knowing the most out of all these women, did not predict her feelings for Scottie, nor his obsessive need to change her into Madeleine. Thus, in this unconscious struggle for knowledge and control, Scottie and the women sit at the bottom of the pyramid while Gavin Elster stands at the top. The film establishes this through the use of different camera angles, such as when Scottie and Gavin meet for the first time. In this scene, when Gavin begins his plan by telling his intricately false story, Scottie sits on a chair while Gavin stands behind him, elevated slightly by a couple steps. The camera stays eye-level with Scottie, but looks up at Gavin. When Gavin says Madeleine's in danger of "someone dead," the camera keeps the low angle and zooms in on Gavin's face. Though the shot initially appears to serve the purpose of dramatizing the moment, once knowing the truth behind everything, it seems like it establishes Gavin's omniscience as he realizes that Scottie starts to fall for his plan. Interestingly, this film technique produces a bit of irony in that, because of Scottie's acrophobia, he metaphorically could never be in that all-knowing position because of his inability to look down from such a height.

Referring back to the counter-arguments to my claims, while Linderman argues that the eye symbolizes Scottie's vertigo and subsequently his inadequacies as a man, I believe it represents his limitations to only ever being at eye-level, unable to take the role of the omniscient lead. In addition, the eye belongs to a woman, which only further feminizes Scottie. This provides proof that Scottie differs from Gavin, because he cannot place himself in this all-knowing position and possess overall control. Though some, like Blakesley, could argue that Scottie and Gavin are indeed alike in their use of women as tools to attain their desires, this is not necessarily true. In fact, the women voluntarily fulfill Scottie's wishes, benefiting from them as well. Midge devotes herself to Scottie as a friend and pseudo-mother, in return gaining some of his affections. The fake Madeleine wanted Scottie to follow her, as per Gavin's instructions. Judy, though seemingly unwilling, allows Scottie to change her instead of just walking away. In the movie, Scottie even says to Judy, "You can go." However, she replies, "No, you wouldn't let me. [And almost to herself] And I don't want to go..." The clear difference between Scottie and Gavin is that the former gives these women a choice, while the latter does not. Though Scottie, as a former detective, should have some of the same attributes as Gavin in terms being in control and gaining knowledge, he instead fails as an example of both his chosen profession and his role as the male protagonist. By presenting this contrasting parallel, *Vertigo* illustrates that the protagonist does not always save day, nor can he always be equal to or better than his adversary.

With that in mind, *Vertigo* has its male lead Scottie wishing not for the role of the male lead, but rather the part of the damsel in distress. Scottie's profession as a detective typically makes people assume that he begins as the knight in shining armor. As in Berman's argument, Scottie remains in a rescue fantasy, in which he feels compelled to rescue his Beauty and slay the Dragon. Scottie then becomes "as lonely as Beauty and…as ruthless and lethal as the Dragon" (Berman). The author Linderman supports this claim, depicting Scottie as a man that has lost his pride and needs to save women in order to regain it. However, a counter-argument can be made to this. Taking the observation that Blakesley uses about the metaphor in opening scene with the police chase, Scottie is the Ego left only with his Id, therefore prone to fulfilling his desires without thinking of the consequences. At that moment, when he hangs off the rooftop, he has a fervent desire for someone to save him, which is ultimately left unfulfilled when the police officer trying to rescue him plummets to his death. As a result, I believe that the entire film revolves around Scottie's ultimate desire to relive the past in order to be saved like a damsel in distress. So, when he meets Madeleine, portrayed as a woman also in need of rescuing, Scottie easily identifies with her. Moreover, he sees her as his chance to take on the role of the damsel in distress and thus makes Madeleine's persona his own in order to fulfill this desire. He throws himself into his work, but consequently becomes so emotionally attached that he loses her and becomes haunted by this failure, as seen at the end of Scottie's dream, where instead of Madeleine's body falling off the bell tower, Scottie's silhouette spirals down. By failing to rescue Madeleine, he fails to rescue himself and so his desires remain unsatisfied.

Thus, Scottie projects this ideal woman onto another in the hopes of finally being rescued. When Scottie needed saving the first time, he froze up due to his vertigo. When he fails the second time, he becomes a blank void in a mental institution. So, when he sees Judy, he looks at her as his last chance at salvation, as seen in his actions when he follows Judy to her hotel, pleading with her and asking personal questions. Additionally, within this scene, a subtle use of visual rhetoric establishes Scottie's connection to Judy. As Judy looks into the mirror, Scottie stands behind her, while the angle of the camera makes it seem as if Scottie too is looking at the mirror. However, instead of his reflection, he sees Judy, almost like he sees himself within her. Thus, Scottie fixates on Judy as his second chance. If he can change Judy into Madeleine, he will have effec-tively "saved" Madeleine from her fate, and thus rescued himself. Ultimately, Scottie looks for a way to satisfy his desires—his Id—and naturally takes the role of the damsel in distress. Yet again, the male lead does not fulfill the role he is typically meant to follow, breaking Hollywood's traditional approach to the portrayal of men and women in films.

Indeed, *Vertigo* uses several film techniques, symbols, and motifs to pro-duce a satire on Hollywood's establishment of gender roles. In the 1950s, films were restricted by the Hays code, a form of censorship that created regulations for directors. Because of the enforced limitations, as one author claims, "… the 1950s reaffirmed male dominance and female subservience [and] women's roles were confined to sex role stereotypes of pretty, amusing or child-like." ("Women in Film"). Characters such as Madeleine do exemplify this in *Vertigo*. However, the film also takes these stereotypes and, instead of placing it in just the women, has the male lead fulfill this role. Scottie portrays the ultimate de-fenseless damsel in need of saving. Perhaps the role reversal meant to stab at the Hays code for limiting a director's creative freedom. Moreover, the 1950s was a time when the film industry began to target the teen market more so than before. And so, in order to appeal to their audience, author Tim Dirks writes "in the period following WWII when most of the films were idealized with conventional portrayals of men and women, young people wanted new and exciting symbols of rebellion. Hollywood responded to audience demands —the late 1940s and 1950s saw the rise of the anti-hero…and anti-heroines." In spite of Hays code, films came out with strong female leads that portrayed women with intellect, bravery, and strength. Hitchcock's film does provide ex-amples of this in the personalities of Midge and Judy—witty and independent women. But, more importantly, *Vertigo* truly takes in the spirit of this new trend by not only having an atypical protagonist who does not follow the guide-lines of a male lead, but also by destroying the stereotype of male supremacy through Scottie. With the uprising of the heroine, the downfall of Hollywood's stereotypes comes about, as *Vertigo* ridicules the idea of set gender roles by reversing them in the film.

At first sight (or viewing), *Vertigo* seems like a commonplace movie, where the kindhearted boy falls in love with the vulnerable girl and puts forth his best effort to save her. However, the film goes into much more depth than that, tak-ing Scottie's initial portrayal as a knight in shining armor and turning him into the damsel in distress. The movie provides several pieces of evidence to support this claim, from Scottie's resemblance to the film's women, to him acting as a foil to the other leading male, and by failing to live up to the characteristic standards of the male protagonist. Ultimately, *Vertigo* breaks down not only the wall of stereotypes, but also the gender barrier closing off the Hollywood industry.

Works Cited

Berman, E. "Hitchcock's Vertigo: The Collapse Of A Rescue Fantasy." *The International Journal of Psycho-Analysis*, 78(1997): 975–988. Web.

Blakesley, David. "Defining Film Rhetoric: The Case of Hitchcock's *Vertigo*." *Defining Visual Rhetorics*. Ed. Charles A. Hill and Marguerite H. Helmers. Mahwah, NJ: Lawrence Erlbaum Associates, 2004. 111–134. Print.

Dirks, Tim. "Film History of the 1950s." *Filmsite*. American Movie Classics LLC. 11 Mar 2009. Web.

Gabbard, Glen O. "*Vertigo*: Female Objectification, Male Desire, and Object Loss." *Psychoanalytic Inquiry*, 18(1998): 161–167. Web.

Linderman, Deborah. "The Mise-en-Abîme in Hitchcock's *Vertigo*." *Cinema Journal*, Vol. 30, No. 4 (Summer, 1991): 51–74. Web.

Vertigo. Dir. Alfred Hitchcock. 1958. With James Stewart, Tom Helmore, and Kim Novak. Paramount, 1958.

"Women in Film." *Green Cine*. 05 Apr 2007. American Movie Classics LLC. 12 Mar 2009. <http://www.greencine.com/central/guide/womeninfilm?page=0%2C3>.

Review Questions

1. Re-read the assignment for the capstone essay. How does the writer use the secondary sources that she cites in order to specify her unique interpretation of *Vertigo*? How does her inclusion of the points of view of other authors strengthen her argument?

2. Locate what you think is the thesis claim or main argument of the essay. Re-write it in your own words. Identify evidence that the author uses to support the thesis claim. What sort of evidence does the author use? Is this evidence relevant and convincing?

3. Identify the examples from the film text that the author analyzes in order to support her argument. Do these passages of close reading of the film move the argument forward? Are these scenes from the film described in sufficient detail? Is their analysis clear and logical? Do the descriptions of the film scenes help advance the author's thesis?

4. Review the organization of the essay. Does the author organize her essay logically? How does her use of historical context frame her interpretation and help to integrate her close textual analysis of the film and her reading of secondary sources?

8.4   Final Comments

A very large percentage of past FIP students say they would recommend a FIP sequence to their friends. A FIP sequence is intellectually challenging but it is also fun. Students attend weekly lectures given by fascinating faculty members and meet separately in discussion sections with well-trained Teaching Associates. TAs lead conversations about the lectures, oversee and explain the writing assignments, publish assignment-specific criteria, or rubrics, and assess the quality of the written assignments. Field trips to unusual sites may even be an occasional part of a FIP course. Be sure to take advantage of professor and TA office hours on a regular basis, particularly when in the process of writing essays.

Remember, as well, to use the many campus-wide resources designed specifically for first-year writers as they work to improve their critical thinking and writing. The campus-wide Peer Tutoring program and workshops or individual appointments at LARC (the Learning and Academic Resource Center) are examples of the kinds of resources available to FIP students.

Because a FIP course enables student writers to become familiar with writing in the disciplines to which the core faculty members belong, it teaches writers how the professionals in these fields research, evaluate, argue, analyze, and structure their dialogues about the issues and questions that are currently informing their disciplines. FIP thereby offers a first good look at the disciplines or majors you may choose as your future focus. A FIP sequence may thus provide students still seeking a major that suits them an excellent introduction to a variety of possible majors.

Because a FIP sequence is specifically designed to promote community-based learning experiences, students often form strong friendships. This is certainly a part of what makes FIP fun. Friendships forged in an intense, focused exploration of the interconnections between linked disciplines may last throughout an entire college career or even longer. A student group formed in FIP's inaugural year met for years following the completion of their sequence to continue debating issues. FIP offers a unique and exciting opportunity, one we know will challenge students to gain new perspectives and rise to new heights.

Appendix A

USING THE UCI LIBRARIES

The **UC Irvine Libraries** are the Langson Library and the Ayala Science Library, located on the main UCI campus, and the Grunigen Medical Library, located at the UCI Medical Center (UCIMC) in Orange.

All of the libraries are open to the public and can be used by any member of the UC Irvine campus community. Each library has a unique collection. Which library you use will depend on your information needs. In some cases, you will use more than one library for the same topic.

A.1 Navigating the Libraries

What if I need help using the services and resources of the Libraries?

University libraries can seem confusing and intimidating at first, but they are designed for use by students like you. Use any or all of the Libraries' "Ask a Librarian" services (ask.lib.uci.edu) to get help getting started or to answer questions as you complete your research. Ask a Librarian services include live chat reference, email reference, personal assistance from librarians at the reference desks in the Langson and Ayala Science Libraries, and individual research consultation appointments.

Library	Provides Services and Resources to Support Research and Teaching in:	Special Emphasis or Unique Collections
Langson	Arts	Government Publications
	Business and Management	Special Collections and Archives
	Education	Southeast Asian Archive
	Humanities	East Asian Collection
	Social Ecology	University Archives
	Social Sciences	
Ayala Science	Biology	One of the largest consolidated science, technology, and medicine libraries in the nation
	Engineering	
	Information and Computer Science	
	Physical Sciences	
Grunigen	Clinical Medicine	Supports doctors and nurses at the Medical Center
	Consumer Health	

What is the best way to find out about the UC Irvine Libraries?

Explore the Libraries' homepage <**http://lib.uci.edu/**>. It contains information about Library hours, locations, borrowing library books, and electronic and print resources available to students, faculty, and staff.

Here are some helpful links that you will find on the Libraries' homepage:

ANTPAC, UCI's online catalog, will help you find books, films, government reports, and other materials that are located in the UCI Libraries. ANTPAC has the most up-to-date information about the status of materials at the UCI Libraries. For example, it indicates whether the material is available, already checked out, or has been ordered.   <http://antpac.lib.uci.edu>

Databases to Get You Started provides links to and brief descriptions of the Libraries' most popular databases and electronic resources. It is a recommended starting point when you begin to search for scholarly information on any topic. <http://www.lib.uci.edu/online/databases_suggest.html>

Subject and Course Guides are directories of recommended resources created by research librarians with subject expertise. These guides provide access to general and specialized resources for beginning and advanced research needs.   <http://libguides.lib.uci.edu/>

Connect from Off-Campus allows currently enrolled students, faculty, and staff to access the Libraries' licensed resources from computers off campus. If you are off campus and need to access any of the Libraries' resources, you will need to sign into the campus Virtual Private Network (VPN) using your UCInetID and password.   <http://www.lib.uci.edu/how/connect-from-off-campus.html>

Why do I need to look for books and journal articles when there is so much information available on the internet?

There are a lot of resources not freely available online that you will be required to use to complete university-level coursework. The Libraries own millions of books and pay for subscription resources that will help you complete your assignments. All of these resources are available free to you because you're a UCI student. Your Writing 39B and 39C instructors will require that you use library resources and scholarly journal articles in order to complete your writing assignments.

➡ *For more help:* **Ask a Librarian** *<http://ask.lib.uci.edu>*

A.2   Steps in the Research Process

Articulate	Ask Five Questions about your topic: • What? • Who? • Where? • Why? • How? **Brainstorm for keywords and synonyms**	
Search/Evaluate **(types of materials)**	**If you need**	**Use**
	Background information, overview	Encyclopedias and dictionaries, textbooks
	Ideas, current information	News magazines, newspapers
	In-depth analysis	Scholarly, peer-reviewed journals
	History, overview	Books
	Population	News magazines, newspapers, books, journals
	Statistics	Government publications, including government web sites

Search	**What resources are available to help you?**
	• Find *books* by using the ANTPAC catalog. Find *articles* by using the resources listed on the "Databases to Get You Started" Guide <http://libguides.lib.uci.edu/databases> and the Subject and Course Guides page. <http://libguides.lib.uci.edu/browse.php> Find *statistics* by using Government Publications.
	• Find federal *public policy* and *pending legislation* by searching the Thomas web site <http://thomas.loc.gov/>
	How do you search the resources?
	• Keyword, Author, Title and Title Word, Subject
	• Truncation (*, #, ?)
	• AND, OR, NOT
Evaluate (results)	**Ask Questions**
	• How is this relevant to my topic?
	• Who wrote or produced this?
	• Who was this written for?
	• Why was it written?
	• Is the material objective?
	• Is the information current?
Locate	**Materials are available in a variety of formats and at a variety of locations:**
	• Use UC-eLinks to find electronic materials
	• ANTPAC catalog
	• Use the ANTPAC catalog to find books and other print materials
Synthesize and Apply	**Write your paper**
	• Use research to connect your ideas and support your argument

➡ *For more help: check the* **Libraries' Begin Your Research tutorial** *at* <http://www.lib.uci.edu/how/tutorials/LibraryWorkshop/begin.html> *or* **Ask a Librarian** <http://ask.lib.uci.edu>

A.3   Searching Article Databases

How can I find information from articles in newspapers, magazines, and scholarly journals?

I know that I can use the Libraries' ANTPAC catalog to find books on my topic. But what about sources that are not books?

Periodicals

A **periodical** is a publication such as a magazine, newspaper, or scholarly journal. Examples of periodicals are *Sports Illustrated, The Los Angeles Times,* or *Tulsa Studies in Women's Literature.* Most periodicals are available electronically, but older issues may be available only in print or on microfiche or microfilm.

You will need to use a **database** that organizes information about our periodicals.

Databases

A **database** is a tool which helps you find information on a topic in a periodical. Examples of article databases available from the UC Irvine Libraries are the Academic Search Complete, Web of Science, and the Access World News databases.

The databases will give you bibliographic, location, and content information about books and articles and may link you to the full text of the article.

Bibliographic information is used to locate the item, as well as citation purposes.

Location information tells you where to locate the item at UCI or electronically.

Content information gives you an idea of what the book or article is about.

You will see ▶ **UC-eLinks** in the databases. This link will take you from information about an article to the actual article if it is available online. If not, the link will take you to information about accessing the article in print or requesting it from another library.

How do I choose a database?

Think about how you're approaching your topic. Do you want information from a business, political, historical, or scientific perspective? That decision will determine which database you should use.

Then, become familiar with the **Databases To Get You Started** section of the Libraries' homepage, which provides links to library databases on a variety of topics. You'll find suggestions for databases to use based on how you're approaching your topic. <http://libguides.lib.uci.edu/databases>

How do I use a database?

Article databases look different from one another, but they all offer similar search features.

Search Methods	When to Use this Method	How it Works
Keyword	• When you have a topic but are not sure how that topic is described in the database	• Looks for words anywhere they appear in the searchable fields of the file
Subject OR Subject Heading	• When you know the exact vocabulary of the database • When you want more precise results than a keyword search	• Looks for words or phrases in the **Subject** or **Descriptor** field of the file

Search Strategies	Use	How it Works
Truncation	When you want to search for variations of a word, e.g., econom* will retrieve economy, economic, economical, etc.	Looks for the letters you type in with any ending
Limit	When you want to limit the results of your search	Typical limits are: • date • language • publication type • refereed publication
AND	When you want all the words you enter to be present in your results (increases precision.)	
OR	When you want any of the words you enter to be present in your results (OR means more.)	
NOT	When you don't want to search a certain word (Warning: can exclude useful information. Use with care.)	

➡ *For more help:* check the **Help** features in the article databases or **Ask a Librarian** <http://ask.lib.uci.edu>.

Appendix B

COMPUTER RESOURCES

Effective use of Information Technology is integral to student success at UCI. You will register for classes, may check out books, turn in papers, or attend virtual office hours via the internet. In all likelihood you will use email to correspond outside of class with your instructor or classmates. You may be assigned an online quiz or evaluation, or may use a class mailing list or discussion list. Many classes have associated web sites that you will need to consult for updates to the class syllabus, assignments, and helpful links to research and writing resources. You may even need to design a web site of your own. This appendix contains information about the computer resources available to you here at UCI.

B.1   Getting Started

B.1.1   Setting Up Your Account

Before you can use UCI's computing resources, you must activate your "UCInetID," a username assigned to you when you entered UCI—usually similar to your name. Activating your UCInetID is easy; just visit <http://activate. uci.edu> and follow the on-screen instructions.

Office of Information Technology (OIT)

Web: http://www.oit.uci.edu
Phone: 949-824-2222
Email: oit@uci.edu

Once you activate your UCInetID, you will be able to access UCI email and other campus services.

B.1.2   Computers on Campus

A chart of the many free computer labs available on the UCI campus is located at <http://www.oit.uci.edu/labs/>. This chart includes locations and hours, as well as hardware and software information.

Not every lab is listed at this web site; many departments have labs available only to majors. Check with your department to find out about labs not listed in the chart.

While most labs are open for student use every day, some labs are available for drop-in use only if a class is not in session. Labs have Windows-based (PC) or Macintosh computers (Mac). Most labs have more software available than is listed on the online chart.

B.2   Email

B.2.1   Accessing Your UCI Email

All UCI students have required email accounts based on their UCInetIDs. Email may be retrieved in several ways:

1. Redirect your UCI email to an alternate account. See "Redirecting Your Email to Another Account" below.

2. Use Webmail to access email via a web interface: <http://webmail.uci.edu/>.

3. Use email programs and up-to-date web browsers to easily access your email.

4. Set up a UCI Google Apps account to use Google Gmail interface instead of UCI Webmail.

➡ *More info: <http://www.oit.uci.edu/email/>.*

Redirecting Your Email to Another Account

If you prefer to use a different email service, you can redirect your UCI email to that account instead. Once you redirect your UCI email, all your UCI mail is automatically delivered to your private account. You will be able to check all your email in the same place and participate in class mailing lists.

➡ *More info: <http://www.oit.uci.edu/email/>*

Disk Quota. Your email is stored on a computer disk with limited space. Every UCI student is allowed 1 GB of space total for email and other folders.

When you exceed this limit, you will not receive any new mail until you delete some messages or files. The best way to avoid disk quota problems is to avoid saving lots of unneeded email messages in your inbox. You can also download email messages to your home computer.

To Check Your Disk Quota

1. Login with your UCInetID: <http://www.oit.uci.edu/email/options/>.

2. If you receive a "Disk Quota Exceeded" message, delete unnecessary email from your email inbox.

➡ *More info: <http://www.oit.uci.edu/email/quota.html>*

B.2.2   Class Mail Lists

In many UCI writing classes, you will be asked to use a class mail list as part of your class work. Common online assignments include online journals, discussion of a text, honing counter-arguments, evaluating online resources, and sharing the results of your research with others in your class.

This section will introduce you to the basics of using class mail lists (also known as "EEE ClassMail Lists"). If you have ever used a discussion list before, you will find that UCI's class mail lists are very similar, but with a few additional features.

➡ *More info: <https://eee.uci.edu/help/maillist/students/>*

Mail List Basics. Class mail lists allow instructors to send email to a "list" of everyone in the class. You do not need to do anything special to be included on the class mailing list. Your UCInetID delivery point address is automatically added to your class mailing list after you register for your course.

Email from the class mail list will arrive in your inbox just as any other email would. You may want to store this email messages in a special folder. Or, you can use the ClassMail Archive <https://eee.uci.edu/mla/> to review all the mail sent to the class mail list.

Your instructor will decide whether the class mail list will be an "announcement list" (only the instructor and assistants can post messages) or a "discussion list" (anyone enrolled in the class can post messages).

Class Discussion Information

1. To send a message to a discussion list, just include the course list address in the **To:** or **cc:** line of your message. Class mail list addresses take the following form: ccode-qyy@classes.uci.edu

2. For **q**, substitute the first letter of the current quarter (f for fall, w for winter, s for spring, y for summer I, m for summer ten-week, z for summer II); for **yy**, substitute the last two digits of the current year; and replace **ccode** with the five-digit course code for your class. For example, if you are taking course code 12345 during the Fall quarter of 2011, send your message to: 12345-f11@classes.uci.edu

3. You will want to add this address to your address book. Please note: If a mailing list is set to "discussion" everybody in your class will get a copy of your email when you send mail to this address.

4. You will know that your message was successfully delivered to the class when you receive a copy in your own inbox. You may also check the ClassMail Archives to see if your message went to the list.

➡ *More info: <https://eee.uci.edu/help/maillist/students/>*

ClassMail Archives <https://eee.uci.edu/mla/>. All the messages sent to EEE class mail lists are automatically archived on the EEE web site. This means that if you have lost an important message from the list, you can go to the archive to find it. It also means that if you are close to exceeding your disk quota, you can save space by not saving all of your class email in your own account. However, please note that some instructors choose to restrict their archives. Check with your instructor if your class's archive does not appear to be available.

> ### Finding ClassMail Archives
>
> You can find the archives for a particular course using a URL like this one: <https://eee.uci.edu/classmail/qyy/ccode/>
>
> For q, substitute the first letter of the current quarter (f for fall, w for winter, s for spring, y for summer I, m for summer ten-week, z for summer II); for yy, substitute the last two digits of the current year; and replace ccode with the five-digit course code for your class. For example, if you are taking a course in the fall quarter of 2011 with a course code of 12345, you would use: <http://eee.uci.edu/classmail/f11/12345/>

B.3   The World Wide Web

UCI writing classes are increasingly using the web. Some writing classes have course materials on the web, others ask you to use the web for research, still others may ask you to create a web site instead of writing a traditional essay. This section will introduce you to some of the web features you may need to use in your writing classes.

B.3.1   The Writing Studio

If you are enrolled in 39A, 39B or 39C, you'll be asked to use an online writing environment called The Writing Studio. Your instructor will enroll you in his/her section at the beginning of the quarter and will let you know how to access the class. For all information concerning the Studio, please ask your Instructor, or visit the Studio at <http://writing.colostate.edu>.

B.3.2   EEE at UCI

The Electronic Educational Environment, or "EEE," is UCI's homegrown learning management system, which offers a variety of web-based tools for learning. The EEE homepage, located at <https://eee.uci.edu/>, is the central location for class web sites. You can also find the ClassMail Archives there, and a number of other useful resources.

Using EEE. The easiest way to find out what electronic resources are available for the classes in which you are enrolled is to login to your MyEEE page. This personalized page provides you with links to your class web sites, your ClassMail Archives, a personal calendar and optional features such as online grades, surveys, and evaluations.

Your classes are automatically added to your MyEEE page. Fall, Winter, and Spring classes are updated every two hours. Summer classes are updated every 24 hours.

> ### To Access Your MyEEE Page
>
> 1. Go to <https://eee.uci.edu/> and click the "Secure Sign In" button.
>
> 2. Enter your UCInetID and password.
>
> 3. Your MyEEE page will be displayed. The current quarter is shown by default, but may be changed to view information from previous quarters.
>
> 4. When you are finished, always click on the "Logout" link and/or exit the web browser entirely. This protects your privacy by ensuring that the next person using the computer cannot access your course information.

B.3.3   Using Google Apps for UCI Students

Google Apps for UCI Students allows you to link a Gmail account with your UCINetID, and then use a series of helpful web-based tools (such as Google Docs, Calendar, etc.).

For more information about how to set this up and what applications are available, please go to <http://www.oit.uci.edu/googleapps/>.

B.3.4   Accessing the UCI Library via Virtual Private Network (VPN)

Academic journals and other research resources are increasingly becoming available online. UCI subscribes to a large number of these journals and resources: for instance, Applied Science and Technology Abstracts and MathSciNet are available to UCI students over the web, as is the Encyclopaedia Britannica.

UCI's subscriptions to these journals make them available to UCI students only. If you are on campus or dialing in through one of UCI's telephone lines, you will have no trouble accessing these journals. If you are accessing these journals through a private ISP, you will need to authenticate your student status through a Virtual Private Network (**VPN**).

VPN authenticates your student status to allow you to view restricted resources and has the added benefit of securely encrypting your web traffic, protecting your privacy.

To Use VPN

1. Go to <http://www.oit.uci.edu/security/vpn/>.

2. Follow the instructions to download and configure the software VPN, or use the online web VPN.

3. After configuring your browser, you will be prompted for your UCInetID whenever you initially attempt to enter a restricted resource.

➡ *More info: For help setting up or using VPN, call the OIT Response Center at 949-824-2222.*

B.3.5   Creating Your Own Web Page

Writing classes are increasingly asking students to create their own web pages as class assignments. Creating your own web page is getting easier all the time as new software tools are introduced. While the details of web page creation are beyond the scope of this brief introduction, we can give you a brief outline of the things needed to create your own web page.

You will first need to be able to format your writing as an HTML (Hypertext Markup Language) file. There are many books available that can teach you the basics (HTML for the World Wide Web with XHTML and CSS: Visual QuickStart Guide, by Elizabeth Castro, is a good place to start).

Additionally, many programs, such as Macromedia Dreamweaver, can do the work for you.

You need a place on the web (a site) to put, or "host," those files.

You need to get your files from your own computer to your web site. FileZilla (for Windows) and Cyberduck (for Mac) are commonly used, free programs for this purpose.

These programs use the FTP or File Transfer Protocol to move files from your local computer to your web space. FTP programs are also available in many computer labs around campus.

B.4   Managing Your Electronic Workload

Sometimes it can seem as if all these electronic resources that are supposed to be making your life easier are in fact just creating more work for you. This is especially true if you are new to working with computers, email, and the web. Here are some tips that may prove helpful to you:

If You Are Having Trouble

1. Ask someone for help.

2. If your class has a web site, make sure that you check it out as early as possible in the quarter. Familiarize yourself with what kind of information is included.

3. Check your email **at least once daily**. If you do not do this, you may miss important announcements and have a backlog of messages to read.

4. Familiarize yourself with the labs around campus for alternatives if one is crowded.

5. If you are working late in the labs, make sure you know the number for the UCI Escorts (824-7233), who will accompany you back to your dorm from anywhere on campus. UCI is a relatively safe campus, but don't take chances.

6. Finally, as with your other work, do not leave your electronic assignments to the last minute.

While every effort is made to ensure that all information is accurate when this book is published, facilities information can change throughout the year and new resources are appearing all the time.

Helpful Web Sites

1. Composition Program: <http://www.humanities.uci.edu/comp/>

2. Electronic Educational Environment (EEE): <https://eee.uci.edu/>

3. UCI Directory: <http://directory.uci.edu/>

4. Humanities Instructional Resource Center (HIRC):
    <http://www.hnet.uci.edu/hirc/>

5. Learning and Academic Resource Center (LARC):
    <http://www.larc.uci.edu/>

6. Libraries: <http://www.lib.uci.edu/>

7. Office of Information Technology (OIT):
    <http://www.oit.uci.edu/>

8. PhUpdate (Update your directory entry):
    <http://www.uci.edu/cgi-bin/phupdate>

9. Virtual Private Networks (VPN): <http://www.oit.uci.edu/security/vpn/>

10. W3School's HTML Tutorial: <http://www.w3schools.com/html/>

Bibliography

Barnet, Sylvan and William E. Cain. *A Short Guide to Writing about Literature*. 9th ed. New York: Longman, 2002. 178–183. Print.

Borges, Jorge Luis. "Funes, the Memorious." *Athenaeum Library of Philosophy*. Web. 4 June 2009.

The Bhagavad Gita. Trans. Stephen Mitchell. New York: Harmony Press. 2000.

"Breaking the News." *C4 Ventures*. 5 March 2005. Web. 13 April 2009.

Bullock, Richard and Francine Weinberg. *The Norton Field Guide to Writing*. 2nd ed. New York: W.W. Norton & Co., 2009. 537–540. Print.

Carroll, Raymond L. "Television Documentary." *TV Genres: A Handbook and Reference Guide*. Ed. Brian G. Rose. Wesport, Conn: Greenwood Press, 1985. 2237–249. Print.

Carroll, Raymond L. "Television News." *TV Genres: A Handbook and Reference Guide*. Ed. Brian G. Rose. Wesport, Conn: Greenwood Press, 1985. 213–228. Print.

Cronon, William. "Introduction: In Search of Nature". *Uncommon Ground: Rethinking the Human Place in Nature*. Ed. William Cronon. New York: Norton. 1996.

Cummings, Corin. "Shades of Journalism: An Apprenticeship in Literary Journalism." *Marlboro College Plan of Concentration*. 1995. Web. 16 April 2009.

Dancyger, Ken. *Broadcast Writing: Dramas, Comedies and Documentaries*. Boston: Focal Press, 1991. 7, 65, 83–85, 95, 119. Print.

de Saint-Exupéry, Antoine. *The Little Prince*. Trans. Katherine Woods. 13 Aug. 2008. *Wikilivres*. Web. 4 June 2009.

Dean, Greg. "Greg Dean's Glossary of Comedy Terms." *Greg Dean's College of Comedy Knowledge*. 2006. Web. 18 April 2009.

Dorf, Jon. "Playwriting 101." *How to Write a Play*. 2009. Web. 17 April 2009.

Douglas, Pamela. *Writing the TV Drama Series: How to Succeed as a Professional Writer in TV.* 2nd ed. Studio City: Michael Wiese Productions, 2007. 7–20. Print.

"Examination of Protozoan Cultures to Determine Cellular Structure and Motion Pattern." 22 Sept. 2004. *NC State University.* Web. 4 June 2009.

Geertz, Clifford. *The Interpretation of Cultures.* New York: Basic Books, 1976. Print.

"Getting to Know Your Textbook." Download. Hanover, New Hampshire: Dartmouth College, 2001. Web. 16 April 2009.

Goodwin, Andrew. *Dancing in the Distraction Factory: Music Television and Popular Culture.* Minneapolis: University of Minnesota Press, 1992. 65. Print.

Hall, Jim. "Beginning Reporting." *Virginia Commonwealth University.* 2001. Web. 15 April 2009.

"How to Become a Radio Personality." *Creative Art Schools.* 2009. Web. 18 April 2009.

Luttmer, Frank. "Academic Papers." *Academic Writing.* 27 April 2001. Web. 16 April 2009.

Mayes, Frances. *The Discovery of Poetry.* 2nd ed. Fort Worth: Harcourt College Publishers, 1994. 6–10. Print.

McIntosh, Heather. "Documentary Conventions." *The Documentary Site.* 2001. Web. 20 April 2009.

Mintz, Lawrence E. "Situation Comedy." *TV Genres: A Handbook and Reference Guide.* Ed. Brian G. Rose. Wesport, Conn: Greenwood Press, 1985. 108–124. Print.

Murata, Margaret. E-mail to Amy Bauer, Associate Professor of Music Theory. UC Irvine. 18 April 2009.

Murray, Susan. "Reality TV (U.S.)." *Museum of Broadcast Communications: Encyclopedia of Television.* 2nd ed. Chicago, IL: Routledge Library (2004) Web. 20 April 2009.

"Nina: Music Video." Online Posting. 24 October 2007. *Forms and Conventions of Music Video.* Web. 21 Jan 2009.

Platt, Wes, Ben Rubenstein, Imperatrix, Andy C. Zhang, Sondra C., Zack, Bert McCracken, Tom Viren, et al. "How to Listen to Music." *WikiHow.* 2009. Web. 19 April 2009.

Preminger, Alex and T.V. F. Brogan, Eds. "Epic." *The New Princeton Encyclopedia of Poetry and Poetics*. Princeton: Princeton UP, 1993. 361–62. Print.

Ramage, John D., John C. Bean, and June Johnson, Eds. "Skill 2: Understand the Different Kinds of Sources." *The Allyn & Bacon Guide to Writing: Brief Edition*. 4th ed. New York: Pearson Longman, 2006. 611–615. Print.

Saavedra, Tony, Jeff Miller, Doug Irving, and Cindy Carcamo. "Pitcher Adenhart was athlete on rise; man in crash with him struggled." 11 April 2009. *The OC Register*. Web. 4 June 2009.

Seaton, Beth. "Reality Programming." *Encyclopedia of Television*. 2nd ed. Chicago, IL: Museum of Broadcast Communications (2008): Web. 20 April 2009.

"Song Lyricists, Music Composition & Lyric Writing." *Songwriters Resource Network*. 2008. Web. 14 April 2009.

"Song Structure and Components." *Song Writing Fever*. Web. 14 April 2009.

Startlett, Carla. "Poetry and Song Lyrics." *How to Write Lyrics*. Web. 14 April 2009.

Strauss, Liz. "Thinking, writing, business ideas." *Liz Straus at Successful Blog*. Web. 15 April 2009.

Sun Tsu. *The Art of War*. Trans. Lionel Giles, 1910. Web. 18 June 2007.

Treitel, Richard. "Definitions of Science Fiction." *What is Science Fiction?* 25 May 1996. Web. 15 April 2009.

Trumbull, Eric W. "Introduction to Theatre." *Northern Virginia Community College*. 4 Jan. 2008. Web. 18 April 2009.

"Using Your Textbook." Download. Hanover, New Hampshire: Dartmouth College, 2001. Web. 16 April 2009.

Vernallis, Carol. *Experiencing Music Video: Aesthetics and Cultural Context*. New York: Columbia UP, 2004. x–xv, 27. Print.

Vogele, Colette, Mia Garlick, and the Berkman Center Clinical Program in Cyberlaw. "Podcasting Legal Guide." *Creative Commons*. Stanford Law School, 2006. Web. 18 April 2009.

Williams, William Carlos. "The Red Wheelbarrow." *Modern and Contemporary Poetry, U. Penn*. 10 Nov. 2008. Web. 4 June, 2009.

"Writing: A Ticket to Work or a Ticket Out." *National Writing Project*. 1 Sept. 2004. Web. 6 July 2009.

Index

C

capstone research project
  First-Year Integrated Program, 282
  précis, 282
causation, 263
cause and effect, 110, 129–131, 151
character, 33
citation. *See* integration
class community, 10, 179
classification, 108, 109, 134, 135,
    136, 148
climax, 33
closure, 53
column, 39
  op-ed, 39
comedy, 29, 48
  black, 56
  film, 56
  musical, 56
  romantic, 56
  screwball, 56
  slapstick, 56
comics. *See* graphic novels
comments, instructor, 88
compare and contrast, 110
comparison, as type of argument, 265
complication, 33
conferencing, 87
connotation, 145
consonance, 31
context, 33, 58, 78, 142, 192–196,
    199–200, 205, 210–213,
    215–216
conventions, 33, 35
  artistic, 51
  documentary, 63
  film, 55
  of scripts, 49
  photography, 52
core text, 220

cost/benefit, 264
coverage (comprehensive), 264
credibility, 143
  of sources, 142
credible sources, 44
critical engagement, 19
critical mass, 18
critical reading, 18, 19, 26, 172, 187
critical thinking, 19

D

defining a problem, 236
definition, 109, 112, 121–125, 134,
    148
  dictionary, 123
demographics, 193
description, 108, 111, 117–121, 123,
    126, 148, 153
  thick, 119
diaries, 36
diegesis, 52
discourse community, 76
documentary, 63
drafting, 86, 162, 165
drama, 47
  film, 56
  television, 62

E

editorials, 39
emails, 43
error patterns, 92
essay
  historical analysis, 244
ethos, 7–9, 28, 44–45, 68–69, 76,
    88–89, 92, 95, 97, 101–102,
    129, 136, 143, 154, 193, 201,
    208–210, 212, 214–215
  academic, 76